JAPANESE COOKERY

JAPANESE COOKERY

ELISABETH LAMBERT ORTIZ

COLLINS

My thanks to Mitsuko (Michie) Endo who taught me the secrets of Japanese home cooking.

First published 1986 by
William Collins Sons & Co Ltd
London · Glasgow · Sydney
Auckland · Johannesburg

British Library Cataloguing in Publication Data
Ortiz, Elisabeth Lambert
    Japanese cookery.
    1.   Cookery, Japanese
    I.   Title
    641.5952   TX724.5.J3

ISBN 0 00 411268 7

Designed by Monica Chia
Drawings by Marion Krupp

Text set in Bembo
by V & M Graphics Ltd, Aylesbury, Bucks
Printed and bound in Great Britain
by Butler & Tanner Ltd, Frome

CONTENTS

There is a Japanese saying that if you truly enjoy a new dish, one you have never eaten before, your life will be lengthened by 75 days. I have not counted up the number of extra days I have earned by a genuine enjoyment of new Japanese dishes, going back to the days when I spent some years in the Far East, through to the present, but I think I have lengthened my life span considerably and enjoyed myself in the process, for Japanese food is surely the most elegantly simple in the world.

It is also entrancingly beautiful, arranged on plates and platters of differing shapes and patterns, and in attractive bowls, to show the ingredients to the most appetizing advantage. The 'picture on the plate' of the *nouvelle cuisine* owes much to the Japanese kitchen, whose aim is to bring out the natural qualities of whatever is being cooked, as well as to display it beautifully.

Because they value natural taste so highly the Japanese like to use foods appearing at their appointed times of spring, summer, autumn and winter. This feeling for nature is called *kisetsukan* and, though modern Japanese supermarkets have very good processed and frozen foods, seasonal feeling still predominates, so that everything is eaten, where possible, at its best. There is also an appreciation of how one's food needs differ as the year moves from winter's cold to summer's heat. It is also a very healthy cuisine, not using animal fats and with very little frying except for *tempura*, when vegetable oil is used. Lots of vegetables and fish are eaten, some poultry and little meat. There are not a great many desserts in the traditional kitchen though modern Japanese have adopted ice-cream and other Western creations.

The kitchen is not a very old one. The Japanese creation story gives us a date of 600 BC for the first Emperor Jimmu Tenno, son of Amaterasu, the Sun Goddess, but Japan was certainly settled much earlier than that by people coming from Korea or Central Asia. The unique quality of the kitchen does not come from its antiquity but from the fact that it developed in almost complete isolation from the rest of the world and, as a result, is fundamentally unlike any other cuisine. From time to time there were contacts that influenced the kitchen. In the middle of the 1st century AD Buddhism was introduced from Korea, reinforcing the Japanese love of vegetables since Buddhists are vegetarians. In the

INTRODUCTION

7th and 8th centuries, at the time of the very advanced T'ang dynasty in China, the kitchen was again influenced. The soy bean (which became the cornerstone of Japanese cooking), China tea and chopsticks were all introduced from China, but by the 9th century contact had been broken. Later, in the 14th century, Zen Buddhism was brought by Japanese student-monks from China, and with it came strict vegetarianism and the ritual of the tea ceremony.

The 16th century saw the arrival of the Portuguese and Spanish. It was the Portuguese who brought in food from the New World like pumpkin, taro, potato and sweet potato, and the idea of frying foods dipped in batter that developed into *tempura*. They also introduced *castera* or *kasutera* (sponge cake), a new idea to the Japanese who had no tradition of cake-making with wheat flour. With the accession in 1867 of Emperor Mutsuhito Meiji to the Imperial throne, Japan moved its capital to Tokyo and opened its doors to the West. French cuisine probably had the most important influence on the kitchen. Vegetarianism dropped out of favour, and the Japanese returned to eating meat, poultry and fish, though meat was still eaten sparingly. Despite these changes the kitchen remains essentially what it has been since its earliest times.

Until recently cooking was done over charcoal. To minimize cooking time, foods – especially vegetables – were cut to expose the maximum surface to the cooking medium (usually stock or water). They were also cut into uniform-sized pieces so that they would all cook in exactly the same time. The resulting shapes

are always attractive, often beautiful, and have the nutritional advantage that both vitamins and flavour are preserved. The pieces are also easy to pick up with chopsticks.

Round vegetables, such as carrots, can be cut in a number of ways: simply sliced as we do in the West; or halved to make half-moons (*hangetsu-giri*), or quartered to give the fan shape of the gingko leaf (*ichogiri*). There is also the clapper cut (*hyoshigi-giri*) named for the wooden blocks clapped together for dramatic emphasis during Kabuki plays. The vegetable is cut into 5 cm (2 in) lengths and these are then sliced lengthways into pieces 1 cm (½ in) thick. These could be sliced crossways into 3 mm (⅛ in) julienne strips, a cut known as *sengiri*. There is a simple diagonal

SENGIRI: Cut into julienne strips, that is, small lengthways strips 3 mm (⅛ in) thick.

cut, *nanamegiri* and *rangiri*, to cut into chunks, in which the vegetable is cut on the diagonal, then given a half or quarter turn and cut on the opposite diagonal into 2.5 cm (1 in) long pieces. This exposes a lot of surfaces to the cooking medium.

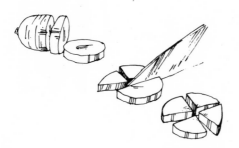

ICHOGIRI: Slice thinly crossways, then quarter into a fan shape.

NANAMEGIRI: Cut on the diagonal.

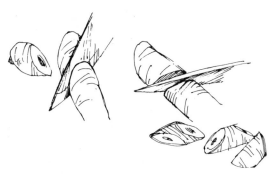

RANGIRI: Cut first on a diagonal, then give a half turn to the vegetable and cut on the opposite diagonal into 2.5 cm (1 in) long pieces.

KIKUKAGIRI: Placing a chopstick on each slice of food to be cut, slice crossways at 3 to 6 mm (⅛ to ¼ in) intervals; then slice in the opposite direction to make little squares.

A very pretty cut is the flower cut (*hana-giri*) in which carrots are shaped to look like plum blossoms, much used as a garnish in spring dishes. The vegetable is trimmed and five, evenly spaced, shallow wedges are cut lengthways. The vegetable is then sliced. Cutting into slivers (*sasagaki*), which is like sharpening a pencil with a knife, is used especially for vegetables like

SASAGAKI: Cut into slivers, like sharpening a pencil with a knife.

burdock root (*gobo*). Other vegetables like small white turnips or slices of Japanese white radish (*daikon*) are cut into chrysanthemum flower shapes (*kikukagiri*) where chopsticks are placed on each side of the vegetable to be cut. It is then sliced crossways at 3 to 6 mm (⅛ to ¼ in)

intervals, then sliced in the opposite direction to make tiny squares, giving a flower-like look. There are the usual cutting techniques of shredding and dicing.

Meat, fish and poultry are also cut into bite-size pieces for quick cooking and convenient eating. There are also some fancy cutting methods more usually encountered in restaurants than in home cooking though the fan cut, *ogi-giri*, used for aubergine and cucumbers, is easy enough to master. A small aubergine is trimmed, halved and quartered. The vegetable is cut into thin, evenly spaced slices, leaving about 1 cm (½ in) uncut at the end to hold the slices together. The fan can then be gently spread out with the fingers.

Sheet paring (*katsura-muki*) requires considerable skill, but anyone who can pare an apple without breaking the skin should manage it. The vegetable, a slice of Japanese white radish (*daikon*), or a large carrot, is peeled round and round in a paper-thin slice to become a single paper-thin sheet.

These cutting techniques are not difficult given good, sharp knives. The Japanese use *hocho* knives, nowadays made from stainless steel with solid brass rivets and fitting, and magnolia wood handles. There is a knife for every purpose: for cutting vegetables, for slicing fish, for boning, and so on. These *hocho* knives are very attractive, excellent knives, but any good knife will do.

Foods are washed more often than in Western cooking, not only before cooking but sometimes to stop the cooking process at a special point.

KNIVES

SERVING PLATTERS

particular order. Traditionally, diners sit on cushions around a low table, about 30 cm (12 in) from the floor. Each person is served the whole meal at once in individual bowls, plates and platters.

Rinsing just-cooked vegetables, such as spinach, in cold water preserves their fresh green colour, a technique probably borrowed from the French. Much attention is paid to small details like cutting off the tips of the tails of prawns because these have a high water content and splutter when fried. This meticulous attention to detail characterizes all Japanese cooking, but it would be unfair to give the impression that the cooking is tedious, or that one needs a stop watch to do it well. So much is prepared ahead of time, cooking time itself is so short, and so many dishes are served at room temperature, that assembling a Japanese meal can, with practice, be quite relaxed. In addition many Japanese dishes can fit happily into a Western meal – starters with drinks, for example, or soups, or *teriyaki* dishes, or *tempura*. It is not necessary to cook an entire meal in order to try out Japanese foods. The bean curd (*tofu*) dishes will fit in anywhere.

The Japanese meal structure is different from our own. There are many one-pot dishes cooked at the table and served with rice and pickles that provide a whole meal. Of these, *sukiyaki* is perhaps the best known. More often, the courses are presented all at once and eaten in no

Unlike the tableware of the West, Japanese dishes are often oblong, square, or fan-shaped and are beautifully decorated. They come in sets of five, not six or twelve to which we are used. Many have a seasonal theme; frosty glass and crystal, for example, are summer favourites. No individual place setting would ever have two matching dishes. Small, rolled up towels, steaming hot in winter, icy cold in summer, are put into small bamboo baskets at each place setting, most refreshing for wiping hands and face, if liked. Chopsticks, usually of bamboo or of lacquered wood, are laid at each place setting with the tips pointing left and resting on small ceramic chopstick rests. Soup is served in covered lacquer bowls, usually red or black. Soup is drunk direct from the bowl, holding it with both hands. As there are a number of courses, only small quantities are served. Since few Westerners can sit happily on cushions, it is usual to have chairs and tables for dining, a custom adopted by many Japanese. For a main meal there is always rice, a soup, a vegetable, salad or pickle dish, fish or shellfish, and a meat or poultry dish. Sometimes a *miso* (bean paste) soup is served as well as a clear soup. Fresh fruit is the dessert favourite.

Sake (Japanese rice wine) is served slightly warmed in tiny *sake* cups with the appetizers or, on more festive occasions, throughout the meal. Wine, especially dry white wine, is becoming increasingly popular. Beer is also very suitable with Japanese food. Green, unfermented tea is

SAKE SET: A flask with cups for drinking *sake*.

served plain in tiny bowls, and is light and delicate in flavour. There is always a teapot on the table. When guests come to call, though not necessarily to dine, they will always be offered tea with a snack. It is not considered impolite to be a little noisy with soup or a bowl of noodles, and it is good manners to lift the bowl with the left hand so that it is nearer the face when negotiating hard-to-manage food like noodles or bean curd.

The recipes in this book have been put into Western categories as this makes it easier for those unfamiliar with Japanese food to find the dish wanted. In Japan, food is classified by the cooking method, so that meat, fish and vegetables are all in the same section. The system of classification is as follows: the Clear Soups (*Suimono*), the Thick Soups (*Shirumono*), Starters (*Zenzai*), Rice and Rice Dishes (*Gohanmono*), Noodles (*Menrui*), Raw Fish (*Sashimi*), Simmered Dishes (*Nimono*), Steamed Dishes (*Mushimono*),

Deep-Fried Dishes (*Agemono*), Grilled Dishes (*Yakimono*), One-Pot Dishes (*Nabemono*), Vinegared Dishes (*Sunomono*), Mixed Foods or Dressed Salads (*Aemono*), Bean Curd Dishes (*Tofu*), Pickles (*Tsukemono*) and Sweets (*Okashi*).

I have written recipes in considerable detail as Japanese cooking methods are often unfamiliar. The technique, for example, of turning up the heat to high for a matter of seconds before leaving the rice to steam in its own retained heat may seem unnecessarily fussy, but it does produce a rice of just the right consistency. The rice holds together so that it can be eaten easily with chopsticks, but it is also nicely fluffy. Many apparently trivial cooking details are in fact vitally important.

Almost all the recipes serve 4 people. They can be halved or doubled successfully. A number of sample menus for breakfasts, luncheons and dinners and for a special party dinner are given on pages 14–15 to help in menu planning.

The one single thing that distinguishes Japanese cooking from all other cuisines is the wide use of many different kinds of seaweeds, often called sea vegetables. Instead of chicken, veal, beef or fish stock, *ichiban dashi*, a very subtle stock known for convenience as *dashi*, is used not only for soups but as a general cooking liquid. It is made from dried kelp (*kombu*) and dried bonito flakes (*hana-katsuo*) and is extremely easy and quick to make; but it does require strict timing as overcooking spoils the flavour. A weaker stock, *niban dashi*, is made from the leftover ingredients of *ichiban dashi* with the addition of a little extra dried bonito. It is used for *miso* (bean paste) soups and for cooking vegetables. The two stocks are known as first and second soup stock. Dried laver seaweed (*nori*), which is sold pressed into thin sheets, is used principally as a garnish. Lobe-leaf seaweed (*wakame*) – a delicate green seaweed, sold dried and packaged – is used in soups and other dishes. *Hijiki* (one of the *Fucales* related to rockweed kelp) is sold packaged as dried flakes and is used in vegetable and bean curd dishes. Instead of gelatine the Japanese use agar-agar (*kanten*) made from *Gelidium amansii* and other related seaweeds. They are all delicately flavoured and easy to use.

The soy bean plays a dominant role in the

Japanese kitchen. It comes in the form of soy sauce (*shoyu*); light soy sauce (*usukuchi shoyu*); bean curd, sometimes called cotton bean curd (*momen tofu*); silky bean curd (*kinugoshi tofu*); grilled bean curd (*yakidofu*); freeze-dried bean curd (*koyadofu*); deep-fried bean curd (*aburaage*); fried bean curd balls (*ganmodoki*); fermented bean paste (*natto*); soy bean flour (*kinako*); and red and white *miso* (bean paste). Despite their common origin, the products of this versatile bean are very different. Bean curd is very high in protein.

Rice is perhaps the most important ingredient in the Japanese kitchen since it is eaten at every meal. *Gohan* (rice) translates as 'honourable food' and signifies not only cooked rice, but food itself. It is considered quite wrong to leave any rice, even a single grain, in one's rice bowl at the end of a meal. The type of rice used is short grain. Rice also produces *sake* (rice wine) – the national drink, also used in cooking – and *mirin* (sweet rice wine), almost exclusively used in cooking.

Noodles, thick and thin – of wheat, buckwheat, devil's-tongue root, and soy bean gelatine – are very popular, especially for lunch dishes. Most of them seem familiar as the wheat noodles approximate spaghetti and noodles.

Though it is not absolutely necessary, since any reasonably well-equipped kitchen will have all that is needed, buying some Japanese cooking equipment is very worthwhile as it will all prove useful in everyday cooking. There is a serrated earthenware mortar (*suribachi*) with a large, very light wooden pestle (*surikogi*) that makes grinding

nuts, sesame seeds, or anything else very easy. Cooking chopsticks, which come tied together in pairs, are used to scrape down the sides of the mortar. The chopsticks are a useful cooking tool for a variety of tasks, such as stirring eggs or checking the oil temperature for deep frying. A wooden spatula (*shamoji*) is useful for stirring

SHAMOJI: A round wooden spatula.

cooked rice, as it does not break the grain. A *donabe*, a flame-proof ceramic casserole, needs only the usual care of starting it off on low, not high, heat. A set of bowls in various sizes is useful

DONABE: A lidded earthenware casserole.

for serving rice, soup and noodles, or tiny ones for sauces and garnishes. A rectangular frying-pan (*tamago-yaki nabe*) is useful for making the rolled omelettes that make splendid accompaniments to drinks or can be served as starters even when a Japanese meal is not being served. A very useful piece of equipment is a grill that can be used on top of the stove. There are double ones for fish, as well as single ones.

SURIBACHI AND SURIKOGI: Earthenware serrated mortar with wooden pestle.

SAKANAYAKI: A top-of-the-stove grill.

HIBACHI: A charcoal grill.

There are a great many shops, some of them mail order, selling Japanese foods and cooking equipment. You will find a list on page 184.

Above all, this is wonderful food, appetizing, healthy, good to look at, a joy to eat.

MENUS

The following are examples of some typical Japanese meals.

BREAKFASTS

Plain Boiled Rice
Gohan

Miso Soup with Noodles and Aubergines
Somen To Nasu No Mishoshiru

Fish Marinated in Bean Paste
Sakana No Misozuke-Yaki

Cucumber Salad
Jabara Kyuri

Chinese Cabbage and Carrot Pickles
Hakusai To Ninjin No Kaorizuke

Plain Boiled Rice
Gohan

Miso Soup with Bean Curd and Lobe-Leaf Seaweed
Tofu To Wakame No Misoshiru

Pickled Smelt
Wakasagi No Nanbanzuke

Spinach Salad
Horenso No Ohitashi

LUNCHEONS

Chilled Noodles with Eggs
Hiyamugi

Grilled Mackerel Fillets
Saba No Shioyaki

Green Asparagus Salad
Green Asparagus No Kimijoyukake

Chicken and Eggs with Rice
Oyako Donburi

Miso Soup with Chrysanthemum Leaves or Spinach
Tofu To Shungiku No Misoshiru

Cucumber and Bean Sprout Salad with Sesame Seeds
Kyuri To Moyashi No Goma-ae

DINNERS

Spring

Plain Boiled Rice
Gohan

Clear Soup with Bean Curd and Lobe-Leaf Seaweed
Tofu To Wakame No Suimono

Glazed Chicken Balls
Toriniku Dango No Terini

Eggs with Bamboo Shoots
Takenoko No Tamago-Toji

Rape Blossoms with Sesame Seeds
Na-No-Hana No Goma-ae

Summer

Batter-Fried Prawns and Vegetables
Tempura

Chicken and Vegetable Salad
Toriniku No Oroshi-ae

Clear Soup with Okra and Ginger
Okura To Hari Shoga No Suimono

Plain Boiled Rice
Gohan

Quick Bean Paste Vegetable Pickles
Sokuseki Misozuke

Autumn

Noodle-Coated Prawns with Fried Sole
Hirame No Kohaku-age To Ebi No Iga-age

Aubergine with Bean Paste
Nasu No Misoni

Plain Boiled Rice
Gohan

Vegetable and Fried Bean Curd Soup
Noppei-jiru

Winter

Deep-Fried Crispy Flounder
Karei No Karaage

Bean Curd, Chicken and Vegetable Custard
Kuya-mushi

Plain Boiled Rice
Gohan

White Radish with *Miso* Sauce
Furofuki

Clear Chicken Soup
Toriniku To Shiraganegi

SPECIAL DINNER

On special occasions, a more formal dinner with a
larger number of dishes will be served. There will be a selection of starters, clear
soup, raw fish (*sashimi*), then dishes using all the traditional cooking methods – a steamed dish,
a grilled dish, a simmered dish and a deep-fried dish such as *tempura*, then salad, plain boiled rice,
miso soup and pickles. Dessert is usually fresh fruit, and green tea is served. In this
elaborate meal, dishes will be chosen to give a balance of foods; fish,
vegetables, meat and poultry will all be represented.

Soup is important in the Japanese kitchen. Clear soup begins almost every meal and the thicker *miso* (bean paste) soups begin the day at breakfast. They also appear towards the end of other meals. *Dashi*, the stock on which the soup is based, is completely different from the chicken and beef stock of the kitchens of the West. It is made from kelp (*kombu*), one of the brown seaweeds which is packaged, dried, in wide flat strands, and *hana-katsuo*, flaked dried bonito, a member of the mackerel family, also sold packaged. *Dashi*, which has a very delicate flavour, takes only minutes to make. There is an even easier way to make it using packaged dried soup stock which needs only the addition of water. This first stock is used to make the clear soups. The kelp and dried bonito flakes are used again to make second soup stock for *miso* (thick soups), to cook vegetables, and for one-pot dishes.

There is an almost infinite variety of clear soups, each with a different garnish that lends flavour to the soup and is also pleasing to the eye. Soups are served in lacquered bowls with lids. They are usually red or black so that the pale gold of the soup with its delicate garnish of vegetable, *tofu* (bean curd), sliced spring onions, chicken or whatever else is used, show off to beautiful advantage. The lidded bowls keep the soup hot, as in a Japanese meal all the dishes are served at once, but any small china bowl will do. And, of course, like all Japanese food, they reflect seasonal feeling.

The *miso* soups, made with the addition of fermented soy bean paste, white or red, are more robust in flavour, with garnishes as varied as those for clear soup. There are clear soups and *miso* soups for every season, depending on the garnishes used. Chopsticks are used to lift out the solids, then one drinks the liquid from the bowl. Spoons are not used and it is not considered impolite to be a little noisy when drinking soup.

FIRST SOUP
STOCK

ICHIBAN DASHI

This is the stock that is used for clear soups and for special dishes where a particularly delicate stock is needed.

10 cm (4 in) square dried kelp (*kombu*)
1 litre (1¾ pints) cold water
15 g (½ oz) dried bonito flakes (*hana-katsuo*)

Wipe the kelp with a damp cloth and cut a 1 cm (½ in) fringe along one side. Pour the water into a medium-sized saucepan, add the kelp and bring the water, uncovered, over moderate heat to just under a boil. Lift out and reserve the kelp (for Second Soup Stock, see below). Bring the water to a boil, stir in the dried bonito flakes. Remove from the heat and allow to stand for 2 or 3 minutes. Strain the stock through a sieve lined with a double thickness of dampened cheesecloth, set over a bowl. Keep the bonito to one side for Second Soup Stock. The stock is now ready to be used.

SECOND SOUP
STOCK

NIBAN DASHI

To make Second Soup Stock (*Niban Dashi*), take the kelp and bonito flakes reserved from making First Soup Stock (see above), and combine in a saucepan with 700 ml (1¼ pints) water and simmer over moderate heat for 4 minutes. Strain and discard the solids. The stock is now ready to be used.

THE CLEAR SOUPS
SUIMONO

CLEAR CHICKEN SOUP

TORINIKU TO SHIRAGANEGI NO SUIMONO

This is a winter soup, but is good at any time of the year.

SERVES 4
125 g (4 oz) skinned and boned chicken breast
cut into 8 diagonal slices
2 teaspoons *sake*
Salt
1 tablespoon *katakuriko, or* cornflour
2 spring onions, trimmed, using white part, cut
lengthways into fine strips
800 ml (1⅓ pints) first soup stock
1 teaspoon soy sauce
1 teaspoon salt
⅛ teaspoon MSG
4 slivers lime peel

Put the chicken into a small bowl with the *sake* and salt to taste. Sprinkle with the *katakuriko* or cornflour, mixing well. Drop the spring onions into cold water and leave to crisp for 5 minutes. Drain, pat dry, and set aside. Bring the stock to a simmer in a medium-sized saucepan, add the chicken and cook, uncovered, for 3 minutes. Add the soy sauce, salt and MSG. Pour into 4 soup bowls, dividing the chicken pieces equally among them. Garnish with the lime peel slivers.

VARIATION: A typical winter version of the soup is garnished with white radish (*daikon*). Omit the lime peel and, instead of slicing the spring onions, chop them finely. Grate 50 g (2 oz) white radish, squeezing it gently to get rid of the excess moisture. Put a small heap of it into each of 4 soup bowls. Make the soup and when it is ready lift out the chicken pieces and place in the bowls at the side of the radish. Sprinkle the finely chopped spring onions over them. Carefully pour the hot soup into the bowls.   SERVES 4.

ANOTHER CLEAR SOUP WITH CHICKEN

TORINIKU NO TSUMIREJIRU

This is a rather more elaborate soup than Clear Chicken Soup (*Toriniku To Shiraganegi No Suimono*), (left).

SERVES 4
125 g (4 oz) skinned and boned chicken breast
1 tablespoon plain flour
2 teaspoons white bean paste (*shiro miso*)
1 jelly mushroom (*kikurage*) soaked in warm water for 10 minutes
950 ml (32 fl oz) first soup stock
2 medium-sized fresh mushrooms, thinly sliced
1 teaspoon salt, or to taste
1 teaspoon light soy sauce (*usukuchi shoyu*)
2 pinches MSG
2 spring onions, using white and green parts, trimmed and sliced diagonally
1 cm (½ in) slice fresh ginger root, peeled and grated

In a food processor or blender reduce the chicken breast to a fluffy purée, or pound it in a mortar (*suribachi*). Add the flour and bean paste, mixing well. Squeeze out the jelly mushroom, slice it very finely and add it to the chicken mixture. Form the mixture into 12 small balls. Heat the stock in a saucepan. Add the mushrooms and the chicken balls and simmer for 2 minutes. Add the salt, light soy sauce, MSG and spring onions and cook just long enough to heat through. Pour into 4 soup bowls with 3 chicken balls in each. Squeeze a little juice from the grated ginger into each bowl.

CLEAR SOUP WITH OKRA AND GINGER

OKURA TO HARI SHOGA NO SUIMONO

This is a summer soup, very light and delicate. Choose small, tender young okra.

SERVES 4
4 small whole okra
4 thin slices fresh ginger
850 ml (1⅔ pints) first soup stock
½ teaspoon salt, or to taste
1 teaspoon light soy sauce (*usukuchi shoyu*)

Drop the okra into a saucepan of briskly boiling, salted water and cook, uncovered, for 5 minutes. Drain and drop the okra into cold water to cool. This gives the vegetable a bright green colour and keeps it crisp. Drain, trim the ends and slice each okra into thin rounds. Soak the ginger for a few minutes in cold water and drain.

In a saucepan, combine the soup stock, salt and light soy sauce, and bring to a simmer. Divide the okra slices and ginger among 4 soup bowls, and pour in the hot stock.

VARIATION 1: Cut 125 g (4 oz) silky bean curd (*kinugoshi tofu*) into small cubes and divide among the bowls with the okra and ginger, then pour on the hot stock.

VARIATION 2: For Clear Soup with Chicken and Okra (*Tori To Okura No Suimono*), omit the ginger. Cut 125 g (4 oz) skinned and boned chicken breast into diagonal bite-size pieces. Season with salt and a few drops of *sake*, then roll in *katakuriko* or in cornflour. Cook in soup stock to cover for 4 minutes. Drain and divide among the soup bowls with the okra slices. Pour on the hot stock, and serve. SERVES 4.

CLEAR SOUP WITH BEAN CURD AND SEAWEED

TOFU TO WAKAME NO SUIMONO

The lobe-leaf seaweed (*wakame*) in this recipe ranks third in the Japanese seaweed harvest coming after *nori* and *kombu*. The dried packaged fronds expand into a delicate green sea vegetable, but the plant loves turbulent water and grows best in strong currents. In Japan, fresh *wakame* is a spring favourite.

SERVES 4
4 × 20 cm (8 in) dried fronds lobe-leaf seaweed (wakame)
1 × 250 to 300 g (8 to 10 oz) piece silky bean curd (kinugoshi tofu)
800 ml (1⅓ pints) first soup stock
Salt
1 teaspoon light soy sauce (usukuchi shoyu)

Soak the seaweed in cold water for 5 minutes, or until soft. Lift out, squeeze lightly and cut away the hard ribs and any tough edges. Chop coarsely and set aside. Slice the bean curd in half horizontally, then cut the two halves into 1 cm (½ in) cubes. Pour the soup stock into a saucepan, season to taste with salt, add the soy sauce, bean curd and seaweed and bring to a simmer. Cook over low heat just long enough to heat the bean curd and seaweed through. Pour into 4 bowls.

VARIATION: For Clear Soup with Okra and Bean Curd (*Tofu To Okura No Suimono*), cook 4 small okra pods in briskly boiling salted water for 5 minutes. Drain, rinse in cold water, drain again, trim the ends and chop finely. Set aside. Heat 800 ml (1⅓ pints) first soup stock with salt to taste and 1 teaspoon light soy sauce (*usukuchi shoyu*). Cut 1 piece of silky bean curd (*kinugoshi tofu*) weighing about 250 g (8 oz) into quarters. Add it to the simmering stock, then remove from the heat and let it stand for a few minutes to heat through. Carefully slide the bean curd into 4 bowls. Top with the okra. Reheat the soup and pour it into the bowls. SERVES 4.

NOODLE AND CUCUMBER SOUP

SOMEN TO KYURI NO SUIMONO

This summer soup is appealing in its fresh simplicity. The clear, amber-coloured soup is garnished with thin wheat noodles and delicate green-edged cucumber slices.

SERVES 4
25 g (1 oz) *somen* (wheat noodles)
50 g (2 oz) sliced, unpeeled cucumber
800 ml (1⅓ pints) first soup stock
1 teaspoon salt, or to taste
1 teaspoon light soy sauce (usukuchi shoyu)
1 tablespoon *sake* (optional)

Drop the noodles into a saucepan of briskly boiling water and cook, uncovered, for 5 minutes. Add 300 ml (½ pint) cold water and bring back to a boil over high heat. Drain, refresh quickly in cold water, drain and set aside.

Using a small spoon, scrape the seeds out of the cucumber, then slice thinly. In a saucepan, combine the soup stock, salt and soy sauce with the *sake*, if liked, and bring to a simmer. Divide the noodles among 4 soup bowls, pour on the stock and float the cucumber slices on top.

VARIATION: For *Somen no Hiyashisuimono* (Noodle Soup with Green Beans), have 8 large, whole, fresh green beans instead of the cucumber. When preparing the soup, drop the beans into boiling salted water and cook, uncovered, for 5 minutes. Drain, refresh quickly in cold water and drain again. Trim the beans and cut each one into 3 diagonal slices. Divide the noodles among 4 soup bowls, add the beans and pour on the hot soup stock. SERVES 4.

VEGETABLE AND FRIED BEAN CURD SOUP

NOPPEI-JIRU

Do not be put off by the long list of ingredients for this hearty winter soup. Many of them are kitchen staples, and the soup is delicious enough to be worth the trouble of seeking the special Japanese ingredients.

SERVES 4
4 dried Japanese mushrooms (*shiitake*)
½ medium carrot, using thick end, scraped
**250 g (8 oz) Japanese white radish
(*daikon*), peeled**
250 g (8 oz) taro, peeled
**125 g (4 oz) salsify *or* scorzonera, scraped and
dropped into cold water**
2 pieces fried bean curd (*aburaage*)
**125 g (4 oz) cooked, packaged fernbrake,
bracken (*warabi*), optional**
175 g (6 oz) devil's-tongue noodles (*shirataki*)
800 ml (1⅓ pints) first soup stock
1 teaspoon salt, or to taste
1 tablespoon soy sauce
Pinch MSG
1 teaspoon arrowroot
1 tablespoon flat parsley, finely chopped

Soak the mushrooms in warm water for 30 minutes. Drain, squeeze out, remove the hard stems and cut into quarters. Thinly slice the carrot and radish. Stack the slices and cut into quarters. Thinly slice the taro. If the slices are large, cut them into quarters. Chop the salsify or scorzonera and return it to the cold water as it discolours very quickly. Rinse the fried bean curd in hot water, halve and cut into 1 cm (½ in) slices. If using the fernbrake or bracken, rinse it and cut it into 2.5 cm (1 in) slices.

Combine all the vegetables in a saucepan of boiling water, and simmer for 2 minutes. Drain and set aside. Drop the noodles into boiling water and cook for 2 minutes. Drain and cut into 2.5 cm (1 in) pieces.

Pour the stock into a saucepan, add the vegetables, bean curd and noodles and simmer, covered, until all the vegetables are soft, 10 to 15 minutes. Season to taste with salt, add the soy sauce and pinch of MSG, and the arrowroot mixed with a teaspoon of cold water. Stir to mix and cook until lightly thickened, about 1 to 2 minutes. Pour the soup into 4 bowls and sprinkle with the parsley.

If fernbrake, bracken (*warabi*) is not available use 250 g (8 oz) spinach, cooked in boiling salted water for 4 minutes, drained, squeezed dry, formed into a roll and cut into 2.5 cm (1 in) slices. Put the spinach into the soup bowls just before adding the hot soup.

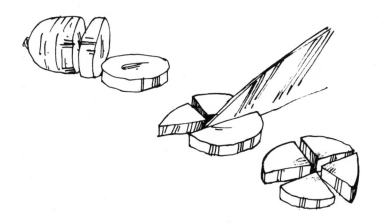

CLEAR FISH SOUP

SHIROMIZAKANA NO SUIMONO

This hearty soup is a cold weather favourite.

SERVES 4
**150 g (5 oz) red snapper, sole, plaice or any
white fish fillets, cut into 8 diagonal slices
Salt
250 g (8 oz) trimmed raw spinach
800 ml (1⅓ pints) first soup stock
1 teaspoon light soy sauce (*usukuchi shoyu*)
Pinch MSG
Piece lime peel**

Drop the fish into a saucepan of boiling, salted water and poach, uncovered, until done, about 4 minutes. Drain and put 2 pieces of fish into each of 4 soup bowls.

Have ready a large saucepan of briskly boiling salted water. Add the spinach, bring back to a boil over high heat and cook for 2 minutes. Drain, refresh in cold water, drain, and squeeze lightly to get rid of the moisture. Chop the spinach coarsely and add to the soup bowls. Heat the stock with the soy sauce and salt to taste. Pour into the soup bowls and garnish with the lime peel cut into V-shapes to represent pine needles.

CLEAR CLAM SOUP

HAMAGURI NO SUMASHI-JIRU

The clams used in Japan differ from the shellfish available in Europe. Fortunately there are satisfactory substitutes. Both live cockles and clams (usually carpet shells, the French *palourdes*) are fine. This is a popular soup for New Year's Day and for wedding feasts. If the opened shellfish are still joined at the hinge it is regarded as a good luck symbol for a happy marriage, woman and man united.

SERVES 4
**12 clams *or* cockles
Salt
1 large spring onion, trimmed
Piece of lime peel
850 ml (1⅔ pints) first soup stock
1 tablespoon *sake*
½ teaspoon light soy sauce (*usukuchi shoyu*)**

Scrub the clams or cockles and rinse under cold running water. Put in a bowl with fresh water and 1 teaspoon salt to 1 litre (1¾ pints) and leave for several hours to disgorge any sand. Discard any clams that are open.

Cut the spring onion into fine 2.5 cm (1 in) strips, put into cold water to crisp, then dry in a kitchen towel. Set aside. Cut the lime peel into 4 V-shapes to represent pine needles, and set aside.

Pour the soup stock into a saucepan. Add the clams, cover and bring to a boil over high heat. Reduce the heat to low and cook just until the clams open, 3 to 4 minutes. Be careful not to overcook lest they become tough and rubbery. Discard any shells that do not open. Off the heat, add the *sake* and soy sauce, taste for seasoning and add a little salt if necessary. Put 3 clams into each of 4 bowls, pour in the soup and garnish with the spring onion and lime peel.

EGG DROP SOUP

KAKITAMA-JIRU

This is a popular soup, served all year round. It is easy to make and looks extremely attractive.

SERVES 4
850 ml (1⅔ pints) first soup stock
1 teaspoon salt, or to taste
1 teaspoon soy sauce
1 tablespoon *katakuriko* or 1 tablespoon
cornflour, mixed with 2 tablespoons cold water
2 eggs, beaten and stirred with 1 tablespoon
***sake*, or soup stock**
Small piece fresh ginger root
Lime peel (optional)
Dried laver seaweed, (*nori*) optional
***Mitsuba* leaves (trefoil), optional**

In a medium-sized saucepan, bring the stock to a simmer, covered. Season with salt and soy sauce and stir in the *katakuriko* or cornflour over low heat and cook, stirring, until the soup is lightly thickened and smooth. Pour the egg mixture through a flat skimmer or a sieve, moving in a circle over the soup. When all the egg has been poured into the soup, cook for a few seconds longer to set the egg threads. Pour the soup into 4 bowls. Grate the ginger and squeeze a few drops of ginger juice into each bowl. Garnish, if liked, with the lime peel cut into 4 V-shapes to represent pine needles. Instead of the lime peel, toast a small sheet of dried laver seaweed (*nori*) on both sides for a few seconds over a gas flame or electric burner, and crumble it over the soup, or garnish with a trefoil leaf.

THE MISO SOUPS
SHIRUMONO

OYSTER AND BEAN CURD
MISO SOUP

KAKI DOFU JIRU

This is a lovely, very special soup and one which makes the oyster season worth waiting for.

SERVES 4
800 ml (1⅓ pints) first soup stock
1 tablespoon red *miso* (bean paste)
4 tablespoons white *miso* (bean paste)
1 piece fried bean curd (*aburaage*)
250 g (8 oz) bean curd (*momen tofu*),
cut into 2.5 cm (1 in) cubes
16 oysters, shelled, rinsed in salted water
25 g (1 oz) Japanese parsley (*seri*)
***or* flat parsley, coarsely chopped**
2.5 cm (1 in) piece fresh ginger root,
peeled and grated
Japanese pepper (*kona sansho*)

Heat the soup stock in a saucepan. Add the bean pastes, mixed until smooth with a little of the stock. Rinse the fried bean curd in hot water, halve lengthways and cut it into 5 mm (¼ in) strips. Add to the soup with the bean curd and the oysters and simmer just until the oysters are plump, about ½ minute. Remove the saucepan from the heat. Add the parsley and pour the soup into 4 bowls with 4 oysters in each bowl. Squeeze a few drops of ginger juice into each bowl, or sprinkle with Japanese pepper.

MISO SOUP WITH NOODLES AND AUBERGINES

SOMEN TO NASU NO MISOSHIRU

Aubergine is a summer favourite in Japan. The type grown there is far smaller than our usual vegetable, though happily the smaller variety is increasingly available in Indian and other ethnic markets.

SERVES 4

2 small aubergines about 7 × 3.5 cm (3 × 1½ in), *or* equivalent slice from a larger aubergine
Salt
800 ml (1⅓ pints) second soup stock
50 g (2 oz) thin wheat noodles (*somen*)
3 tablespoons white *miso* (bean paste)
2 spring onions, finely chopped, using white and green parts
Japanese pepper (*kona sansho*) *or* seven-flavour spice (*shichimi-togarashi*)

Trim the aubergines and halve them lengthways. Cut into 5 mm (¼ in) diagonal slices. If using a slice of a larger aubergine, cut into equivalent size pieces. Put the vegetable to soak in a bowl with 1 tablespoon salt to 1 litre (1¾ pints) cold water, and weight down with an inner wooden lid (an *otoshibuta*) or a plate or saucer for 15 minutes. Drain and rinse in fresh cold water, drain again and put into a saucepan with the soup stock. Simmer, covered, over moderate heat until tender, about 5 minutes. Add the noodles and simmer for 2 minutes longer. Add the *miso* mixed until smooth with a little of the soup stock, stir and cook just long enough to bring the soup back to a simmer. Pour into 4 soup bowls, and garnish with the spring onions and the Japanese pepper or seven-flavour spice.

THICK PORK SOUP

BUTAJIRU

This is another of the richly satisfying winter soups using popular winter foods like burdock and Chinese leaves. Salsify (oyster plant) and scorzonera are excellent substitutes for the hard-to-find burdock. White sweet potato, not the orange variety known as Louisiana yam, is used.

SERVES 6 to 8

375 g (12 oz) lean, boneless pork, coarsely chopped
250 g (8 oz) salsify *or* scorzonera, scraped and dropped into cold water
1 medium carrot, scraped
250 g (8 oz) sweet potato, peeled
1 large potato, peeled and dropped into cold water
7 cm (3 in) slice Japanese white radish (*daikon*) peeled *or* 2 small white turnips, peeled
2.5 cm (1 in) slice fresh ginger root, peeled and thinly sliced
950 ml (32 fl oz) second soup stock, *or* water
6 tablespoons white *miso* (bean paste)
4 tablespoons red *miso* (bean paste)
3 spring onions, cut into 1 cm (½ in) slices
Japanese pepper (*kona sansho*) *or* seven-flavour spice (*shichimi-togarashi*)

Put the pork into a colander or sieve and pour boiling water over it. Drain, rinse in cold water quickly, drain again and set aside.

Cut the salsify or scorzonera and carrot *rangiri*, that is cut on a diagonal, give the vegetable a quarter turn and slice again on the diagonal. Cut the sweet potato, potato, radish or turnips into 1 cm (½ in) slices. Stack the slices and cut in half. Put the pork into a large saucepan with the second soup stock or water, add the vegetables and ginger, bring to a simmer and cook, covered, for 10 minutes. Combine the bean pastes in a bowl, and mix until smooth with a little stock from the saucepan. Stir the mixture into the soup and cook at just under a simmer for 1 hour or until the vegetables are tender. When the soup is ready, add the spring onions and cook for a minute longer. Pour into 6 or 8 soup bowls. Serve with *sansho* powder or *shichimi-togarashi* on the table to be added as liked.

MIXED VEGETABLE *MISO* SOUP

KENCHINJIRU

This is a hearty winter soup using a number of vegetables as well as bean curd and *miso* (bean paste). It is a flexible dish and if one vegetable is not available, another can be substituted according to taste. In Japan, burdock is used in the soup but this vegetable is seldom, if ever, available here. Salsify (also called oyster plant) or scorzonera, both members of the Daisy Family like burdock, make excellent substitutes.

SERVES 4

4 dried Japanese mushrooms (*shiitake*)
125 g (4 oz) spinach
Salt
4 small taro, peeled and thinly sliced *or* 1
medium potato about 125 g (4 oz) peeled and
thinly sliced
10 cm (4 in) carrot, scraped
1 cake bean curd (*momen tofu*) about 250 g (8 oz)
2 tablespoons vegetable oil
700 ml (1¼ pints) second soup stock
4 tablespoons red *miso* (bean paste)

Soak the mushrooms in warm water for 30 minutes. Squeeze out, remove the hard stems and cut into quarters.

Wash the spinach and drop it into a large saucepan of briskly boiling salted water, bring back to a boil over high heat, and cook for 1 minute. Drain and rinse quickly in a colander under cold running water. Drain again and form into a roll on a bamboo mat (*sudare*), or on a kitchen towel, roll up and squeeze out the moisture. Cut into 2.5 cm (1 in) slices. Set aside.

Cut the carrot into 4 slices *rangiri*, that is cut on a diagonal then give the carrot a quarter turn and slice again on the diagonal. Cook the carrot and taro, or potato, in boiling salted water for 5 minutes. Drain and set aside. Rinse the bean curd, then pat it dry and crush it in a kitchen towel. Heat the oil in a saucepan, add the bean curd and stir-fry over high heat for 1 or 2 minutes. Add the carrot and taro or potato slices, and the mushrooms and stir-fry for 30 seconds longer. Add the soup stock and simmer until the vegetables are tender, 10 to 15 minutes. Mix the bean paste with a little stock, and stir it into the soup. Cook just long enough to heat through. Divide the spinach among 4 soup bowls and pour the hot soup over them making sure there is some of each vegetable in all the bowls.

MISO SOUP WITH BEAN CURD AND LOBE-LEAF SEAWEED

TOFU TO WAKAME NO MISO-SHIRU

This spring soup is enhanced by the addition of the delicate *wakame* seaweed and cubes of bean curd balancing the robust flavour of bean paste (*miso*).

SERVES 4
**6 × 20 cm (8 inch) fronds lobe-leaf seaweed
(*wakame*)
300 g (10 oz) bean curd (*momen tofu*)
800 ml (1⅓ pints) second soup stock
4 tablespoons red *miso*
1 teaspoon soy sauce
1 spring onion, using white and green parts,
finely chopped**

Soak the seaweed in cold water for 10 minutes. Drain, squeeze lightly and cut away any hard ribs and tough sections and chop coarsely. Set aside. Cut the bean curd into 16 cubes and put 4 into each of 4 soup bowls. Warm the soup stock in a saucepan. Take out about 150 ml (¼ pint) and mix the *miso* until smooth. Stir into the soup stock with the seaweed and soy sauce and heat through without letting it boil. Pour into the soup bowls and sprinkle with the spring onion.

VARIATION 1: If liked, silky bean curd (*kinugoshi tofu*) can be used instead of ordinary *tofu*, and a mixture of red and white *miso* (2½ tablespoons white to 1½ red) can be used for a more delicate flavour. The soup can be garnished with *hana-katsuo* (dried bonito flakes) sprinkled on at the last minute, using about 2 tablespoons.

VARIATION 2: For *Miso* Soup with Shungiku (*Tofu To Shungiku No Misoshiru*), substitute the edible chrysanthemum (*shungiku*) for the seaweed, or substitute spinach using 500 g (1 lb) of cleaned and trimmed spinach or chrysanthemum leaves. Drop the vegetable into a large saucepan of briskly boiling salted water, bring back to a boil and blanch for 1 minute, rinse in cold water and drain. Arrange the vegetable on a bamboo mat (*sudare*) or a kitchen towel, roll up and squeeze out the moisture. Form into a roll and cut into 1 cm (½ in) slices. Make the soup as in the principal recipe, using either type of bean curd, and either red *miso* or a mixture of red and white. Add the vegetable and the bean curd, cut into cubes, to the soup and heat through very gently. Pour into bowls and serve. SERVES 4.

MISO SOUP WITH MIXED VEGETABLES

SATSUMA-JIRU

This rich, thick soup takes its name from the region of Satsuma, now called Kyushu. A comforting winter soup, it allows for considerable variation. Potato and pumpkin may both be used as substitutes for sweet potato and salsify and, if liked, a piece of fried bean curd (*aburaage*) halved and cut into crossways slices, may be added. White pepper and cayenne pepper can be used as a garnish instead of seven-flavour spice, (*shichimi-togarashi*).

SERVES 4
**250 g (8 oz) skinned and boned chicken,
or lean boneless pork cut into 1 cm (½ in) pieces
2 dried Japanese mushrooms (*shiitake*)
2.5 cm (1 in) slice Japanese white radish (*daikon*),
peeled
1 medium carrot, scraped
125 g (4 oz) white sweet potato, peeled
1 salsify *or* scorzonera, scraped, cut into slivers
(*sasagaki*), and dropped into cold water
900 ml (1½ pints) second soup stock
2 tablespoons red *miso* (bean paste)
1 tablespoon white *miso* (bean paste)
1 spring onion, using white and green parts,
coarsely chopped
Seven-flavour spice (*shichimi-togarashi*)**

Drop the chicken or pork pieces into a small saucepan of briskly boiling water, blanch for 10 seconds, drain and set aside.

Put the mushrooms into a bowl of warm water and soak for 30 minutes. Drain, squeeze out, and cut away the hard stems. Cut into quarters and set aside. Thinly slice the radish, carrot and sweet potato, stack the slices and cut them into quarters (*ichogiri*), which is to look like a gingko leaf, fan shaped.

Pour the soup stock into a saucepan and add the chicken or pork. Bring to a simmer and cook, covered, for 10 minutes. Add the mushrooms, radish, carrot, sweet potato and salsify or scorzonera, and cook until the vegetables are tender, about 15 minutes. Mix the bean pastes until smooth with a little soup stock, then stir into the soup and heat through without letting the mixture boil. Pour the soup into 4 soup bowls distributing the solids among them. Sprinkle with the spring onion and serve with the seven-flavour spice on the table.

Starters, appetizers, hors d'oeuvre, whatever they are called, are very versatile dishes as they can be served to accompany pre-lunch or pre-dinner drinks, as part of a meal, or as picnic food. These small dishes can often be prepared ahead of time and are usually easy to make with few hard-to-find ingredients. They provide an admirable chance to experiment with Japanese food as they can be served as the prelude to a Western meal. Their presentation can also demonstrate the Japanese attitude to the seasons, which depends not just on the choice of seasonal foods but on presenting the foods in a setting appropriate to the time of year, a frosty-looking crystal plate for a summer hors d'oeuvre for example.

When the starters are served as picnic food, they are called *bento* and packed into *bento* boxes, often lacquered and of great beauty, perhaps cherished family antiques, though everyday ones are often made of plastic. *Bento* are served at room temperature, and without sauces. When served as starters or to accompany drinks, they are called *zenzai* and may be served either hot or at room temperature, and accompanied by sauces.

Meat, poultry, seafood and vegetables are all used and are traditionally served with *sake*, though nowadays many Western drinks are considered appropriate.

STARTERS AND ACCOMPANIMENTS

SKEWERED CHICKEN

TORINIKU NO KUSHIAGE

SERVES 4
**300 g (10 oz) skinned and boned
chicken breast
4 large spring onions, trimmed, using
only white part
Salt
Plain flour
1 large egg
Vegetable oil
Dipping sauces**

Cut the chicken breast into 24 slices, about 2.5 cm (1 in) long. Put into a bowl and sprinkle with salted flour to coat lightly. Cut each of the spring onions into 4 slices as nearly as possible 2.5 cm (1 in) long. Put into a bowl and sprinkle with salted flour to coat lightly. On each of 8 bamboo skewers, thread 3 pieces of chicken and 2 pieces of spring onion. Set aside.

Break the egg into a bowl and stir with chopsticks until well-blended but not foamy. Stir in 125 ml (4 fl oz) water, then sift in 75 g (3 oz) flour, stirring with chopsticks to mix to a light batter.

Heat 5 to 7 cm (2 to 3 in) oil in a *tempura* pan or a heavy frying-pan and heat the oil until bubbles form on wooden chopsticks stirred in the oil, or to 180°C (350°F) on a frying thermometer. Dip the skewers in the batter, coating the chicken and spring onions thoroughly, then drop into the oil. Cook for 4 or 5 minutes, turning once, until the batter is very lightly browned. Lift out and drain on the rack of the *tempura* pan, or on paper towels.

Arrange 2 skewers on each of 4 plates and serve with Japanese pepper (*kona sansho*) mixed with a little salt in a small bowl, a little Japanese or English dry mustard mixed with soy sauce in a small bowl, and citrus vinegar (*ponzu*) as dipping sauces. Eat by hand holding the end of the skewer.

GRILLED CHICKEN LIVERS

TORIKIMO NO KUSHIYAKI

SERVES 4
**300 g (10 oz) chicken livers
4 large spring onions, trimmed, using
only white part
3 tablespoons soy sauce
2 tablespoons *mirin*
1 tablespoon *sake*
2 teaspoons sugar
Japanese pepper (*kona sansho*)**

Rinse the chicken livers and pat them dry with paper towels, and cut them in half. Cut the spring onions into 4 slices each. Thread the liver and spring onions alternately onto eight 12 cm (5 in) skewers. Set aside.

Combine the soy sauce, *mirin*, *sake* and sugar in a small saucepan, stir and bring to a boil. Remove from the heat and set aside to use as a glazing sauce.

Heat a grill and cook the chicken livers over or under high heat for 1 minute on each side. Spoon or brush the glazing sauce over the livers and grill for ½ minute longer. Repeat until the sauce is used up. Sprinkle the skewers with Japanese pepper and arrange 2 skewers to a plate. Slide the livers and spring onion slices off the skewers and eat with chopsticks.

BEEF WITH GINGER

GYUNIKU NO TSUKUDANI

This is a great favourite for picnic boxes. It can also be served as a main dish.

SERVES 4
**300 g (10 oz) lean beef (rump, topside or chuck)
in one piece
5 cm (2 in) piece fresh ginger root, peeled and
thinly sliced
75 ml (3 fl oz) water
3 tablespoons soy sauce
2 tablespoons *mirin*
2 tablespoons *sake*
1 teaspoon sugar
¼ teaspoon MSG**

Using a very sharp knife, cut the beef into thin slices, then chop it coarsely.

Combine the rest of the ingredients in a medium-sized saucepan and bring to a simmer over moderate heat. Simmer for 2 to 3 minutes to blend the flavours. Add the beef and continue to cook, uncovered, over low heat until the liquid has evaporated and the beef is tender, about 15 minutes. The meat should be quite moist, not dried out.

Serve at room temperature or very lightly chilled on small plates or dishes.

PRAWN SUSHI

EBI NO KIMI-ZUSHI

Instead of the usual vinegared rice, scrambled eggs flavoured with vinegar are used to make the base for cooked, marinated prawns.

MAKES 6 PIECES
**6 large, raw, unshelled prawns, heads removed
50 ml (2 fl oz) rice vinegar, plus 1 tablespoon
1½ tablespoons sugar
½ teaspoon salt
3 large eggs
1 egg yolk
⅛ teaspoon MSG**

Shell the prawns and devein them (that is, remove the intestinal vein with a toothpick) leaving the tail and last segment of the shell intact. Insert toothpicks along the inside curves from the tail end to straighten the prawns. Drop them into a saucepan of briskly boiling water and cook just until they are pink, about 2 minutes. Drain, remove the toothpicks and cut the prawns along the undersides three-quarters of the way through. Open them out and flatten them lightly with the flat blade of a large knife. In a bowl, mix the 50 ml (2 fl oz) rice vinegar with 1 tablespoon of the sugar and ¼ teaspoon of the salt. Add the prawns and leave to marinate for 1 hour. Drain and set aside.

In a small saucepan, combine the eggs, egg yolk, tablespoon of vinegar, ½ tablespoon of sugar, ¼ teaspoon salt and ⅛ teaspoon MSG. Stir to mix with chopsticks, then cook, stirring constantly, over moderate heat until the egg is set but not hard. Remove from the heat and push through a fine sieve into a bowl, or process in a blender or food processor for 3 or 4 seconds, or until very light. Divide the egg into 6 equal pieces and squeeze each gently to form an oval patty. Arrange the prawns on the egg patties, cut side down. Arrange on a plate in a radiating pattern.

BEAN CURD WITH TWO TOPPINGS

DENGAKU

Bean curd, topped with red or white bean paste, makes a delicately flavoured accompaniment to drinks. In Japan the white bean paste would be garnished with a leaf of the Japanese pepper plant (*sansho*) for a very pretty effect. For an even more delicate dish, use silky bean curd (*kinugoshi tofu*) instead of ordinary (cotton) bean curd (*momen tofu*). Both are popular cold weather snacks.

SERVES 4 or 8

**2 cakes bean curd (*momen tofu*) each weighing
about 250 g (8 oz)
3 tablespoons white *miso* (bean paste)
3 tablespoons sugar
2½ tablespoons *mirin*
1 tablespoon *sake*
3 tablespoons red *miso* (bean paste)
Poppy seeds**

Rinse the bean curd cakes in cold water, then wrap in a kitchen towel. Place on a flat surface and cover with a chopping board or a plate and leave for 20 to 30 minutes to press out excess moisture. Unwrap and cut each bean curd cake into 4 lengthways slices then in half crossways, making 16 pieces. Transfer the bean curd to a shallow bowl and put into a steamer over boiling water. Cover, turn heat to low and steam for 10 minutes.

In a small saucepan over very low heat, mix together the white bean paste, 2 tablespoons of the sugar, 1 tablespoon of the *mirin* and ½ tablespoon of the *sake*. Stir until the mixture is smooth and heated through but do not let it boil. Set aside.

In another small saucepan over very low heat, mix together the red bean paste, the remaining tablespoon of sugar, 1½ tablespoons *mirin*, and ½ tablespoon of *sake*. Stir until the mixture is smooth and heated through but do not let it boil. Set aside.

Remove the bean curd pieces from the steamer and run bamboo skewers lengthways through them, 2 to a skewer. Spread half the skewered tofu with the red *miso* mixture, the other half with the white. Sprinkle the red with poppy seeds. Place 1 skewer with 1 red and 1 white *miso*-topped piece of bean curd on each of 8 plates. Eat from the skewers. Serves 8. For heartier appetites double the servings for 4.

The prepared tofu may be run under a moderately hot grill for 3 to 4 minutes and served hot. The tofu pieces may be deep fried and then spread with topping, or baked in a 190°C (370°F), gas mark 5 oven for 10 minutes.

JELLIED FISH AND VEGETABLE LOAF

SHIROMIZAKANA NO KANTEN-YOSE

This is a popular summer dish and looks very attractive served on small glass plates. It can be made ahead of time and refrigerated. Agar-agar (*kanten*) can be bought in bar form, or in flakes, powder or strands.

SERVES 6

7 g (¼ oz) bar agar-agar (*kanten*)
or **3 tablespoons flakes**
475 ml (16 fl oz) first soup stock
2 dried jelly mushrooms (*kikurage*)
**2.5 cm (1 in) slice thick end of carrot, scraped
and cut into julienne strips**
4 medium-sized whole raw green beans
250 g (8 oz) sole, flounder or other white fish
1 tablespoon soy sauce
2 tablespoons *mirin*
½ teaspoon salt
⅛ teaspoon MSG

If using bar agar-agar, rinse in cold water, squeeze dry and shred with the fingers into a medium-sized saucepan. Pour in the soup stock and let it stand for at least 1 hour. If using flakes, simply add to the soup stock, stir and let stand for 1 hour.

Put the mushrooms into a bowl with warm water to cover and soak for 15 minutes. Drain and slice thinly. Drop the carrot into boiling water and cook for 4 minutes. Drain and set aside. Trim the beans and drop into boiling water and cook for 4 minutes. Drain and add to the mushrooms and carrot. Cut the fish into diagonal strips about 1 cm (½ in) wide. Set aside.

Simmer the soaked agar-agar and stock over moderate heat, stirring frequently, until it has dissolved, about 3 minutes. Stir in the soy sauce, *mirin*, salt, MSG and fish. Cook for 2 to 3 minutes longer, skimming if necessary. Remove from the heat and add the reserved mushrooms, carrot and beans. Set the pan in a bowl of cold water for a minute or two to cool it slightly. Have ready a loaf pan about 10 × 15 cm (4 × 6 in) rinsed in cold water, and pour in the contents of the saucepan. Put in a cool place, or in the refrigerator, to set. To serve, unmould and cut into 1 cm (½ in) slices.

VARIATION: Use chicken breast or shrimps or prawns instead of fish. If the shellfish is frozen, thaw it thoroughly and add it to the agar-agar mixture with the vegetables. Large prawns can be cut into 1 cm (½ in) pieces.

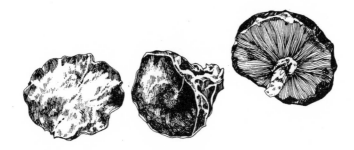

MUSTARD-STUFFED LOTUS ROOT

KARASHI RENKON

Fresh lotus roots may be hard to find in local markets but the tinned lotus root is a very good substitute and can be found in Japanese and Chinese shops. The root has a pattern of holes running its length which makes it easy to stuff.

SERVES 4

1 medium-sized lotus root (*renkon*), about 18 cm (7 in)
2 teaspoons rice vinegar
375 ml (13 fl oz) second soup stock
¼ teaspoon soy sauce
¼ teaspoon salt
2 teaspoons *mirin*
3 tablespoons dry Japanese or English mustard
3 tablespoons white *miso* (bean paste)
1 teaspoon sugar
1 large egg yolk plus 1 small egg
⅛ teaspoon MSG
50 g (2 oz) plain flour
Vegetable oil

Peel the lotus root and drop it into a saucepan of briskly boiling water and the vinegar. Simmer for 5 minutes. Drain. In the saucepan, combine the soup stock, soy sauce, salt and *mirin*. Add the lotus root and simmer, uncovered, for 5 minutes, or until the lotus root is tender. There should be enough liquid to cover the root. Lift out onto a plate and allow to cool.

In a mediuum-sized bowl, mix the mustard to a thick paste with 2 to 3 tablespoons hot water. Add the bean paste, sugar, egg yolk and MSG and mix until smooth. Using chopsticks and fingers, stuff the mustard mixture into the holes that run the length of the vegetable in a flower pattern.

Break the egg into a small bowl and stir with chopsticks to mix. Stir in 1 tablespoon of cold water, then add the flour, mixing lightly with the chopsticks to a batter. Coat the lotus root with the batter.

In a *tempura* pan or a heavy frying-pan, heat enough oil to cover the lotus root until bubbles form on chopsticks stirred in the oil, or to 180°C (350°F) on a frying thermometer. Put the batter-coated lotus root into the oil and fry for about 5 minutes, turning 2 or 3 times, until it is lightly coloured. Lift out, drain on paper towels and cut into 1 cm (½ in) slices. Arrange the slices on 4 small plates.

VARIATION: For Stuffed Mushrooms (*Karashi Shiitake*), stuff medium-sized mushrooms with the mustard mixture, coat with batter and deep-fry for 2 or 3 minutes, or until the batter is golden.

ASPARAGUS WITH MALTED BEAN PASTE

ASPARAGUS NO MOROMIZOE

This is a springtime dish looked forward to when fresh asparagus comes into the market. *Moromi miso*, malted bean paste sold ready prepared in Japanese markets, adds a delicious flavour to the vegetable.

SERVES 4
12 medium-sized stalks green asparagus
Salt
1 tablespoon light soy sauce (*usukuchi shoyu*)
2 tablespoons malted bean paste (*moromi miso*)

Rinse the asparagus stalks in cold water and cut off the hard ends. Fill a saucepan large enough to hold the asparagus comfortably with salted water. Bring to a boil, add the asparagus and cook over fairly high heat, uncovered, for 8 minutes, or until tender. Be careful not to overcook the asparagus; it should be slightly crisp to the bite. Lift out onto a *zaru* (bamboo plate or strainer) or onto a chopping board, and fan vigorously for 2 to 3 minutes to cool. This keeps the asparagus an attractive bright green in colour. Lowering the asparagus briefly into a bowl of cold water, then lifting it out to drain, will achieve the same result. Pour the soy sauce over the asparagus and arrange on 4 platters or plates.

Divide the bean paste among the platters, placing ½ tablespoon on top of the stalk in the centre. To eat, spread the bean paste with chopsticks over the whole length of the stalks.

VARIATION: For *Saya-ingen No Moromizoe*, Green Beans with Malted Bean Paste, cook 250 g (8 oz) whole green beans, trimmed, in boiling salted water, uncovered, for 6 minutes. Drain and refresh quickly in cold water, then arrange in bundles on 4 plates and top with bean paste. SERVES 4.

DEEP-FRIED STUFFED MUSHROOMS

SHIITAKE NO TSUMEAGE

Fresh Japanese mushrooms are not at present widely available but local mushrooms make an excellent substitute.

SERVES 4
12 medium-sized mushrooms
125 g (4 oz) peeled and cleaned raw shrimp *or* prawns; *or* frozen, thoroughly defrosted
Salt
***Katakuriko* flour, *or* cornflour *or* arrowroot**
25 g (1 oz) plain flour
125 ml (4 fl oz) water
Vegetable oil
75 ml (3 fl oz) second soup stock
2 tablespoons *mirin*
3 tablespoons soy sauce
50 g (2 oz) grated white radish (*daikon*)

Quickly rinse the mushrooms, pat dry, and remove the stems. Chop the shrimp or prawns to a paste with the back of a knife or reduce to a purée in a blender or food processor. Season to taste with salt. Sprinkle the inside of the mushrooms with *katakuriko*, cornflour or arrowroot and shake out to remove the excess. Stuff with the shrimp or prawn mixture.

In a bowl, combine the flour with 20 g (¾ oz) of the *katakuriko* flour, or cornflour or arrowroot. Using chopsticks, stir in 125 ml (4 fl oz) water, mixing lightly to a batter.

Heat 5 to 7 cm (2 to 3 in) oil in a *tempura* pan or a heavy frying-pan and heat the oil until bubbles form on wooden chopsticks stirred in the oil, or to 180°C (350°F) on a frying thermometer. Coat the mushrooms with the batter and fry, a few at a time, until lightly golden, about 2 minutes, turning them once or twice. Drain on the rack of the *tempura* pan or on paper towels.

In a small saucepan, combine the soup stock, *mirin* and soy sauce. Bring to a boil over moderate heat, and pour into a small bowl. Lightly squeeze out the grated radish. Make a mound of the radish and put it on to a platter with the mushrooms. To eat, dip the mushrooms into the sauce and eat with the radish.

NOODLE-COATED PRAWNS

EBI NO SHIBAAGE

This is a very glamorous-looking appetizer and quite easy to make with the prawns looking like little bundles of twigs. There is a more elaborate version, *Igaguri* (Noodle-coated Prawns with a Chestnut Stuffing), in which the appetizer looks like a wild chestnut. This tastes so good it is worth the rather finicky effort required.

SERVES 4
**4 medium-sized fresh prawns, unpeeled, heads removed
Salt
1 teaspoon *sake*
Cornflour
1 large egg yolk, lightly beaten
25 g (1 oz) thin wheat noodles (*somen*)
4 strips, 1 × 10 cm (½ × 4 in), dried laver seaweed (*nori*)
Vegetable oil**

Devein the prawns and peel, leaving the tails on. Cut a small lengthways slit at the head end of the prawn on the underside so it can be straightened out. Sprinkle with a little salt and the *sake*. Dip in cornflour and shake to remove the excess. Dip into the egg yolk, coating thoroughly. Break the noodles into pieces the same length as the prawns and roll each prawn in the pieces lengthways, then put a strip of seaweed round each bundle and stick it in place with a little egg yolk.

Pour about 7 cm (3 in) oil into a *tempura* pan or heavy frying-pan and heat the oil until bubbles form on wooden chopsticks stirred in the oil, or to 180°C (350°F) on a frying thermometer. Using tongs, drop the shrimp bundles into the hot oil and cook for about 2 minutes, or until the noodles are golden. Drain on the rack of the *tempura* pan or on paper towels. Serve on small plates.

If frozen prawns are used, defrost thoroughly before preparing.

VARIATION: For Noodle-coated Prawns with a Chestnut Stuffing (*Igaguri*), simmer 4 whole cooked chestnuts with 1 tablespoon sugar in water to cover for 15 minutes. Drain and set aside. In a food processor or blender combine 250 g (8 oz) peeled prawns (if frozen thoroughly defrosted) with 1 large egg white, 1 tablespoon plain flour, ¼ teaspoon salt (or to taste), and 1 teaspoon *mirin*. Process until the mixture is light and smooth. Mould the prawn mixture round the chestnuts then roll them in 25 g (1 oz) thin wheat noodles (*somen*) broken into 2.5 cm (1 in) pieces. The noodles should stick out like thorns. Fry as for Noodle-coated Prawns. SERVES 4.

GRILLED SCALLOPS WITH JAPANESE PEPPER

TAIRAGAI NO SANSHO YAKI

SERVES 4
4 large scallops, without roe
2 tablespoons soy sauce
1 teaspoon *mirin*
1½ tablespoons *sake*
Japanese pepper (*kona sansho*)

Rinse the scallops in cold water and pat them dry with paper towels. Halve them horizontally. Combine the soy sauce, *mirin* and *sake* in a small saucepan, bring to a simmer over moderate heat to blend the flavours. Remove from the heat and cool. Add the scallops and marinate for 5 minutes. Lift out and pat dry with paper towels. Thread onto a skewer.

Grill the scallops over or under fairly high heat, about 12 cm (5 in) from the heat, basting frequently with the soy mixture, and using a pastry brush. Grill the scallops for about 4 minutes, turning several times. Put the cooked scallops into 4 small bowls and sprinkle with Japanese pepper, or serve on a large platter for guests to help themselves with chopsticks.

Nothing is more important in Japanese cuisine than rice. It is eaten at any meal — morning, noon and night — as well as in between. *Gohan*, which translates as 'honourable food', means both a meal and cooked rice. The principal grain crop in Japan, rice is planted in spring and harvested from the end of summer into autumn. There is no green as vivid as the green of paddies (rice fields) in early summer when the young shoots form rippling carpets of vegetation.

It is a short-grain rice and is not cooked with every grain separate since it would be impossible to eat with chopsticks. It is closer to Chinese rice in consistency, not sticky but holding together nicely. Japanese shops and supermarkets in Britain and elsewhere sell a type of Japanese rice that is grown in California and can be cooked very successfully if the precise instructions for cooking are followed faithfully. *Shinmai* or new rice, the first of the crop marketed in late summer, is highly esteemed. It is cooked in the same way but needs less water and a shorter cooking time.

Rice that has been kept on a kitchen shelf for some time may even need soaking in cold water for half an hour before cooking. With practice, perfect rice is easy to attain. An essential is a straight-sided, fairly heavy, medium-sized saucepan with a very tight-fitting lid. A Japanese electric rice cooker takes the guesswork out of cooking rice and is a sound investment. It keeps rice warm for hours, making it possible to cook in advance.

RICE (GOHAN) AND SUSHI

PLAIN BOILED RICE

GOHAN

SERVES 4
275 g (9 oz) short-grain rice
550 ml (18 fl oz) water

Wash the rice very thoroughly in several changes of cold water, stirring with the fingers, until the water is clear. Drain in a sieve for 30 minutes unless a recipe specifies a longer time. Put the rice into a medium-sized, heavy saucepan with a tightly fitting lid and pour in the water. Cover and bring to a boil over high heat, reduce the heat to moderate and cook for 5 minutes longer, then reduce it to very low and cook for 15 minutes. Turn the heat up to high for 10 seconds, then let the rice stand, off the heat, for 10 minutes. When ready to use, stir the rice with a wooden spatula (*shamoji*) and serve. If the rice is not to be served immediately, cover it with a kitchen towel, then the saucepan lid, until ready to use. It will keep warm for 15 to 20 minutes. Serve in individual bowls.

To SERVE 6, use 375 g (12 oz) rice to 725 ml (24 fl oz) water. To SERVE 3, use 175 g (6 oz) rice to 350 ml (12 fl oz) water.

To reheat leftover rice, put the rice into a steamer over simmering water, cover and steam for 5 minutes. An improvised steamer can be made by putting a colander in a large heavy pot with about 5 cm (2 in) water, covering the pot tightly and setting in on moderate heat.

RICE WITH GREEN PEAS

ENDO GOHAN

This is a spring dish and a very pretty one, the green of the peas in attractive contrast to the white rice.

SERVES 6
375 g (12 oz) short-grain rice
40 g (1¹/₂ oz) sweet (sticky or glutinous) rice
½ teaspoon salt, or to taste
2 teaspoons *mirin, or* 1 tablespoon *sake*
125 g (4 oz) freshly shelled green peas,
or **frozen, thoroughly thawed**

Mix the rice and sweet rice together and wash thoroughly in several changes of cold water until the water is clear. Drain in a sieve for at least 1 hour. Put the rice into a medium-sized, heavy saucepan with a tightly fitting lid, pour in 600 ml (1 pint) water, the salt, *mirin* or *sake*, and the peas. Stir to mix, cover and bring to a boil over moderate heat. Cook for 5 minutes, then reduce the heat to very low and cook for 15 minutes longer. Turn the heat to high for 10 seconds, then let the rice stand, off the heat, for 10 minutes. Stir with a wooden spatula (*shamoji*) to mix the peas evenly in the rice, and serve in individual bowls as the rice course.

RICE WITH BAMBOO SHOOTS

TAKENOKO GOHAN

This is a spring dish when fresh bamboo shoots are in season. Fortunately, tinned bamboo shoots, an admirable substitute, are available all year making it possible to enjoy this delicious and healthy luncheon dish at any season.

SERVES 4
375 g (12 oz) short-grain rice
125 g (4 oz) boned and skinned chicken breast
250 g (8 oz) tinned whole bamboo shoots
1½ pieces fried bean curd (*aburaage*)
2 tablespoons *sake*
3 tablespoons soy sauce
10 cm (4 in) square kelp seaweed (*kombu*)
Small sheet dried laver seaweed (*nori*) (optional)

Thoroughly wash the rice and let it drain in a sieve for 1 hour.

Chop the chicken breast coarsely and put it into a bowl. Cut the bamboo shoots into julienne strips, about 0.5 × 2 cm (¼ × ¾ in) and add to the bowl. Rinse the bean curd in hot water, and cut it into julienne strips the same size as the bamboo shoots, and add to the bowl. Pour the *sake* and soy sauce over the chicken mixture and let it stand for about 15 minutes, stirring 2 or 3 times.

In a saucepan, combine the rice and chicken mixture. Clean the seaweed with a damp cloth and bury it in the rice. Pour in 500 ml (17 fl oz) cold water. Cover and bring to a boil over high heat. Just before the water boils, remove the seaweed and reserve it to make second soup stock. Lower the heat to moderate and cook the rice for 5 minutes longer, then reduce the heat to very low and cook for 15 minutes. Turn the heat high for 10 seconds and let the rice stand, off the heat, for 10 minutes. Toast the laver seaweed over a gas flame or electric burner for a few seconds and crush in a piece of cheesecloth, if using.

Serve the rice mixture in large bowls (*donburi*) and garnish with the crushed seaweed.

RICE WITH CHESTNUTS

KURI GOHAN

This is another of the mixed rice dishes that makes a good light luncheon and is traditionally served in a *donburi*, a large china bowl. Sweet rice, sometimes called sticky or glutinous rice, is often added to this recipe. It is a matter of taste.

SERVES 4
475 g (15 oz) short-grain rice
12 large, or 16 medium-sized, chestnuts, peeled, *or* tinned whole chestnuts
10 cm (4 in) square kelp seaweed (*kombu*)
725 ml (24 fl oz) water
1 tablespoon *sake*
2 tablespoons *mirin*
½ teaspoon salt, or to taste
¼ teaspoon black sesame seeds, toasted

Thoroughly wash the rice and drain in a sieve for 1 hour. If using sweet rice (*mochigome*) substitute 40 g (1½ oz) of short-grain rice for the same amount of sweet rice. Mix the two lots of rice together, wash and drain as for short-grain rice.

Cut the chestnuts into 2 or 3 pieces according to size. Put the rice into a saucepan with the kelp, cleaned with a damp cloth and cut on one side into a 1 cm (½ in) fringe. Bury the kelp in the rice. Add the water, *sake*, *mirin* and salt, cover and bring to just under a boil over high heat. Remove the kelp and reserve it for making second soup stock. Cook the rice over moderate heat for 5 minutes, then reduce the heat to very low and cook for 15 minutes longer. Turn the heat to high for 10 seconds, and then let the rice stand, off the heat, for 10 minutes. Mix lightly with a wooden spatula (*shamoji*) and serve in large bowls. Top with the toasted sesame seeds.

CHICKEN AND EGGS WITH RICE

OYAKO DONBURI

The literal translation of this is 'parents and children rice', a charming culinary joke referring to the garnishes on the rice which are chicken and egg. A companion dish, *Gyutama Donburi* ('Strangers and Children') see page 45, is made with beef, thinly sliced and cut into 1 cm (½ in) strips. The *donburi* of the title is a large, china bowl frequently used for dishes of this type where rice is served with a topping and a sauce. It is marvellous for a quick lunch, or as an impromptu dish for unexpected guests. Any leftovers of fish, meat or vegetable can be used.

SERVES 4
275 g (9 oz) short-grain rice
175 g (6 oz) skinned and boned chicken breast
4 dried Japanese mushrooms (*shiitake*)
2 large spring onions, trimmed, using white and green parts, *or* ½ sheet dried laver seaweed (*nori*)
350 ml (12 fl oz) second soup stock
3 tablespoons soy sauce
3 tablespoons *mirin*
4 large eggs

Cook the rice according to the recipe for Plain Boiled Rice (*Gohan*), page 40.

Cut the chicken breast diagonally into thin slices. Soak the mushrooms in warm water for 30 minutes. Drain, remove the stems, squeeze out lightly and cut into 1 cm (½ in) slices. Cut the spring onions into very fine 2.5 cm (1 in) strips.

In a bowl, combine the soup stock, soy sauce and *mirin*, stirring to mix. Pour ¼ of the stock into a small frying-pan. Add ¼ of the chicken and 1 mushroom and simmer for 2 or 3 minutes. Meanwhile break 1 egg into a bowl and stir with chopsticks until it is thoroughly blended but not foamy. Pour the egg into the frying-pan in a thin, slow stream to cover the surface of the pan. Chopsticks, held about 5 cm (2 in) apart at the front of the bowl, can be used to slow the flow of the egg if necessary. Cook until the egg is set, about 30 seconds. Slide the contents of the pan into a deep saucer or shallow bowl and set aside. Repeat with the remaining ingredients, using one quarter each time.

Stir the cooked rice with a wooden spatula (*shamoji*) and divide it among 4 large bowls (*donburi*). Top each bowl with the chicken and egg mixture. Sprinkle with the chopped spring onions. Instead of spring onions, ½ sheet *nori* seaweed, toasted for a few seconds over an open flame then crumbled, can be used.

If preferred, the rice can be served in the bowls, then the stock, chicken and eggs can be cooked all together in a larger frying-pan instead of in 4 lots, and divided among the bowls.

RICE WITH EGGS, CHICKEN AND MANGETOUT

SOBORO GOHAN

This is a very attractive dish for a picnic. The *soboro* in the title refers to the technique of cooking the eggs until they are in tiny curds. Green beans, cut into 1 cm (½ in) diagonal slices, may be used instead of the mangetout, and the amount of vegetable may be doubled, in which case the amount of soup stock should be proportionately increased.

SERVES 4
275 g (9 oz) short-grain rice
3 tablespoons soy sauce
Salt
4 large eggs
2 teaspoons sugar
3 tablespoons *mirin*
2.5 cm (1 in) piece peeled ginger root
1 tablespoon *sake*
250 g (8 oz) skinned and boned chicken breast or thigh
12 mangetout
50 ml (2 fl oz) second soup stock

Cook the rice according to the recipe for Plain Boiled Rice (*Gohan*), page 40, adding 1 tablespoon of the soy sauce and ½ teaspoon salt.

While the rice is cooking, break the eggs into a bowl and stir with chopsticks until they are well-blended but not foamy. Stir in ¼ teaspoon of salt, or to taste, 1 teaspoon of the sugar and 1 tablespoon of the *mirin*. Have 5 or 6 chopsticks ready. Pour the egg mixture into a small, fairly shallow saucepan and cook over moderate heat. As soon as the eggs begin to set on the bottom of the pan, remove from the heat and stir quickly, about 4 times, round the pan with the bunch of chopsticks held in one hand. Return the saucepan to the heat for about 30 seconds, and repeat the process up to about 10 times until the eggs are *soboro*, that is in tiny curds. Scrape the eggs out of the saucepan into a bowl and set aside. Rinse out and dry the saucepan.

Grate the ginger root, gather it together and squeeze out the juice until there is 1 teaspoon. Pour the ginger juice with the remaining 2 tablespoons of soy sauce, 2 tablespoons of *mirin* and the *sake* into the saucepan. Chop the chicken coarsely and grind it in a food mill or food processor, or chop it very finely by hand. Divide the chicken into 4 lots and add them, one at a time, to the saucepan. Cook over moderate heat, stirring frequently with chopsticks, until all the liquid has evaporated.

Drop the mangetout into boiling salted water and blanch for 1 minute. Drain. Add the soup stock, 1 teaspoon sugar and ¼ teaspoon salt to the saucepan. Add the mangetout and cook, uncovered, over moderately high heat until all the liquid has evaporated.

Turn the hot rice out into a large shallow bowl or platter and gently pat the surface even. Spread half the surface with the eggs, the other half with the chicken. Arrange the mangetout in a row down the centre of the bowl or platter. Serve in bowls.

VARIATION: For Three-Colour *Soboro* (*Sanshoku Soboro*), drop 125 g (4 oz) peeled and deveined prawns into boiling salted water and cook for 2 minutes. If using frozen prawns, thoroughly defrost but do not cook further. Reduce the prawns to a purée in a food processor or blender, or grind until smooth in a Japanese mortar, a *suribachi*. Add 2 teaspoons *sake*, 1 teaspoon each *mirin* and sugar, ¼ teaspoon salt and ⅛ teaspoon soy sauce. Mix together, then put into the top of a double boiler over simmering water and cook, stirring, until all the liquid has evaporated.

Put this prawn *soboro* over ⅓ of the rice, the chicken over another ⅓ and the egg over the final ⅓. Make a line of mangetout down the side of the dish. Garnish with red or pink pickled ginger. SERVES 4.

CHICKEN-LOOKING-LIKE-PHEASANT WITH RICE

TORINIKU NO KIJAYAKI DONBURI

This is another of the rice dishes that are so good for lunch or supper. This one has the sort of highly poetic name the Japanese enjoy and the chicken meat does indeed look like pheasant.

SERVES 4
**275 g (9 oz) short-grain rice
1 whole large chicken breast (two halves), skinned and boned
3 tablespoons *sake*
5 tablespoons soy sauce
⅛ teaspoon MSG
4 large spring onions, trimmed, using white and green parts
Japanese pepper (*kona sansho*)**

Cook the rice according to the recipe for Plain Boiled Rice (*Gohan*), page 40.

Cut the chicken into thin diagonal slices, and put it into a bowl with 2 tablespoons of the *sake*, 3 tablespoons of the soy sauce, and the MSG, mixing lightly. Marinate for 15 minutes, then lift out and grill for ½ minute on each side. Repeat the process 2 or 3 times, dipping the chicken slices in the marinade, until the chicken is lightly browned and looking like pheasant. Set aside. Reserve any marinade.

Halve the spring onions crossways, and grill until browned, turning frequently. Dip in the marinade and cut into 2.5 cm (1 in) pieces. Set aside with the chicken.

Divide the cooked hot rice among 4 large china bowls (*donburi*) and top with the chicken and spring onions. Pour any leftover marinade into a small saucepan with the remaining *sake* and soy sauce. Heat and pour over the chicken and rice.

RICE WITH BEEF

GYUDON

The beef topping makes this a pleasantly robust dish for lunch or supper.

SERVES 4
**375 g (12 oz) short-grain rice
250 g (8 oz) lean beef such as flank or skirt steak
175 g (6 oz) devil's-tongue noodles (*shirataki*)
4 large spring onions, trimmed, using white and green parts
1 grilled bean curd (*yakidofu*)
250 ml (8 fl oz) second soup stock
4 tablespoons soy sauce
4 tablespoons *mirin*
⅛ teaspoon MSG**

Cook the rice according to the recipe for Plain Boiled rice (*Gohan*), page 40.

Cut the beef crossways into thin slices. Drop the noodles into briskly boiling water for 1 minute, drain and cut into 4 cm (1½ in) pieces. Slice the spring onions diagonally. Halve the bean curd and cut into 1 cm (½ in) slices. In a saucepan, combine the soup stock, soy sauce, *mirin*, and MSG. Bring to a simmer and add the beef, noodles, spring onions and bean curd, and simmer over moderate heat for 3 minutes, skimming if necessary.

Stir the cooked rice with a wooden spatula (*shamoji*) and divide among 4 large bowls. Top with the beef mixture.

RICE WITH BEEF AND EGGS

GYUTAMA DONBURI

This is the companion dish of *Oyako Donburi* (Chicken and Eggs with Rice, literally 'parents and children'), page 42, and is the other half of the culinary joke as it translates into 'strangers and children'. An ideal lunch dish.

SERVES 4
275 g (9 oz) short-grain rice
250 g (8 oz) lean beef such as flank
or skirt steak
4 dried Japanese mushrooms (*shiitake*)
12 thin slices Japanese fish sausage (*kamaboko*)
10 sprigs trefoil (*mitsuba*), or ½ bunch watercress,
***or* equivalent amount of spinach**
3 tablespoons soy sauce
3 tablespoons *mirin*
7 (¼ oz) dried bonito flakes (*hana-katsuo*)
4 large eggs

Cook the rice according to the recipe for Plain Boiled Rice (*Gohan*), page 40.

Thinly slice the beef, then cut it into 1 cm (½ in) strips. Soak the mushrooms in warm water for 30 minutes. Drain, remove the stems, squeeze out lightly and cut into thin slices. If trefoil is available, stack the stems and cut across into 3 pieces. Trim the cress or spinach, if using, and cut crossways into 5 cm (2 in) pieces. Set these ingredients aside with the fish sausage.

In a saucepan, combine 350 ml (12 fl oz) water, soy sauce, *mirin* and dried bonito flakes. Bring to a simmer over moderate heat and simmer for 1 minute. Strain into a bowl through a sieve lined with dampened cheesecloth. Rinse out and dry the saucepan and return the strained stock to it. Bring to a simmer, add the fish sausage, beef and mushrooms and simmer for 3 minutes. Skim if necessary. Add the trefoil, or watercress or spinach.

Break the eggs into a bowl and stir with chopsticks until they are well-blended but not foamy. Have the liquid in the saucepan at just under a simmer. Holding a pair of chopsticks about 5 cm (2 in) apart at the front of the bowl to slow the flow of the eggs, pour the eggs in a thin stream to cover the whole surface of the saucepan. Cook until the eggs are set, about 30 seconds.

Stir the rice with a wooden spatula (*shamoji*) and divide it among 4 large bowls. Ladle the beef and egg mixture over the rice and pour in the soup. The topping can be divided into 4 and the eggs cooked separately. A small frying-pan is best for this.

RICE WITH DEEP-FRIED PRAWNS AND GREEN BEANS

TENDON

This could be described as *tempura* on rice. It makes a very splendid lunch or supper dish, both healthy and hearty. It invites improvisation. Fish or squid may be added, or chicken used instead of prawns. Any vegetable may be used instead of green beans, and dried Japanese mushrooms (*shiitake*) or fresh mushrooms make a welcome addition. It can be as hearty, or as elegant, as appetite dictates.

SERVES 4
275 g (9 oz) short-grain rice
1 small egg
25 g (1 oz) plain flour
8 very large prawns, unpeeled, heads removed
4 large or 8 small green beans
Vegetable oil
125 ml (4 fl oz) first soup stock
50 ml (2 fl oz) soy sauce
50 ml (2 fl oz) *mirin*
⅛ teaspoon MSG

Cook the rice according to the recipe for Plain Boiled Rice (*Gohan*), page 40.

Break the egg into a bowl and stir with chopsticks until it is well-blended but not foamy. Stir 2 tablespoons water into the egg. Sift the flour into the egg mixture, stirring lightly with chopsticks to mix to a batter. Set aside.

Peel and devein the prawns, leaving the last segment of the shell and the tail on. Make a small, shallow slit in the underside of the prawn at the head and bend the tails back slightly to straighten the prawn. Japanese cooks always cut the ends off the tails of prawns when using them for *tempura* as they say this part of the tail has water in it and will splutter in the hot oil, so cut off the ends of the tails. Cut the beans into 2 or 3 diagonal slices according to their size.

Heat 5 cm (2 in) vegetable oil in a *tempura* pan or a heavy frying-pan and heat the oil until bubbles form on wooden chopsticks stirred in the oil, or to 180°C (350°F) on a frying thermometer. Dip the prawns in the batter and fry for 2 minutes, turn and fry for 1 minute longer or until a light golden. Drain on the rack of the *tempura* pan or on paper towels. Make 4 bundles of the beans, dip in the batter and fry until the batter is golden. Lift out and drain.

Make a dipping (*tentsuyu*) sauce. Combine the soup stock, soy sauce, *mirin* and MSG in a small saucepan, stir to mix and heat through.

Divide the cooked hot rice among 4 large china bowls (*donburi*), top with the prawns and beans and pour the sauce over them.

RICE AND OYSTERS IN SOUP

KAKI-ZOSUI

Oysters make this into a luxury dish even though it uses leftover rice. It is soupy, but too solid to be a soup, and is one of the few Japanese dishes that is eaten with a spoon. In Japan it could be eaten for breakfast, lunch, dinner, or as an in-between snack.

SERVES 2 .

275 g (9 oz) leftover cooked rice
1 large spring onion, trimmed and using white and green parts
725 ml (24 fl oz) first soup stock
12 oysters, rinsed and drained
½ teaspoon salt, or to taste
1 teaspoon light soy sauce (*usukuchi shoyu*)

Spoon the cooked rice into a sieve and rinse quickly under cold running water. Leave to drain. Cut the spring onion into 2.5 cm (1 in) pieces crossways, then slice them finely lengthways. Put into a bowl of cold water to crisp for about 10 minutes, drain and pat dry in a kitchen towel.

Combine the rice and soup stock in a saucepan, bring to a simmer and cook, uncovered, for 3 minutes. Add the oysters, salt and light soy sauce and cook just long enough to plump the oysters, about 1 minute. Serve in a large china bowl (*donburi*) and eat with chopsticks and a soup spoon.

VARIATION 1: Rice and Oysters (*Kakimeshi*) is a less soupy version of the dish, using freshly made rice. Make 1 recipe of Plain Boiled Rice (*Gohan*), page 40; adding 2 tablespoons of *sake* and 1 tablespoon of light soy sauce (*usukuchi shoyu*) to the rice when cooking, and at the same time season to taste with salt, about ½ teaspoon. When the cooked rice is removed from the heat, add 2 dozen (24) shucked oysters, folding them gently into the rice with a wooden spatula (*shamoji*). Return the rice to the heat for 1 minute, then let it stand, covered, for 10 minutes before serving. Serve in large china bowls (*donburi*) and eat with chopsticks in the usual way. SERVES 4.

VARIATION 2: For an equally delicious, though less expensive, dish substitute scallops for the oysters. Use half the number of scallops as oysters. SERVES 2.

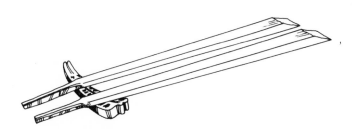

SUSHI

Sushi is one of the most attractive features of the Japanese kitchen. Based on subtly flavoured vinegared rice with a multitude of toppings which include sliced raw fish, shellfish, fish roe, omelette strips and vegetables, it is a great favourite as an accompaniment to drinks, as a first course, as a main course, for picnics and for parties. There are even small restaurants, *sushiya*, and bars devoted to *sushi*.

The vinegared rice is sometimes stuffed into little bags of fried bean curd; there is also pressed *sushi* with various toppings, *sushi* rolled in sheets of dried laver seaweed (*nori*) and sliced, and vinegared rice salad. Handmade *sushi* (*Nigiri-Zushi*), the *sushi* of the *sushiya*, is the most popular type with little patties of rice topped with slices of raw fish on which a little Japanese green horseradish (*wasabi*) has been spread. The patties are dipped in soy sauce and eaten by hand. Some are wrapped in dried laver seaweed (*nori*). A lacquered tray with an assortment of *nigiri-zushi* with the translucent white of sole, red of snapper, deeper and darker red of fresh tuna, the delicate pink of cooked prawns, and the black of *nori* wrapped round salmon 'caviar' (roe) make a lovely and very appetizing picture. The bite-size morsels are hard to resist and it is worth doing the comparatively small amount of work required for making *sushi*, and worthwhile finding a good source for really fresh fish. Japanese supermarkets sometimes have counters where *sushi* fish, ready sliced, can be bought. With a little planning it is perfectly possible to enjoy *sushi* at home. It has the added merit of being served at room temperature. The expertise of the makers of *sushi* in a restaurant or bar is very impressive and though the home cook cannot expect to equal their dexterity, a very creditable imitation can easily be achieved.

The vinegared rice is the key to successful *sushi*. It is essential to use rice vinegar, as any other type lacks its subtle and delicate flavour. It is also essential to use the right type of rice, Japanese short-grain, as long-grain rice will not hold together in a patty but will break apart into separate grains. The rice must be cooled quickly by fanning. Perhaps the most important rule in making *sushi* is to keep the hands moistened with vinegared water to prevent the rice from sticking to the fingers when pressing it into shape.

RICE WITH VINEGAR DRESSING

SUSHI

SERVES 4 to 8
375 g (12 oz) short-grain rice
7 cm (3 in) square kelp seaweed (kombu)
725 ml (24 fl oz) water
50 ml (2 fl oz) rice vinegar
1 tablespoon sugar
2 teaspoons salt
½ teaspoon MSG

Thoroughly wash the rice in several changes of water until the water runs clear, and drain in a sieve for 1 hour. Transfer the rice to a heavy saucepan with a tightly fitting lid. Wipe the seaweed with a damp cloth, then cut with scissors along one side into a 1 cm (½ in) fringe. Bury the seaweed in the rice, pour in the water, cover, and bring to a boil over high heat, removing the seaweed just before the water boils, or it will flavour the rice too strongly. Immediately reduce the heat to moderate and cook the rice for 5 minutes. Reduce the heat to very low and cook for 15 minutes. Turn the heat to high for 10 seconds, then let it stand, covered, for 10 minutes.

Combine the vinegar, sugar, salt and MSG in a small saucepan and heat through, stirring to mix. Turn the rice out into a large, shallow dish into which a little of the vinegar mixture has been poured. In Japan a *sushioke* (*bandai*), a large, round wooden dish, would be used. Pour the vinegar little by little over the rice, mixing it with a wooden spatula (*shamoji*) and fanning it vigorously to cool it quickly and to make it glisten. It is a good idea to have a helper to do the fanning.

Cover the rice with a cloth until ready to use. It can be left at room temperature for several hours if necessary.

HANDMADE SUSHI

NIGIRI-ZUSHI

This is the *sushi* of the *sushiya*, the small restaurants that specialize in the dish. The rice and fish may be prepared ahead of time as the rice can stand, covered, at room temperature for some hours. The sliced fish must be refrigerated and the dish assembled only at the last minute. The more guests to be served, the greater can be the variety of fish, but it is perfectly possible to settle for one or two kinds.

SERVES 4
as a main course,
SERVES 8 to 12
as an appetizer
375 g (12 oz) short-grain rice
500 g (1 lb) cleaned assorted fish and shellfish
using any of the following: sole, plaice, striped
bass, sea bass, red snapper, bream, abalone,
squid, octopus, clams, sea urchins, scallops and
salmon caviar (roe)
6 medium-sized uncooked prawns
Salt
1 teaspoon rice vinegar
1 tablespoon Japanese green horseradish (*wasabi*)
Soy sauce

Cook the rice and season it with vinegar according to the recipe for Rice with Vinegar Dressing (*Sushi*), page 48.

Fillet the fish, then cut it into 5 mm (¼ in) diagonal slices about 5 × 2.5 cm (2 × 1 in). 375 g (12 oz) should give about 24 slices. Abalone, squid, and octopus can be eaten raw if they are very fresh. If preferred, the slices can be cooked for about 1 minute in boiling water. Scallops need only to be thinly sliced and clams can be butterflied, that is cut ¾ way through lengthways and opened out. Remove the intestinal vein from the prawns with a toothpick but do not peel the prawns. Skewer the prawns lengthways on the underside with toothpicks to stop them curling when cooked. Drop them into briskly boiling salted water with the vinegar, and cook only until they turn pink, about 1½ minutes. They should be undercooked. Drain, remove the toothpicks and peel the prawns. Cut along the underside ¾ way through, then open and lightly flatten the prawns. Mix the green horseradish powder to a paste with a little water in a bowl and set aside.

Wet the hands in water to which a little rice vinegar has been added, and form about 2 tablespoons *sushi* rice into an oblong patty about 5 × 2.5 cm (2 × 1 in). Spread a little horseradish down the centre of a piece of fish and put the fish, horseradish side down, on top of the rice. Top patties of rice with the prawns but do not use any horseradish. If liked, make little cylindrical patties of rice, top with salmon roe and surround with a strip of dried laver seaweed (*nori*). Use a dab of horseradish to hold the seaweed in place. Arrange the *sushi* on a large platter and place it in the centre of the table.

Put chopsticks, a tiny bowl of soy sauce and a tiny bowl with some horseradish at each place setting. To eat, dip one end of the *sushi* in soy sauce, using either chopsticks or fingers. Add more horseradish if liked. *Sake* or green tea are traditional accompaniments but chilled dry white wine is an accepted alternative. A little pickled ginger may be eaten with the *sushi* if liked.

MANY GARNISHED VINEGARED RICE

CHIRASHI-ZUSHI

This is a sort of rice salad with a number of ingredients mixed into the rice. It is a flexible dish. Thoroughly defrosted cooked prawns can be added, as can cooked carrot and bamboo shoots, as well as green beans and fresh white crab meat. It is an admirable dish for using up what is on hand.

SERVES 4

375 g (12 oz) short-grain rice
1½ tablespoons *mirin*
15 g (½ oz) dried gourd strips (*kanpyo*)
Salt
4 dried Japanese mushrooms (*shiitake*)
2.5 cm (1 in) lotus root (*renkon*)
2 teaspoons rice vinegar
12 mangetout
2 large eggs
Vegetable oil
150 ml (¼ pint) second soup stock
2 tablespoons sugar
2 tablespoons soy sauce
4 slices pickled ginger root
1 sheet dried laver seaweed (*nori*)

Cook the rice according to the recipe for Rice with Vinegar Dressing (*Sushi*), page 48.

Sprinkle the dried gourd strips with salt and rub lightly. Wash in cold water, and squeeze out. Put into a saucepan of boiling water and blanch for 1 or 2 minutes. Drain, fold up and cut into 1 cm (½ in) pieces. Place on a platter.

Soak the mushrooms in warm water for 30 minutes, drain, squeeze out and cut away the hard stems. Cut the mushrooms into thin slices and add to the platter.

Peel the lotus root and slice it thinly. Simmer in water to cover and the vinegar for 5 minutes. Drain and add to the platter.

Drop the mangetout into boiling, salted water and blanch for 2 minutes. Drain, cut into diagonal slices and add to the platter.

Break the eggs into a bowl, add a pinch of salt and stir with chopsticks until they are well-blended but not foamy. Heat a rectangular omelette pan (*tamago-yaki nabe*) or an 18 to 20 cm (7 to 8 in) frying-pan and pour in just enough oil to film the surface. Pour in ¼ of the eggs, tilting the pan so that the egg covers the whole surface. As soon as the omelette is lightly browned on the underside, flip it over and cook for a few seconds longer to brown the other side. Lift out onto a chopping board. Make 3 more omelettes in the same way and stack them on the first omelette. Cut the omelettes in half, then into thin cross-ways strips. Add to the platter.

Pour the soup stock into a small saucepan. Add ½ teaspoon salt and the sugar. Bring to a simmer, add the mangetout and simmer for 1 minute. Lift out the vegetable with a slotted spoon and return it to the platter. Add the lotus root to the pan and simmer for 2 minutes. Lift out with a slotted spoon to the platter. Add the soy sauce and the dried gourd strips and simmer for 5 minutes. Add to the platter. Put the mushrooms into the pan and simmer over moderate heat until all the liquid has evaporated, about 5 minutes. Add to the platter with the ginger root slices. Toast the seaweed on both sides for a few seconds over a gas flame or electric burner. Crush in a piece of cheesecloth or crumble with the fingers, and put into a small bowl.

Divide the rice among 4 large china bowls (*donburi*) and top with the ingredients on the platter in an attractive way. Put a small heap of crushed seaweed in the centre of each bowl. If liked, turn the rice out into a very large bowl. Reserve a few slices of lotus root and omelette and some mangetout for a garnish. Gently fold all the ingredients into the rice, top with the reserved omelette, lotus root and mangetout. Sprinkle with the seaweed or make a heap of it in the centre of the bowl.

GARNISHED RICE

KAMAMESHI

Ideally this should be cooked in a *donabe*, the fireproof earthenware casserole used for one-pot dishes, but it can be cooked in a heavy saucepan. In Japan it is a favourite station lunch to be eaten on the train, in which case it comes in small individual casseroles which the traveller gets as a bonus. The medley of ingredients used results in a very flavourful, robust dish.

SERVES 4
**250 g (8 oz) skinned and boned chicken breast
2 teaspoons soy sauce
12 prawns, shelled and deveined with tails left on; if frozen, thoroughly defrosted
4 tablespoons *sake*
4 medium-sized fresh mushrooms, halved
1 large spring onion, using white and green parts, cut into fine 2.5 cm (1 in) strips
375 g (12 oz) short-grain rice
475 ml (16 fl oz) first soup stock
Salt to taste**

Halve the chicken breast lengthways, then cut into 1 cm (½ in) diagonal slices. Pour 1 teaspoon of soy sauce over the prawns, mixing gently. Pour 1 teaspoon of the *sake* over the mushrooms and mix. Put the spring onion to crisp in a bowl of cold water.

Wash the rice thoroughly and drain in a sieve for 1 hour. Put the rice into a large earthenware casserole or a heavy saucepan and pour in the stock, the rest of the *sake*, the remaining teaspoon of soy sauce, and salt to taste. Add the chicken, prawns and mushrooms with any liquid to the rice, folding in lightly. Cover and bring to a simmer over moderate heat, lower the heat and cook for 15 minutes. Remove from the heat and let stand for 5 minutes. Add the scallions, cover and let stand for another 5 minutes. Serve in large bowls.

If liked, clams may be used instead of prawns, and Japanese dried mushrooms (*shiitake*), soaked in warm water for 30 minutes, stems removed and quartered, may be used instead of fresh mushrooms.

PINK RICE WITH RED BEANS

SEKIHAN

This is a festival dish and is served at birthdays, weddings, anniversaries, and on any other similar happy occasion. The dried beans used in this dish, adzuki, *azuki* in Japan, have been cultivated for thousands of years in China, Korea and Japan. They are readily available in health food shops.

SERVES 6 to 8
**50 g (2 oz) red adzuki (*azuki*) beans
500 g (1 lb) sweet (sticky or glutinous) rice (*mochigome*)
1 teaspoon black sesame seeds
1 teaspoon salt**

Wash and pick over the beans and put them into a saucepan with 250 ml (8 fl oz) water and bring to a boil over moderate heat. Remove from the heat and drain. Add 700 ml (1¼ pints) water to the saucepan and simmer, covered, over low heat for 30 minutes. Drain, reserving the cooking water.

Thoroughly wash and drain the rice, then put it to soak in the reserved water from the beans for 8 hours or overnight. The bean water will give the rice an attractive pink colour. Drain the rice for at least 30 minutes in a sieve set over a bowl. Reserve the soaking water. Mix the rice and beans together.

Line a steamer with a kitchen cloth and add the beans and rice. Pat smooth, then poke 5 holes in the mixture with the fingers. Bring the water in the steamer to a boil, and steam over high heat for 40 to 50 minutes, or until the rice and beans are done. During the cooking period, sprinkle the rice mixture 3 or 4 times with the reserved soaking water, using your fingers. It is not necessary to use up all the water.

In a small frying-pan, toast the sesame seeds over moderate heat until they begin to jump. Put them into a small bowl and mix with the salt.

Serve the rice in bowls, or on small plates and sprinkle with the sesame seed mixture. The rice mixture can be made into rice balls, can be reheated in the steamer if necessary, and can be eaten cold.

PRESSED VINEGARED RICE WITH CRAB

KANI-ZUSHI

A rectangular wooden box with a removable top and bottom, an *oshiwaku*, is used to press the vinegared rice and its garnishes into a firm cake that can be sliced into individual servings. Available in most Japanese shops, the boxes come in various sizes. If you do not have the size of box indicated in a recipe, distribute the garnish according to the size of box you have. A square cake tin with a removable bottom is the best substitute if an *oshiwaku* is not available.

Sushi may be kept refrigerated overnight if necessary. Traditionally it would be wrapped in a dried bamboo leaf, but aluminium foil does just as well. Pressed *sushi* is good for picnics, and as an accompaniment to drinks. Many different toppings can be used. Here are two traditional ones: *Kani-Zushi* (Pressed Vinegared Rice with Crab) and *Hako-Zushi* (Pressed Vinegared Rice with Prawns and Salmon).

SERVES 4 to 8
375 g (12 oz) short-grain rice
**250 g (8 oz) cooked white crab meat, fresh,
frozen or tinned**
2 tablespoons lemon juice
2 large eggs
1 teaspoon sugar
¼ teaspoon salt, or to taste
Vegetable oil
25 g (1 oz) freshly cooked green peas
Pickled red ginger, thinly sliced

Cook the rice according to the recipe for Rice with Vinegar Dressing (*Sushi*), page 48.

Pick over the crab and remove any shell or cartilage. Sprinkle with the lemon juice and a little salt. If there is any claw meat, set it aside for a garnish, otherwise reserve enough crab meat to garnish 4 *oshiwaku*. Stir the remaining crab meat into the rice, mixing lightly.

Break the eggs into a bowl and stir with chopsticks until they are well-blended but not foamy. Stir in the sugar and ¼ teaspoon salt. Heat a rectangular omelette pan (*tamago-yaki nabe*) or an 18 to 20 cm (7 to 8 in) frying-pan and pour in just enough oil to film the surface. Pour in ¼ of the eggs, tilting the pan so that the egg covers the whole surface. As soon as the omelette is lightly browned on the underside, flip it over and cook for a few seconds longer to brown the other side. Lift out onto a chopping board. Make 3 more omelettes in the same way and stack them on the first omelette. Roll the omelettes and cut into very thin slices making a pile of golden threads.

Pack a dampened *oshiwaku* (about 7 × 15 cm, 3 × 6 in) with the *sushi* rice, pressing down firmly with the lid. There will be enough rice for 4 boxes. Arrange ¼ of the eggs, the reserved crab meat and the peas on top of the rice, and again press down firmly with the lid. The success of the dish lies in firm pressing. Remove the bottom of the box and press out the rectangle of decorated rice using the lid, which fits inside the box, to do so. Put the rice on a flat platter. Wash the box thoroughly in vinegared water after each use or the rice will stick. Repeat, using up all the ingredients. Let stand for 20 minutes to firm up the rice which otherwise may crumble when cut.

If using a square cake tin with a removable bottom, oil the tin lightly. It will probably be large enough to take all the rice in one go. Pack in the rice, pressing firmly with hands moistened with vinegared water. Arrange the eggs, reserved crab meat and peas on top of the rice. Cover with a sheet of greaseproof paper and a tin of the same size on top, and weight down for 10 minutes. Remove the weight and tin and greaseproof paper, remove sides of tin and slide onto a platter. Let it stand for 20 minutes to firm up the rice.

To serve, slice in half lengthways, using a very sharp knife wiped with a damp cloth, then cut crossways into squares. Arrange on 4 small plates, garnish with pickled ginger, and eat with chopsticks or by hand. Serve with soy sauce.

STUFFED RICE BALLS

ONIGIRI

These easy-to-make rice balls are sometimes called *omusubi* and are a great favourite for *bento*, the lacquered lunch boxes that are a feature of both picnics and train travel in Japan, and even turn up at intermission time in *Kabuki* theatres. Salt-cured salmon, dried bonito flakes (*hana-katsuo*) and pickled plums (*umeboshi*) are the most popular fillings. Others include the salted roes of cod or salmon, tinned sea urchin (*uni*) paste, Beef with Ginger (*Gyuniku No Tsukudani*) and Cooked Kelp (*Kombu No Tsukadani*) which can both be bought ready-prepared.

SERVES 4
125 g (4 oz) fresh salmon fillet with skin
Salt
375 g (12 oz) short-grain rice
1 sheet dried laver seaweed (*nori*)
4 small pickled plums (*umeboshi*)
7 g (¼ oz) dried bonito flakes (*hana-katsuo*)
Soy sauce

Prepare the salmon for salt-cured salmon a day ahead. Sprinkle the fish on both sides with salt, cover lightly and refrigerate for 24 hours. Rinse quickly in cold water and pat dry with paper towels. When ready to cook, grill the fish under moderate heat, skin side down, for 5 minutes, turn and grill skin side for 3 minutes. Remove skin and any bones, and break with chopsticks into pieces about 1 cm (½ in) square. Set aside.

Cook the rice according to the recipe for Plain Boiled Rice (*Gohan*), page 40.

Toast the seaweed on both sides for a few seconds over a gas flame or electric burner, then cut with scissors into 5 cm (2 in) squares. Remove the stones from the pickled plums. Divide the dried bonito flakes between 2 bowls, mixing one with soy sauce.

To make the rice balls, check that the rice is cool enough to handle. It should still be warm. Wet the hands and sprinkle with a little salt to stop the rice from sticking to them. Take about a tablespoon of rice and flatten it in the palm of the hand. Put a plum in the centre. Form it into a ball, pressing it firmly into shape. It will be about 6 cm (2½ in) in diameter. Continue with the other plums. If only large plums are available, quarter or halve them. Continue making rice balls, stuffing with the salmon, making 4 and wetting the hands and sprinkling them with salt from time to time. Press the seaweed squares on the tops and bottoms of the rice balls, then press again to fit the squares round the balls. Arrange on a tray with salmon-stuffed balls at one end and plum at the other.

Continue to make rice balls using the bonito mixed with soy sauce as the stuffing and rolling the balls in the plain bonito. Place these on the tray. If there is any leftover rice, mix it with any leftover salmon, finely shredded to make pink and white rice balls. Eat with fingers or chopsticks. Serve always at room temperature, never chilled.

VINEGARED RICE ROLLED IN SEAWEED

NORIMAKI-ZUSHI

This is a great favourite with children, especially for birthdays, and is one of the dishes made to celebrate *Hina Matsuri*, the Dolls' Festival, on March 3. This is an old festival, sometimes called Girls' Day. It dates from the 8th-century Heian Court when girls were given elaborately dressed dolls. A *sushi* dish is very appropriate for a festival as the character for '*su*' means happiness and the character '*shi*' means purpose, so a happy purpose dish is one for any festive occasion. Serve *Norimaki-Zushi* as a main course for lunch, as a first course, or as an accompaniment to drinks. Served at room temperature, it can be made ahead of time for parties.

SERVES 6 to 8 (according to appetite)
375 g (12 oz) short-grain rice
4 Japanese dried mushrooms (*shiitake*)
Sugar
2 tablespoons plus 1 teaspoon soy sauce
10 × 23 cm (9 in) pieces dried gourd strips
(*kanpyo*)
Salt
150 ml (¼ pint) second soup stock
1 tablespoon *mirin*
3 tablespoons light soy sauce (*usukuchi shoyu*)
125 g (4 oz) raw tuna
2 large eggs
Vegetable oil
250 g (8 oz) spinach
4 sheets dried laver seaweed (*nori*)
Pickled red ginger

Cook the rice according to the recipe for Rice with Vinegar Dressing (*Sushi*), page 48.

Soak the mushrooms in cold water to cover for 30 minutes. Lift out of the water, squeeze lightly and cut away the tough stems. Simmer in the water in which they have soaked, uncovered, over moderate heat for 5 minutes. Add 1 tablespoon sugar and 2 tablespoons of soy sauce. Reduce the heat to low and simmer, turning from time to time, until the liquid has evaporated. Cool, squeeze out any moisture, and cut into 1 cm (½ in) diagonal strips. Put in a heap on a large plate.

Sprinkle the gourd strips with salt and rub lightly. Soak in cold water for a few minutes, drain and put into a small saucepan with cold water to cover. Simmer for 2 to 3 minutes. Drain, and return to the saucepan with the soup stock, 1 tablespoon each of sugar and *mirin*, cover with an inner wooden lid (*otoshibuta*), or a saucer or plate, and simmer over low heat for 10 minutes. Add the light soy sauce and simmer for 5 minutes longer, uncovered. Cool, squeeze out and put onto the plate with the mushrooms.

Slice the raw tuna into pieces about 7 × 0.5 cm (3 × ¼ in) and put onto the plate.

Break the eggs into a bowl with a pinch of salt and stir with chopsticks until well-blended but not foamy. Lightly oil an omelette pan and make an omelette. Cool, lift out and cut into thin strips. Add to the plate.

Cut away any coarse stems from the spinach and wash it. Drop it into a saucepan of boiling, salted water, bring back to a boil over high heat and cook for 1 minute. Drain and squeeze dry. A bamboo mat (*sudare*) is useful for this, or use a kitchen towel. Form into a roll and sprinkle with the teaspoon of soy sauce. Add to the plate.

To assemble the dish divide all the ingredients on the plate into 4 portions. Lay a bamboo mat (*sudare*) on a wooden chopping board. Toast a sheet of seaweed on both sides over a gas flame or electric burner and lay it on the bamboo mat. Wet the hands with rice vinegar and pat ¼ of the rice evenly over the seaweed, leaving a 1 cm (½ in) border along the bottom. Starting from the top about 3.5 cm (1½ in) from the edge, arrange ¼ of the spinach on top of the rice in a horizontal row. Next to the spinach make a row of omelette strips, then gourd strips, then tuna, then mushrooms. Roll up the seaweed using the bamboo mat to help, pressing lightly but firmly to make a neat cylinder. Let it rest 2 to 3 minutes, then unroll and set aside.

Tap the ends of the roll on the chopping board to firm them up. Repeat with the remaining ingredients to make 4 rolls. Using a sharp knife wiped with a damp cloth, cut into 2 cm (¾ in) slices, about 9 to a roll. Arrange on individual platters, garnish with pickled ginger.

VARIATION: For *Kappa-Maki*, omit the spinach, omelette, gourd strips, mushrooms and tuna. Peel a 10 cm (4 in) slice of cucumber, halve it and scrape out the seeds. Cut lengthways into 5 mm (¼ in) strips. Have ready some Japanese green horseradish (*wasabi*). Spread a little of this across the middle of ¼ of the rice spread on a half sheet of *nori*. Top with the cucumber and roll up in the usual way. Continue with the rest of the cucumber.   SERVES 6 to 8.

VARIATION 2: For *Tekka Maki*, make as above but substitute raw fish, as for *Nigiri-Zushi*, cut into 7 × 0.5 cm (3 × ¼ in) pieces for the cucumber. Roll up in the usual way.   SERVES 6 to 8.

VARIATION 3: For *Norimaki-Zushi* made with sole, put 125 g (4 oz) skinned and boned fillet of sole into a small saucepan with water just to cover, and simmer over moderate heat for 2 minutes. Lift out the fish and drain on a piece of cheesecloth, squeezing out the moisture and breaking up the fish. Discard the water in the saucepan and return the fish to it with 2 tablespoons *sake*, 1 teaspoon sugar, 2 tablespoons *mirin* and salt to taste. Cook, stirring with 5 or 6 chopsticks held in a bunch in one hand, over low heat until the mixture is dry and grainy. This is *soboro* and can also be made with prawns. Use it in place of the raw tuna when making the master recipe. If liked, serve with soy sauce.   SERVES 6 to 8.

Norimaki-Zushi can be served together with *Nigiri-Zushi*, page 49, making a very festive platter.

FRIED BEAN CURD STUFFED WITH VINEGARED RICE

INARI-ZUSHI

These little bags of fried bean curd are a great favourite for children's picnics and birthday parties. They make a fine accompaniment to drinks. They are easy to make and can be prepared ahead of time.

SERVES 4
175 g (6 oz) short-grain rice
10 slices fried bean curd (*aburaage*)
150 ml (¼ pint) second soup stock
4 tablespoons *mirin*
1 tablespoon sugar
4 tablespoons light soy sauce (*usukuchi shoyu*)
Pickled red ginger, thinly sliced
Pickled cucumber

Cook the rice and season it with vinegar according to the recipe for Rice with Vinegar Dressing (*Sushi*), page 48.

Rinse the bean curd slices in hot water to remove the oil. Squeeze lightly, pat dry and cut in half giving 20 little bags. In a saucepan, combine the soup stock, *mirin* and sugar, bring to a boil, add the bean curd bags, and simmer, uncovered, until the liquid is reduced to half, about 5 minutes. Add the light soy sauce and continue to simmer over moderate heat until all the liquid is absorbed. Be careful not to let the bean curd burn. Transfer the bean curd bags to a colander to drain any remaining moisture, and when they are cool enough to handle press lightly to get rid of any remaining moisture. Stuff each bag with rice to make a little package, pressing down firmly with the fingers. Turn the ends of the bags over and lay with the turned-side down to keep the package closed.

Arrange 5 of the bags on each of 4 small oblong platters, or other small dish. Garnish the right-hand front side of the dish with red ginger or cucumber pickles or both. Eat with chopsticks or by hand at room temperature.

VARIATION: Instead of plain vinegared rice, use the garnished rice from *Chirashi-Zushi* (page 50).

The Japanese have a wide variety of noodles, readily available in shops specializing in Japanese foods and also sometimes in health food shops. Packaged noodles made from wheat flour or buckwheat can be bought dried. The wheat-flour noodles include thick noodles (*udon*), thin ones (*somen*), broad flat ones (*kishimen*). Buckwheat noodles are called *soba*. They can also be bought fresh as *nama udon* either cooked or uncooked, in the refrigerator section. These fresh noodles are easy enough to make at home with either wheat flour or buckwheat.

More exotic are *harusame* or bean gelatine noodles, usually called cellophane noodles. The Japanese name translates into 'spring rain' and demonstrates the Japanese talent for seeing the beauty of the seasons everywhere. With a little imagination it is possible to see that the noodles are like spring rain when it falls with the sun shining through it. *Shirataki* is made from the root of an aroid called devil's tongue or snake palm in English, and 'shining waterfall' in Japanese.

The noodle dishes, though they can be eaten at any time, are superb for lunch. A steaming bowl can be very comforting on a bleak winter's day, and chilled noodle dishes are cooling and refreshing in hot weather. They take very little time and effort to prepare. The ready-cooked noodles are heated briefly in hot water needing no cooking at all. They are also good for you. Once the philosophy of the Japanese kitchen is understood, toppings for noodle dishes may be freely improvised.

NOODLE DISHES = HOT AND COLD

TO COOK DRIED NOODLES

To cook thick wheat-flour noodles (*udon*) or broad, flat wheat-flour noodles (*kishimen*), put the noodles into a large saucepan full of briskly boiling water and bring back to a boil over moderate heat. Add 250 ml (8 fl oz) cold water and bring back to a boil again. Repeat this process twice more, adding 3 lots of water in all. Test to see if the noodles are done; if not, boil for 2 minutes and test again. Be careful not to overcook as the noodles will be mushy and not pleasantly firm to the bite. Drain the noodles and rinse quickly under hot running water. Drain again. The noodles are now ready to serve.

If the noodles are to be cooked ahead of time and reheated, or if they are to be served chilled for summer dishes, rinse in cold water. To reheat the noodles simply pour boiling water over them, let them stand for 1 minute, drain and serve. Uncooked fresh noodles are cooked in the same way.

To cook thin wheat-flour noodles (*somen*), vari-coloured thin wheat-flour noodles (*hiyamugi*) and buckwheat noodles (*soba*), cook in the same way but add 250 ml (8 fl oz) cold water twice instead of 3 times.

For fresh, cooked, thick wheat-flour noodles (*nama udon*), put the noodles into a saucepan and pour boiling water over them. Let them stand for a few minutes to heat them through. Separate the noodles gently with chopsticks while still in the water. Drain and serve.

SOY DIPPING SAUCE FOR NOODLES

TENTSUYU SAUCE

SERVES 4
250 ml (8 fl oz) second soup stock
75 ml (3 fl oz) soy sauce
75 ml (3 fl oz) *mirin*

Combine all the ingredients in a small saucepan and bring to a simmer over moderate heat. Simmer for 1 minute, then remove from the heat, and cool. Pour into a small bowl.

BROTH FOR NOODLES

KAKEJIRU

SERVES 4
1 litre (1¾ pints) second soup stock
125 ml (4 fl oz) light soy sauce (*usukuchi shoyu*)
125 ml (4 fl oz) *mirin*
Salt to taste
Pinch MSG

Combine the ingredients in a saucepan, bring to a simmer, taste for seasoning and set aside, off the heat, until ready to use.

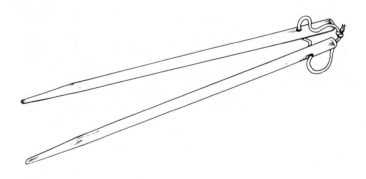

HOMEMADE NOODLES, WHEAT-FLOUR OR BUCKWHEAT

TEUCHI UDON OR SOBA

Fresh noodles are always popular and can be bought in Japanese supermarkets or shops. They are, however, very easy to make at home and not at all time-consuming. Buckwheat noodles (*soba*) need to be handled more delicately than wheat-flour noodles. Mixing wheat flour into the buckwheat makes this easier. If the buckwheat is very coarse, put it into a food processor and process it for 30 seconds.

SERVES 4 to 6
**500 g (1 lb) plain flour *or* 375 g (12 oz) buckwheat plus 125 g (4 oz) strong white (bread) or plain flour
1 tablespoon salt
175 ml (6 fl oz) warm water**

Sift the flour for *udon* into a large bowl, or if making buckwheat noodles sift the two flours together. Dissolve the salt in warm water. Make a well in the centre of the flour and gradually add the warm water, mixing to a firm dough. Add a little more water if necessary, but keep the dough firm. Form the dough into a ball, turn it out onto a lightly floured board or flat surface

and knead it until it is smooth and elastic. Form it into a ball again, return it to the bowl, cover with a damp cloth and let it stand in a warm place for 1 hour. Knead it again for 5 minutes on the floured board, then roll out the dough 3 mm (⅛ in) thick into a rectangle. Fold the dough back and forth over itself in 5 cm (2 in) folds, concertina fashion, dusting it with a little flour to prevent it from sticking. Cut the dough cross-ways with a very sharp knife into 4 mm (⅙ in) slices for *udon* and 3 mm (⅛ in) slices for *soba*. Separate the strips of dough shaking to remove any excess flour.

Have ready a very large saucepan of boiling water. Add the noodles and bring back to a boil over moderate heat. Add 250 ml (8 fl oz) cold water. Repeat this process twice more, 3 times in all. Cook for 2 minutes longer or until the noodles are tender but still firm to the bite. Drain and rinse under cold running water, then drain again. The noodles are now ready to use, either heated or cold in a summer dish.

The noodles will keep, refrigerated in a plastic bag, for 3 or 4 days.

FRESH NOODLES WITH A MIXED GARNISH AND EGGS

ODAMAKIMUSHI

This winter dish is complete as a meal in itself. *Kamaboko* fish sausage may be used but *naruto-maki* is preferred because its pink and white colours are an attractive foil to the other ingredients.

SERVES 4
4 large raw unpeeled prawns *or* large frozen cooked prawns, thoroughly defrosted
250 g (8 oz) skinned and boned chicken either breast or thigh
2 teaspoons light soy sauce (*usukuchi shoyu*)
4 dried Japanese mushrooms (*shiitake*)
2 medium-sized spring onions
4 × 2.5 cm (1 in) slices fish sausage, preferably *naruto-maki*
4 × 200 g (7 oz) packages fresh noodles (*nama udon*)
4 large eggs
1 recipe Broth for Noodles (*Kakejiru*), page 58
Lime peel (optional)

If using uncooked prawns, peel and devein but leave the tails on. Peel the cooked prawns and leave the tails on. Cut the chicken into diagonal, bite-sized pieces. Put chicken into a bowl with 1 teaspoon of light soy sauce and mix well. Soak the mushrooms for 30 minutes in warm water, cut away the hard stems and squeeze to remove the excess liquid. Cut the spring onions into 3.5 cm (1½ in) crossways pieces, then slice finely lengthways.

Sprinkle the fresh noodles with the remaining teaspoon of soy sauce and separate gently with the fingers. Divide the noodles among 4 large china bowls (*donburi*). Arrange the prawns, chicken, mushrooms, spring onions and fish sausage on top of the noodles in an attractive pattern.

Break the eggs into a bowl and stir with chopsticks until they are well-blended but not foamy. Make the broth and let it cool. Stir the eggs into the broth, and pour equal amounts into each of the 4 bowls.

Set the bowls in a steamer over boiling water and partially cover each bowl. A saucer will do. Steam for 15 to 20 minutes. Lift out the bowls and garnish, if liked, with a small piece of lime peel. Eat with chopsticks and a soup spoon.

NOODLES WITH POACHED EGGS

TSUKIMI UDON

Translated literally, this is 'looking-like-the-moon noodles'. The noodles are the clouds and the poached egg, with the white filming the yolk, is the moon. To the poetic imagination the dish can be seen to look like the moon on a cloudy night.

SERVES 4
1 recipe Broth for Noodles (*Kakejiru*), page 58
300 g (10 oz) spinach, trimmed
Salt
375 g (12 oz) thick noodles (*udon*) or 4 × 200 g (7 oz) packages fresh noodles (*nama udon*)
4 large eggs
Dried laver seaweed (*nori*)
Seven-flavour spice (*shichimi-togarishi*)

Make the broth and set it aside. Wash the spinach and drop it into a large saucepan of briskly boiling salted water. Bring back to a boil over high heat and cook for 2 to 3 minutes. Drain, then rinse in cold water and drain again. Put on a bamboo mat (*sudare*) or kitchen towel, roll up and squeeze out the excess moisture. Form into a roll. Cut into 4 slices.

Heat the noodles according to the recipe To Cook Dried Noodles (page 58). Divide among 4 large, heated bowls, preferably with covers. Reheat the broth, pour it over the noodles, put a slice of spinach on top at the side. Break an egg into each bowl and cover with the lid, or a saucer, so that the egg poaches lightly. Garnish with a small square of dried laver seaweed toasted until crisp over a gas flame or electric burner. Season to taste with seven-flavour spice.

BUCKWHEAT NOODLES ON BAMBOO PLATES

ZARU SOBA

This summer dish, wonderfully refreshing on a hot summer's day, is traditionally served in a *zaru*, a flat bamboo basket sieve or colander, used as a plate, which is both practical and pretty as the noodles can be completely drained.

SERVES 4
1 recipe Soy Dipping Sauce (*Tentsuyu*), page 58, using first soup stock
2 large spring onions, trimmed, using white and green parts
300 g (10 oz) buckwheat noodles (*soba*)
1 tablespoon green horseradish powder (*wasabi*)
2 sheets dried laver seaweed (*nori*)

Make the dipping sauce in a bowl and place it in a larger bowl of cold water with a few ice cubes. It should be very lightly chilled. Pour into 4 small soup bowls, and put one at each place setting.

Finely chop the spring onions and put them into 4 tiny bowls. Place alongside the dipping sauce.

Cook the noodles according to the recipe To Cook Dried Noodles (page 58) and chill in cold water. Drain and divide among 4 bamboo plates (*zaru*). Mix the horseradish to a paste and put a small mound beside the noodles. Toast the seaweed for a few seconds over a gas flame or electric burner and crumble in a piece of cheesecloth or the fingers and sprinkle over the noodles.

To eat, stir a little of the horseradish into the sauce. This is very hot, so the amount used is a matter of taste. Add the spring onions to the sauce. Dip the noodles into the sauce before eating.

BROAD NOODLES WITH EGG AND CHICKEN

TOJIKISHIMEN

This is a very satisifying, well-flavoured dish, robust enough to appease any cold weather appetite.

SERVES 4

**1.1 litre (2 pints) Broth for Noodles (*Kakejiru*),
page 58**
250 g (8 oz) skinned and boned chicken breast
1½ tablespoons *katakuriko, or* cornflour
3 large eggs, stirred
8 spinach leaves
375 g (12 oz) broad, flat noodles (*kishimen*)
**2 large spring onions, trimmed, using white
and green parts, finely chopped**
Seven-flavour spice (*shichimi-togarashi*)

Pour the broth into a large saucepan. Cut the chicken into bite-size diagonal pieces and add to the saucepan. Simmer over moderate heat until the chicken is tender, about 4 minutes. Mix the *katakuriko* or cornflour with a little water and stir into the broth. Simmer until it is lightly thickened, a minute or two. Holding a pair of chopsticks against the side of the bowl to slow the flow, pour the stirred eggs into the saucepan in a thin stream to cover the whole surface of the pan. Cook the spinach in boiling water for 2 minutes, drain, squeeze out and chop coarsely. Set aside.

Cook the noodles according to the recipe To Cook Dried Noodles (page 58) and divide among 4 large china bowls (*donburi*). Top with the spinach, then pour in the chicken, egg and broth mixture. Sprinkle with the spring onions and seven-flavour spice. Eat with chopsticks.

VARIATION: For Thick or Buckwheat Noodles with Egg and Vegetables (*Tamago Toji Udon* or *Soba*), use either thick noodles (*udon*) or buckwheat noodles (*soba*), instead of broad, flat noodles (*kishimen*). Omit the chicken, *katakuriko* or cornflour, and spinach. For the garnish choose any favourite vegetable such as green peas (50 g, 2 oz), cooked or green beans (50 g, 2 oz) cut into 1 cm (½ in) diagonal slices, and 1 sheet dried laver seaweed (*nori*) toasted on both sides for a few seconds over a gas flame or electric burner and crumbled with the fingers or in a piece of cheesecloth. Increase the large spring onions from 2 to 4. In Japan a special long white onion, *negi*, would be used. Very tender young leeks or large spring onions are the best substitutes. Slice the spring onions, or 2 very young leeks, thoroughly washed and trimmed, into 2.5 cm (1 in) diagonal slices and cook in the broth for 3 minutes. Add the eggs as in the main recipe. Divide the noodles among 4 large china bowls, pour in the broth with the egg topping, and garnish with peas or beans and the seaweed. SERVES 4.

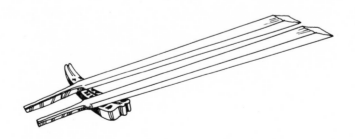

CHILLED NOODLES WITH PRAWNS

HIYASHI SOMEN

There is an easy way to deal with the problem of how to grate white radish (*daikon*) with dried hot red chilli pepper. Peel the radish, then poke a hole with chopsticks in the centre, and stuff the pepper inside. Grate the radish, grating the chilli at the same time. The Japanese have a poetic way of describing the resulting colours. They call it *momiji-oroshi*, 'looking like autumn leaves', appropriate even though this is a summer dish with the noodles afloat in water and ice cubes.

SERVES 4

300 g (10 oz) thin wheat-flour noodles (*somen*)
8 large uncooked prawns, preferably with shells on *or* 8 large cooked frozen prawns, thoroughly defrosted
1 tablespoon *sake*
Salt
½ medium-sized cucumber
5 cm (2 in) slice white radish (*daikon*), peeled
1 large or 2 small dried hot red chilli peppers, seeded
2 medium-sized spring onions, trimmed, using white and green parts
1 recipe Soy Dipping Sauce (*Tentsuyu*), page 58, using first soup stock

Cook the noodles according to the recipe To Cook Dried Noodles (page 58), drain and set aside.

If using uncooked prawns, drop them into a small saucepan of boiling salted water, add the

sake and cook just until they turn pink, about 2 minutes. Drain and peel when they are cool enough to handle, leaving the tails on. If using cooked prawns, put into a bowl and sprinkle with the *sake*. Set aside.

Trim the cucumber but do not peel it. Using a vegetable peeler or a small serrated spoon, scrape the seeds out of the cucumber and cut it into 5 mm (¼ in) slices. Drop into boiling salted water and cook for 1 minute. Drain and set aside.

Using chopsticks, poke a hole in the centre of the radish and stuff in the chilli pepper. Grate the radish and put it into a small bowl. Set aside. Chop the spring onions and put them into another small bowl. Set aside.

Make the dipping sauce and chill it lightly. Pour it into 4 medium-sized bowls, preferably glass. Set aside.

To assemble the dish put the noodles into a deep serving bowl, preferably cut glass, pour in cold water barely to cover the noodles and add some ice cubes. Arrange the prawns on top of the noodles in a decorative pattern and surround with the cucumber slices. Put the bowl in the centre of the table, with the bowls of radish and spring onions. Set a bowl of dipping sauce at each place. To eat, put some of the spring onions and radish into the sauce. Using chopsticks lift out some of the noodles and dip in the sauce. Dip the cucumber slices and prawns in the same way.

CHILLED NOODLES WITH EGGS

HIYAMUGI

When appetites flag in sultry summer heat this is the perfect lunch or dinner dish. The white noodles with their sprinkling of pink and green ones are so fresh and pretty that the Japanese say the sight of the dish makes one feel cooler immediately.

SERVES 4

1 recipe Soy Dipping Sauce (*Tentsuyu*), page 58, using first soup stock and ⅛ teaspoon MSG
300 g (10 oz) thin wheat-flour noodles (*hiyamugi*)
2 large spring onions, trimmed, using white and green parts
½ medium-sized cucumber
1 large tomato, peeled
2 large eggs, hard-boiled and halved lengthways
Seven-flavour spice (*shichimi-togarashi*), *or* hot ground red chilli (*togarashi-ko*)

Make the dipping sauce and chill it lightly. Pour it into 4 medium-sized bowls, preferably glass.

Cook the noodles according to the recipe To Cook Dried Noodles (page 58) and put into a large bowl, preferably cut glass. Cover with cold water and add a few ice cubes to chill the noodles thoroughly. Chop the spring onions and put them into cold water for a few minutes to crisp. Drain, pat dry and put into a bowl.

Peel the cucumber in alternate strips lengthways, then slice thinly on the diagonal. Cut the tomato into 4 slices and poke out the seeds with chopsticks. Drain the noodles and return them to the bowl. Arrange the cucumber slices round the edge of the bowl on top of the noodles with the tomato slices at even intervals between them. Arrange the eggs, cut side up, in a flower pattern in the centre of the bowl. Put the noodles in the centre of the table and put a bowl of dipping sauce at each place with the spring onions in 4 tiny bowls beside the sauce.

To eat, add a little spring onion to the dipping sauce and season to taste with either of the peppers. Dip the noodles, and the garnishes into the sauce. If preferred the noodles and garnish can be served in individual bowls with a bowl of dipping sauce at the side.

NOODLES WITH BEAN PASTE

MISO UDON

This is a hearty winter dish served in generous proportions.

SERVES 4 to 6

500 g (1 lb) chicken thighs with bone
4 medium-sized fresh mushrooms, *or* 4 dried Japanese mushrooms (*shiitake*)
2 large spring onions, trimmed, using white and green parts
4 × 200 g (7 oz) packages fresh, thick, cooked wheat-flour noodles (*nama udon*)
8 tablespoons red *miso* (bean paste)

Chop the chicken, with the bone, into approximately 2.5 cm (1 in) pieces, or have the butcher do it. Put the chicken into a large saucepan with 1.1 litre (2 pints) water and bring to a simmer, covered, over moderate heat. Reduce the heat to low, skim if necessary and cook until the chicken is tender, about 30 minutes.

If using fresh mushrooms, wipe the caps with a damp cloth, trim the stems and cut into quarters. If using dried mushrooms, soak for 30 minutes in warm water, drain, remove the hard stems and cut into quarters. Slice the spring onions thinly. Heat the noodles according to the recipe To Cook Dried Noodles (page 58). Set aside.

When the chicken is tender, add the bean paste mixed until smooth with a little of the chicken stock. Add the mushrooms and spring onions, and simmer very gently for 2 minutes. Add the noodles and simmer for 1 minute longer. Serve in large china bowls (*donburi*).

Uncooked fresh or dried noodles may also be used.

VARIATION: For a simpler dish, omit the chicken and the red *miso* (bean paste). Serve the noodles in second soup stock with the mushrooms and spring onions and have ready bowls of the two dipping sauces so that diners can dip the noodles in the sauce.

NOODLES WITH FRIED BEAN CURD

KITSUNE UDON

These are sometimes called Fox Noodles, perhaps because the fox, not very highly thought of in Japanese folklore, is known to have an inordinate passion for bean curd.

SERVES 4

4 pieces fried bean curd (*aburaage*)
175 ml (6 fl oz) second soup stock
2 tablespoons soy sauce
2 tablespoons *mirin*
1 tablespoon sugar
1 recipe Broth for Noodles (*Kakejiru*), page 58
375 g (12 oz) thick noodles (*udon*)
2 medium spring onions, trimmed using white and green parts
Seven-flavour spice (*shichimi-togarashi*)

Rinse the fried bean curd pieces in hot water and cut into triangles or 1 cm (½ in) slices. Pour into a small saucepan with the soup stock, soy sauce, *mirin* and sugar and simmer until most of the liquid has been absorbed, about 10 minutes. Set aside.

Make the broth (*kakejiru*) and set aside, keeping hot.

Cook the noodles according to the recipe To Cook Dried Noodles (page 58) and divide among 4 large bowls (*donburi*). Top with the reserved bean curd and any liquid. Slice one of the spring onions into 1 cm (½ in) pieces and add to the noodles. Finely chop the other spring onion. Pour the hot broth over the noodles and garnish with the chopped spring onion and seven-flavour spice.

VARIATION 1: For Buckwheat Noodles with Fried Bean Curd (*Kitsune Soba*), use buckwheat noodles (*soba*) instead of thick noodles (*udon*).

VARIATION 2: For Fox Noodles, Osaka-style (*Osaka Kitsune Udon*), add 4 dried Japanese mushrooms (*shiitake*), soaked for 30 minutes in warm water and hard stems cut out, and cut into 1 cm (½ in) slices, to the bean curd when it is cooking. Cut 375 g (12 oz) skinned and boned chicken breast into 1 cm (½ in) diagonal slices. Put into a small saucepan with enough of the broth to cover and simmer for 4 minutes, or until tender. Lift out of the broth and add to the noodles with the bean curd and mushrooms. Pour the broth back into the saucepan with the rest of the broth. Finish the dish as in the main recipe.

GARNISHED CASSEROLE NOODLES

NABEYAKI UDON

This is a hearty winter dish of noodles and mixed garnishes cooked in a lidded earthenware casserole (*donabe*). Since these come in many sizes, cook in 4 small or 1 large casserole. An electric frying-pan can also be used.

SERVES 4
375 g (12 oz) thick noodles (*udon*)
1 recipe Broth for Noodles (*Kakejiru*), page 58
4 dried Japanese mushrooms (*shiitake*)
10 cm (4 in) fish sausage (*kamaboko*)
250 g (8 oz) skinned and boned chicken breast
3 medium-sized spring onions, trimmed, using white and green parts
4 large eggs
Seven-flavour spice (*shichimi-togarashi*)
***or* ground hot red pepper (*togarashi-ko*)**

Cook the noodles according to the recipe To Cook Dried Noodles (page 58). Drain and set aside.

Make the Broth for Noodles and set aside. Soak the dried mushrooms for 30 minutes in warm water. Drain, cut away the tough stems and squeeze gently to remove the excess moisture. Put into a small saucepan with 125 ml (4 fl oz) of the broth and simmer over low heat until the mushrooms are tender, about 15 minutes. Set aside.

Cut the fish sausage into 8 slices. Cut the chicken breast into bite-size diagonal slices. Cut the spring onions into 2.5 cm (1 in) diagonal slices.

Divide the noodles among 4 individual lidded earthenware casseroles (*donabe*) and arrange the mushrooms, fish sausage, chicken and spring onions on top of the noodles. Pour in the heated broth and bring each casserole to a boil over moderate heat. Remove from the heat. Make a hollow in each casserole and break an egg into each nest. Cover and let the casserole stand until the egg is set, about 2 minutes. Serve in the casseroles with seven-flavour spice or ground hot red pepper to taste.

VARIATION: Fresh mushrooms may be used instead of *shiitake*; 125 g (4 oz) spinach, cooked and chopped, or edible chrysanthemum leaves (*shungiku*), cooked and chopped, may be added. Prawn *tempura* or pieces of fried fish may be added instead of, or as well as, the chicken breast. The dish may be prepared in one large casserole or electric frying-pan in which case the eggs should be added after the ingredients have been served into 4 large heated soup bowls so as not to break the eggs or overcook them. Fresh noodles (*nama udon*) may be used instead of dried noodles.

CHICKEN WITH BUCKWHEAT NOODLES

TORINANBAN

This is a well-flavoured, quickly made lunch dish, light yet satisfying and good at any time of year.

SERVES 4

375 g (12 oz) skinned and boned chicken breast
125 ml (4 fl oz) plus 1 tablespoon soy sauce
1 tablespoon *sake*
300 g (10 oz) trimmed spinach
Salt
6 medium-sized spring onions, trimmed, using white and green parts
950 ml (32 fl oz) first soup stock
50 ml (2 fl oz) *mirin*
300 g (10 oz) buckwheat noodles (*soba*)
Seven-flavour spice (*shichimi-togarashi*)
***or* 1 tablespoon freshly grated ginger root**

Slice the chicken breast diagonally into bite-size pieces and put into a bowl. Add the tablespoon of soy sauce and the *sake*, mix gently and set aside.

Wash and drain the spinach and drop it into a large saucepan of briskly boiling salted water. Bring back to a boil over high heat and cook for 2 to 3 minutes. Drain, rinse quickly in cold water and drain again. Put the spinach on a bamboo mat (*sudare*), or use a kitchen towel, roll up and press out the excess moisture. Form into a roll, cut into 4 slices and set aside.

Cut 4 of the spring onions diagonally into 2.5 cm (1 in) pieces. Finely chop the remaining 2 spring onions and put into a small bowl.

In a saucepan combine the remaining soy sauce and the *mirin* and bring to a simmer. Add the chicken and any liquid and simmer gently for 3 minutes. Add the sliced spring onions and simmer for 1 minute longer.

Cook the noodles according to the recipe To Cook Dried Noodles (page 58), and divide among 4 large bowls (*donburi*). Arrange the chicken pieces and sliced spring onions on top with a slice of spinach at the side. Pour in the hot broth. Serve with seven-flavour spice or grated ginger and the chopped spring onions.

VARIATION: Instead of buckwheat noodles use thick or thin or freshly-made noodles.

No country on earth has a richer harvest of seafood, or makes a better use of it, than Japan. There is an astonishing variety of fish and shellfish in the waters surrounding the group of islands that make up the country. This is due partly to the Japan current which creates an environment rich in the minerals that nourish the plankton, prime food for marine life, and to the great depth of the waters around the islands which abound in shallow bays and inlets, ideal for fishermen. The Japanese are a seafaring people who crossed the ocean to reach their islands in the first place, and they have never lost their love of the sea and their love of its harvest, very evident in the kitchen where seafood plays an important role. We, in contrast, do not have as rich a harvest from the sea, but it is possible to find excellent substitutes for special fish and, of course, we have many types of fish in common, like mackerel, salmon and sole.

A unique feature of the kitchen is *sashimi*, raw fish which has a fresh, delicate flavour, never fishy. The secret lies in the absolute freshness of the fish. *Sashimi* can be served as a first course, or as a main course. One fish, or several varieties, can be served and suitable fish include sole, bream, tuna, sea bass, salmon trout, rainbow trout, mackerel, flounder, red snapper, squid and octopus, which vary in both taste and texture. The thinly sliced fish is served with various condiments and dipping sauces, gracefully presented, like all Japanese food.

Tempura – batter-fried seafood and vegetables – belong to the group of Japanese dishes called *agemono* (fried things). It was introduced into Nagasaki by Portuguese priests in the 16th century. As devout Catholics, they observed the four lots of fast days, the Ember Days, called by their Latin name *Quattour Tempora*, when they ate seafood instead of meat, prawns being a particular favourite. These they had batter-coated and deep-fried. The Japanese adopted the cooking method, improved and lightened the batter, expanded the range of foods to include many fish, shellfish and vegetables, and called them *tempura*. They invented a special pan with a ledge to drain the fried foods, which are cooked at a lower temperature than our deep frying, and not until brown, just golden. Though a *tempura* pan is ideal, and is useful for other frying, any deep, heavy frying-pan will do, using paper towels for draining. *Tempura* should be served as soon as possible after it is cooked. The oil in the pan should be skimmed after each batch of food is fried.

FISH · SHELLFISH ·

TEMPURA · SASHIMI ·

BATTER-FRIED PRAWNS AND VEGETABLES

TEMPURA

The secret of successful *tempura* lies in the batter which should be made at the last minute, lightly mixed and slightly lumpy. It is also very important not to crowd the *tempura* pan, or frying-pan, as this reduces the temperature of the oil which should be kept constant. The result is a soggy batter instead of a light, crisp one. The oil must be skimmed after each batch of *tempura* is fried to remove any bits of batter which otherwise might burn.

The dish is flexible. There must be prawns, but other ingredients can include scallops, squid, and any white fish such as sole or smelts. Suitable vegetables include mushrooms, spring onions, carrots and celery cut into julienne strips, sweet potato, green beans, small aubergine and sweet green peppers. *Tempura* should be served as soon as it is cooked, then dipped in a special sauce, *tentsuyu*, served at room temperature. *Tempura* should never be fried until it is brown. The cooked batter should be light gold, fried for about 2 minutes on each side. The sauce can be made ahead of time and all the ingredients prepared and set out so that the dish is neither difficult nor time-consuming to make.

SERVES 4

**8 large uncooked, unshelled prawns, if frozen
thoroughly defrosted
125 g (4 oz) white fish such as sole, cut into four
7 × 3.5 cm (3 × 1½ in) pieces
1 squid, about 250 g (8 oz), body sac only
12 large green beans
7 cm (3 in) slice from top of a large carrot
1 sweet green pepper
1 small aubergine, about 175 g (6 oz)
4 medium-sized fresh flat mushrooms
1 small bamboo shoot (optional)
1 lotus root (optional)
5 cm (2 in) square dried laver seaweed (*nori*)
5 cm (2 in) slice white radish (*daikon*)
Grated fresh ginger root (optional)**

FOR THE DIPPING SAUCE (*Tentsuyu*):
**50 ml (2 fl oz) *mirin*
175 ml (6 fl oz) soy sauce
7 g (¼ oz) dried bonito flakes (*hana-katsuo*)
⅛ teaspoon MSG**

FOR THE BATTER:
**1 large egg
125 ml (4 fl oz) water
125 g (4 oz) plain flour
Vegetable oil for deep frying**

Peel and devein the prawns leaving the last segment of shell and the tail on. Make a small, shallow slit on the underside of the prawns at the head end to prevent them curling when fried. Gently straighten the prawns by bending the tails back slightly. Cut off the ends of the tails as this part has water in it which would splutter in the hot oil.

Rinse the fish and pat it dry with paper towels. Rinse the cleaned squid and pat it dry. Cut it open so that there are 2 pieces, then score all over the outside with a sharp knife in a criss-cross pattern. Cut into squares of about 3.5 cm (1½ in). Set the prawns, fish and squid aside in groups of 4 portions.

Prepare the vegetables. Trim the beans and cut them into 2 or 3 diagonal slices. Scrape the carrot and cut it into thin lengthways strips. Remove the stem and seeds, and cut the pepper into strips about 2.5 × 5 cm (1 × 2 in). Cut the aubergine into thin lengthways strips. Wipe the caps of the mushrooms and remove the stems. Cut the bamboo shoot, if using, into thin slices. Peel the lotus root, if using, and cut it into thin slices. Divide these ingredients into groups of 4 portions to be cooked separately.

Peel and grate the radish. Squeeze it out lightly, then place it in mounds on 4 very small individual dishes. Grate the ginger, if using, and place little mounds of it beside the radish.

Make the sauce. In a small saucepan, bring the *mirin* to a boil. Add the water, soy sauce and bonito flakes and bring back to a boil over moderate heat. Strain, add the MSG and pour into 4 small bowls.

Make the batter. Break the egg into a bowl and stir with chopsticks until it is well-blended but not foamy. Add the water, stirring to mix. Sift the flour into the egg and water mixture, stirring with chopsticks to mix lightly. It does not matter if it is slightly lumpy.

Heat 5 to 7 cm (2 to 3 in) oil in a *tempura* pan or heavy frying-pan to 180°C (350°F) on a frying thermometer, or until bubbles form on wooden chopsticks stirred in the oil. Another test is to drop a small piece of batter into the oil. If it rises immediately to the surface, the heat is right.

Dip the prawns, fish and squid in the batter. Make little bundles of the beans and carrots and dip these in batter. All the other ingredients are dipped, slice by slice in the batter except the squares of seaweed which are coated on one side only. Fry the ingredients until golden, turning once, for about 2 minutes, being careful not to overcrowd the pan. Drain on the rack of the *tempura* pan or on paper towels spread on a bamboo plate (*zaru*), or on paper towels. Continue until all the ingredients are cooked.

Arrange the *tempura* on 4 plates. Put the seaweed batter-side down. The effect is very pretty as the colours show through to some extent – with pink prawns, orange carrot, green beans, white sweet potato, black seaweed, and so on. To eat, add a little grated ginger to the radish (if liked), add the radish to the sauce and mix. Using chopsticks dip each piece of *tempura* into the sauce.

PICKLED SMELT

WAKASAGI NO NANBANZUKE

SERVES 4

**12 small smelt, cleaned with heads and
tails left on
Salt
Plain flour
Vegetable oil for deep frying
125 ml (4 fl oz) rice vinegar
3 tablespoons sugar
⅛ teaspoon MSG
2 dried hot red chilli peppers, seeded**

Sprinkle the fish with salt and set them aside for 30 minutes. Pat dry with paper towels and coat lightly with flour.

Heat 5 to 7 cm (2 to 3 in) oil in a *tempura* pan or heavy saucepan to 180°C (350°F) on a frying thermometer, or until bubbles form on wooden chopsticks stirred in the oil. Add the smelt, a few at a time, and fry, turning once, for about 5 minutes or until the fish are golden brown. Drain on the rack of the *tempura* pan or on paper towels and transfer to a shallow dish.

In a small saucepan, combine the vinegar, sugar and MSG and heat until warm, stirring to dissolve the sugar. Chop or crumble the chillies and add to the mixture. Pour the mixture over the fish and refrigerate for 2 or 3 days turning from time to time. Serve at room temperature as an appetizer or main course. Eat with chopsticks, picking up the whole fish.

MIXED VEGETABLE FRITTERS

KAKIAGE

These delicate vegetable fritters make a perfect ending to a *tempura* meal, using the leftover batter. They can of course be made independently using the recipe for *tempura* batter. It is very flexible, giving a wide choice of vegetables, though carrot, green beans and onion are nearly always included. Fresh *shiitake* mushrooms would be used in Japan. Either use fresh mushrooms, thinly sliced, or soak dried *shiitake* mushrooms in warm water for 30 minutes, cut away the hard stems, and cut into 1 cm (½ in) slices. If using burdock root which is not usually available fresh, either use it tinned, or substitute salsify or scorzonera. Lotus root is not always available fresh but can be bought tinned.

SERVES 4
125 g (4 oz) burdock root (*gobo*), fresh or tinned, *or* use salsify or scorzonera
50 g (2 oz) lotus root (*renkon*)
1 medium carrot
25 g (1 oz), about 8 medium-sized, green beans
4 medium-sized fresh mushrooms
6 edible chrysanthemum leaves (*shungiku*) (optional)
50 g (2 oz) slice white sweet potato
1 recipe *tempura* batter, page 70
1 teaspoon grated fresh ginger root (optional)
1 recipe Dipping Sauce (*Tentsuyu*) for *tempura*, page 70
White radish (*daikon*) and ginger root as for *tempura*, page 70

If using fresh burdock, salsify or scorzonera roots, scrape under running water with the back of a knife. Cut into 3.5 cm (1½ in) slices, then slice very finely lengthways and drop into cold water as these roots discolour very quickly.

Peel the lotus root, cut into slices as for the burdock, then cut into fine julienne strips. Put into another bowl of cold water.

Scrape the carrot and cut into 5 cm (2 in) julienne strips. Trim the beans and slice into 5 cm (2 in) diagonal pieces. Set aside with the carrot strips. Trim the mushroom stems, slice thinly and add to the carrot and beans.

Peel the sweet potato and cut into 1 cm (½ in) slices. Cut into julienne strips and put into a bowl of cold water.

Have ready the *tempura* batter. Stir in the grated ginger root. If using chrysanthemum leaves, coat the underside of the leaves with batter. Set aside, batter-side up.

Drain the vegetables that are soaking and put into a bowl with all the other vegetables. Mix together lightly, then add them to the *tempura* batter.

Heat 5 to 7 cm (2 to 3 in) vegetable oil in a *tempura* or heavy frying-pan to a temperature of 180°C (350°F) on a frying thermometer, or until bubbles form on wooden chopsticks stirred in the oil. Add the chrysanthemum leaves to the pan, batter-side down, and fry for 30 seconds. Lift out and drain on the rack of the *tempura* pan, or on paper towels. Add the mixed vegetables and batter to the pan by generous tablespoons and fry for about 1 minute on each side, turning once, until golden. Drain on the rack of the *tempura* pan or on paper towels, and serve with the dipping sauce and the condiments of radish and ginger. Eat with chopsticks. Add a little ginger to the radish, if liked, and stir into the dipping sauce. Dip the fritters into the sauce.

VARIATION: A simpler version of Mixed Vegetable Fritters is Deep-Fried Peas (*Endo No Kakiage*), using 250 g (8 oz) fresh peas, or if frozen then thoroughly defrosted, combined with 1 recipe *tempura* batter and dropped by scant tablespoons into a *tempura* pan or heavy frying-pan, deep-fried in the usual way, and served with dipping sauce and grated radish. SERVES 4

NOODLE-COATED PRAWNS WITH FRIED SOLE

HIRAME NO KOHAKU-AGE TO EBI NO IGA-AGE

The prosaic English is very different from the romantic Japanese name for this dish which signifies a wild chestnut (the noodle-coated prawns), a chestnut leaf turning gold (the fish), and the maple leaf turning to flame in autumn (white radish grated with dried chilli pepper). The name of the dish is poetic, the dish itself is a very appetizing example of *tempura*, with the puffed-up noodles coating the prawns.

SERVES 4
375 g (12 oz) fillet of sole
Plain flour
1 large egg, separated
2 tablespoons *katakuriko or* cornflour
8 large uncooked, unshelled prawns, if frozen
thoroughly defrosted
50 g (2 oz) bean gelatine noodles (*harusame*)
5 cm (2 in) slice Japanese white radish (*daikon*)
2 dried, hot red chilli peppers
Vegetable oil for deep frying
4 teaspoons soy sauce

Cut the sole into 4 equal-sized pieces, and sprinkle with flour, shaking to remove the excess. Beat the egg white until stiff, add the *katakuriko* or cornflour, and mix well with chopsticks. Dip the fish into the egg white mixture. Stir the egg yolk with chopsticks, then spoon it over the fish pieces and set aside.

Rinse the prawns, shell and devein but leave on the tail and the last segment of shell. Cut the tips of the tail off as they contain water which makes the prawns splutter when fried. Roll the prawns in flour and dip into the remaining egg white. Cut the noodles into 2.5 cm (1 in) pieces using kitchen shears as they are quite tough. Coat the prawns with the noodles and set aside.

Peel the radish and seed the chillies. Poke a hole in the centre of the radish and stuff with the chillies. Finely grate the radish and lightly squeeze out the excess liquid. Set aside.

Heat 5 to 7 cm (2 to 3 in) oil in a *tempura* pan, or a heavy frying-pan and heat the oil to 180°C (350°F) or until bubbles form on wooden chopsticks stirred in the oil. Fry the fish for 1 minute on each side, lift out and drain on the rack of the *tempura* pan or on paper towels. Fry the prawns in the same way, lift out and drain.

Arrange the fish on 4 medium-sized plates with the prawns in front. At the right-hand side in front, put a small pile of grated radish, and pour 1 teaspoon of soy sauce over each mound of radish.

VARIATION: For a simpler dish, Prawns in Bean Gelatine Noodles (*Ebi No Harusame-age*), just cook the noodle-coated prawns of the main recipe. The noodles, *harusame*, literally 'spring rain', are sometimes called cellophane noodles. The prawns in their puffed-up coating make a very impressive accompaniment to drinks. Sprinkle the prepared prawns with a little salt, a little MSG and 1 tablespoon *sake* and let them stand for 30 minutes. Roll them in the starch or cornflour, then dip in the egg white and coat thoroughly with the noodles. Deep-fry as above. Take care not to overcrowd the pan and cook the prawns only until the noodles are very lightly coloured. They really need no sauce but can be served with *tempura* dipping sauce, if liked. SERVES 4.

SALT-GRILLED
SEA BREAM

KODAI NO SHIOYAKI

This is a *yakimono* dish in which the fish to be grilled is salted then skewered in such a way that when it is served it looks as if it had come straight from sea to plate. The fish, with its crisp skin and delicate flesh, does not need any elaborate garnishes. Red pickled ginger is an admirable accompaniment, so is lemon, or a little soy sauce. A *hibachi* is ideal for this sort of cooking and can turn a picnic into a feast.

SERVES 4

**4 small sea bream *or* similar medium-sized fish,
scaled and cleaned, with head and tail left on
Salt
Pickled red ginger (beni-shoga)**

Wash the fish, pat dry with paper towels and sprinkle generously with salt, inside and out. Set aside for 30 minutes. Rinse off the salt and pat dry. Skewer each of the fish, entering the fish just under the eye, taking the skewer through the middle of the fish and coming out at the tail. Put a second skewer through the fish starting 2.5 cm (1 in) below the first skewer. If necessary tie the mouth of the fish shut with a piece of kitchen string. Sprinkle the tail and fins heavily with salt to prevent them burning. This is called cosmetic salting. Salt the fish lightly.

Put the fish on the oiled rack of a preheated grill and grill, under or over the heat, for about 5 minutes on each side, or until golden brown.

Carefully remove the skewers and place the fish on individual oblong platters or plates with the head to the left. Remove the kitchen string from the mouth. Garnish with a little pickled ginger placed at the right-hand front side of the platter. The skewers will have forced the fish into curves so that they appear to be swimming.

FISH MARINATED IN
BEAN PASTE

SAKANA NO MISOZUKE-YAKI

This is an unusual technique for flavouring a dish. It is also economical as the bean paste can be used again for making Quick Bean Paste Vegetable Pickles (*Sokuseki Misozuke*) page 168. Mackerel, red snapper, bluefish or any similar fish can all be used.

SERVES 4

**4 small bream, cleaned and scaled
Salt
300 g (10 oz) red *miso* (bean paste)
3 tablespoons *sake*
Pickled red ginger (beni-shoga)**

Wash and dry the fish, and sprinkle them lightly on both sides with salt. Set aside. In a bowl mix the bean paste with the *sake* to make a smooth paste. Spread half the bean paste mixture on a glass or enamel dish large enough to hold the fish in a single layer. Cover the bean paste with a piece of cheesecloth cut to fit the dish, and arrange the fish on top. Cover with another piece of cheesecloth, and spread this with the rest of the bean paste mixture. Cover the dish firmly with aluminium foil or plastic wrap and refrigerate for at least 2 days, or up to 5 days for a more pronounced flavour.

When ready to cook the fish, remove the cheesecloth and lift out the fish. The bean paste need not be discarded. It can be scraped off the cheesecloth and stored in a container in the refrigerator for another use. Do not wash the fish. Wipe off any bean paste with a cloth. Grill the fish under moderate heat for about 4 minutes on each side. They will have been flavoured by the bean paste. Arrange the fish on 4 individual dishes and garnish with the ginger.

MACKEREL AND BEAN CURD CAKES

SATSUMA-AGE

This dish is in the style of Satsuma as it was called in the Edo era, in the southern part of Kyushu. It can be made with a variety of fish, not just mackerel. Blue fin tuna (tunny) and sardine fillets are popular.

SERVES 4

1 bean curd (*momen tofu*) weighing about 250 g (8 oz)
1 burdock root, fresh or tinned, about 30 cm 12 in), *or* use salsify or scorzonera
375 g (12 oz) mackerel fillets, *or* tunny, *or* sardine fillets
1 tablespoon white *miso* (bean paste)
1 teaspoon each sugar, salt and soy sauce
2 tablespoons *sake*
1 large egg
2 teaspoons *katakuriko* starch, *or* cornflour
1 teaspoon finely chopped fresh ginger root
1 tablespoon black sesame seeds
Vegetable oil for deep frying
Pickled red ginger (*beni-shoga*) (optional)

Slide the bean curd into a shallow pan of boiling water for about 10 seconds only, lift out and drain in a colander. Put into a piece of cheesecloth and squeeze out the moisture. Rub through a sieve and set aside.

Scrape the burdock root if using fresh, or salsify or scorzonera, under cold running water with the back of a knife, cut it into slivers (*sasagaki*) then drop into cold water as it discolours very quickly.

Check that there are no tiny bones in the fish and if there are, pull them out with tweezers. Chop coarsely, then put into a Japanese mortar (*suribachi*) and pound to a smooth paste, beating with the wooden pestle until the fish is light and fluffy, or reduce to a light, fluffy purée in a food processor. Add the bean curd and mix well. Add the bean paste, sugar, salt, soy sauce and *sake*, mixing well. Break the egg into a bowl and stir with chopsticks until it is well mixed but not foamy. Add it to the fish mixture, little by little, pounding constantly until the mixture has increased in bulk and is very light, or add it to the food processor little by little with the machine running. Drain the burdock root and stir it into the fish mixture with the *katakuriko* or cornflour, ginger and sesame seeds. Divide into 8 slightly flattened oval cakes.

Heat 5 to 7 cm (2 to 3 in) vegetable oil in a *tempura* pan or frying-pan to 180°C (350°F) on a frying thermometer, or until bubbles form on wooden chopsticks stirred in the oil. Carefully slide in the fish cakes. They will rise to the surface in a minute or two. Cook only for about 2 minutes longer, or until they are golden. Cook them in batches so as not to overcrowd the pan. Drain on the rack of the *tempura* pan or on paper towels. Eat at room temperature garnished with pickled ginger, if liked.

SOLE SIMMERED IN *SAKE*

KAREI NO NITSUKE

A richly flavoured stock with *sake* is used for this easy-to-cook *nimono* (simmered) dish. A winter favourite, it is a summer favourite too when it is served chilled. The sauce chills into a delicious aspic.

SERVES 4
8 small sole or plaice, each weighing about 250 g (8 oz), cleaned and with head, tail and fins left on
200 ml (7 fl oz) second soup stock
50 ml (2 fl oz) *sake*
4 tablespoons *mirin*
5 tablespoons soy sauce
1 teaspoon salt
8 fresh hot green chilli peppers

Wash and dry the fish. Using a very sharp knife, score diagonally across in both directions at 2.5 cm (1 in) intervals to form a diamond pattern. Do this on both sides of the fish, making very shallow cuts.

In a saucepan, or lidded frying-pan large enough to hold the fish comfortably, combine the soup stock, *sake*, *mirin*, 4 tablespoons of the soy sauce, and salt and bring to a boil over moderate heat. Add the fish, dark-skinned side up, bring back to a boil, skim, then cover with an inner wooden lid (*otoshibuta*) or use a plate, cover with the saucepan lid and simmer for 10 minutes over moderate heat, shaking the pan from time to time so that the fish do not stick.

Cut the stems from the peppers and slit them lengthways taking care not to cut them through.

Scrape out the seeds. Put peppers into a small saucepan with the remaining tablespoon of soy sauce, bring to a boil, then remove from the heat.

Arrange the fish on 4 platters, oblong if possible, dark-skinned side up and head facing left. Garnish with the chillies placing them at the right-hand front of the fish. Pour 1 tablespoon or so of the simmering liquid over each fish. Eat with chopsticks using them to cut the fish into convenient portions.

VARIATION: For another sole or plaice dish cooked with *sake, Karei No Sawani* (Simmered Sole), have 1 large sole or plaice weighing about 500 g (1 lb) cleaned, scaled and cut into 4 crossways slices. Score the skin of each piece with an H-cut on the diagonal. Pour 475 ml (16 fl oz) boiling water very gently over the fish, then rinse in cold water. Finely chop 4 medium-sized spring onions. Combine 250 ml (8 fl oz) second soup stock, 5 tablespoons *sake*, 2 tablespoons *mirin* and 2 tablespoons light soy sauce (*usukuchi shoyu*) in a saucepan large enough to hold the fish comfortably. Bring to a boil, add the fish, dark-skinned side up, cover with an inner wooden lid (*otoshibuta*) or use a plate, and the saucepan lid and simmer for 6 minutes over moderate heat. Remove the inner lid or plate, add the spring onions, cover and simmer for 2 minutes longer. Add 1 teaspoon ginger juice squeezed from grated fresh ginger. Put the fish into 4 individual bowls and pour the sauce over them. Serve hot. SERVES 4.

MACKEREL WITH GRATED WHITE RADISH

SABA NO OROSHINI

This attractive, well-flavoured dish takes only a brief time to prepare. The technique is suitable for any round-bodied oily fish.

SERVES 4
**4 mackerel fillets weighing about
375 g (12 oz) in all
Plain flour
Vegetable oil
125 g (4 oz) grated white radish (*daikon*)
2 medium-sized spring onions, trimmed, using
white and green parts
350 ml (12 fl oz) first soup stock
5 tablespoons soy sauce
3 tablespoons *mirin*
2 teaspoons sugar**

Cut the mackerel fillets into 2.5 cm (1 in) diagonal slices and coat lightly with flour. Let them stand for a few minutes. Heat 5 to 7 cm (2 to 3 in) vegetable oil in a *tempura* pan or heavy frying-pan to 180°C (350°F) on a frying thermometer or until bubbles form on chopsticks stirred in the oil. Fry the mackerel pieces, turning once, for 2 to 3 minutes, or until lightly browned. Lift out and drain on the rack of the *tempura* pan or on paper towels.

Lightly squeeze out the grated radish. Cut the spring onions into 4 diagonal slices. In a small saucepan, combine the soup stock, soy sauce, *mirin* and sugar and bring to a boil. Add the mackerel, grated radish and spring onions and bring back to a boil, uncovered, over moderate heat. Remove from the heat immediately and serve in bowls with the sauce poured over the fish. Eat with chopsticks.

VARIATION: An interesting variation is Mackerel Cooked in *Sake* (*Saba No Nitsuke*) which can also be used for any oily fish. Cut the fillets into diagonal slices as above, salt them lightly and let stand for 1 hour. Rinse and pat dry. Put them into a saucepan large enough to hold them comfortably in a single layer, skin side uppermost. Add 250 ml (8 fl oz) *sake* and bring to a boil over moderately high heat. Add 4 tablespoons soy sauce, 3 tablespoons *mirin* and 2 tablespoons fresh ginger root cut into julienne strips. Bring to a simmer, and skim, if necessary. Cover with an inner lid (an *otoshibuta*) or use a plate and cook over moderate heat for 10 minutes or until the liquid has reduced by about a half. Divide the fish among 4 bowls and pour the sauce over. SERVES 4.

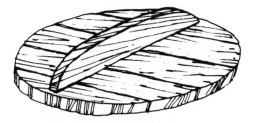

MACKEREL WITH RED BEAN PASTE

SABA NO MISONI

The robust flavour of the red *miso* (bean paste) sauce is just right for the equally robust flavour of the mackerel.

SERVES 4
4 small mackerel fillets, each weighing about 75 g (3 oz)
2.5 cm (1 in) slice fresh ginger root
250 ml (8 fl oz) first soup stock
1 tablespoon sugar
50 ml (2 fl oz) *sake*
5 tablespoons red *miso* (bean paste)
2 medium-sized spring onions, trimmed, using white and green parts

Cut the fish into 2.5 cm (1 in) diagonal slices. Peel the ginger and cut it into julienne strips. Set fish and ginger aside.

In a saucepan large enough to hold the fish in a single layer, combine the soup stock, sugar and *sake* and simmer, stirring, until the sugar has dissolved. Add the fish and the ginger and cover with an inner wooden lid, an *otoshibuta*, or use a plate. Simmer over low heat for 5 minutes or until the fish is done. In a bowl mix the bean paste with a little of the soup stock until it is smooth and add it to the saucepan, mixing gently. Simmer over low heat for 10 minutes.

Thinly slice the spring onions and crisp for a few minutes in cold water. Drain and squeeze out the moisture in a cloth.

Arrange the fish on 4 plates and pour the sauce over it. The sauce should be moderately thick. If it is too thick, thin with a little soup stock. Garnish with the spring onions.

GRILLED MACKEREL FILLETS

SABA NO SHIOYAKI

This is a simple, very pleasant way of cooking mackerel. The accompanying white radish (*daikon*) and soy sauce enhance the flavour of the fish.

SERVES 4
2 × 175 g (6 oz) mackerel fillets with skin on
Salt
75 g (3 oz) white radish (*daikon*), finely grated
1 tablespoon soy sauce

Cut the fillets in half crossways and sprinkle lightly all over with salt. Leave for 5 minutes, then rinse in cold water and pat dry with paper towels. Sprinkle again with salt very lightly on both sides, then cut a shallow cross in the skin of each piece to prevent the fish curling when it is being cooked. Do not cut deeper than the skin.

Grill the fish over or under moderate heat until lightly browned on both sides, about 10 minutes. Put the fish on 4 plates, skin-side up. Lightly squeeze out the radish and put a mound on each plate beside the fish. Pour the soy sauce over the radish. Eat with chopsticks, putting a little radish on each bite.

FOIL-WRAPPED MACKEREL

SABA NO GINSHIYAKI

In Japan, fresh local mushrooms (*nama-shiitake*) would be used. These are a pretty brown and give a colour contrast that enhances the appearance of the dish. Dried Japanese mushrooms (*shiitake*), soaked for 30 minutes in warm water, squeezed out and with the tough stems removed, may be used instead, or fresh local mushrooms.

SERVES 4
375 g (12 oz) mackerel fillets
2 tablespoons *mirin*
3 tablespoons soy sauce
½ teaspoon sugar
8 medium-sized flat mushrooms
4 whole chestnuts, tinned in syrup
16 cooked gingko nuts, tinned or bottled
1 lemon, cut into 4 wedges

Cut the mackerel into 4 pieces and put into a bowl. Mix the *mirin* with 2 tablespoons of the soy sauce over the fish and leave it to marinate for 30 minutes, turning once or twice. Put the mushrooms into a bowl. Mix the sugar with the remaining tablespoon of soy sauce and pour over the mushrooms.

Cut aluminium foil into eight 30 × 25 cm (12 × 10 in) pieces. Use 2 sheets of foil, one on top of the other for each serving. Brush the top sheet with oil, leaving an unoiled margin of 2.5 cm (1 in). Place a piece of mackerel, skin-side up, in the centre of the foil. Top with 2 mushrooms, 1 chestnut and 4 gingko nuts. Repeat with the rest of the ingredients. Fold the top pieces of foil over to make neat packages, then wrap the second

pieces of foil over the first, twisting the ends. Put the packages on a baking sheet and bake in a preheated 180°C (350°F), gas mark 4 oven for 8 to 10 minutes. Put a package on each of 4 plates and garnish with a lemon wedge. To eat, unwrap the packages, squeeze lemon juice over the fish and eat with chopsticks.

VARIATION 1: Many types of fish can be baked in foil and the dishes varied by using different garnishes. For Trout Baked in Foil (*Masu No Ginshiyaki*), wash and dry 4 small rainbow trout and make 3 diagonal cuts in the skin on one side. Brush the foil pieces with oil and place a trout on each. Season with salt and sprinkle each fish with 2 teaspoons *sake*. Fold up as in the main recipe and bake in a preheated 180°C (350°F), gas mark 4 oven for 20 minutes. Serve with a garnish of lemon wedges and pickled red ginger. SERVES 4.

VARIATION 2: Fillets of any white fish such as sole, plaice or flounder can be used for Fish Baked in Foil (*Sakana No Ginshiyaki*). Have 4 fillets of any of the above fish weighing about 375 g (12 oz) and arrange on pieces of oiled aluminium as in the main recipe. Pour 2 teaspoons *sake* on each package of fish and top the fish with 3 tinned or bottled cooked gingko nuts, 2 medium-sized flat mushrooms, stems trimmed, and salt to taste. Bake in a preheated 180°C (350°F), gas mark 4 oven for 15 minutes, about. Serve with a garnish of lemon wedges, and a little soy sauce if liked. SERVES 4.

MACKEREL WITH HOT RED CHILLI PEPPERS

SABA NO NANBAN-NI

Mackerel is a favourite fish in Japan and is cooked in a number of imaginative ways, this one like the sole and trout in the same way as *tempura* without the batter coating. The use of hot chillies, green or red, is interesting as these were introduced into Japan only in the mid-16th century by Portuguese traders. The Japanese cultivate, among others, a type of chilli known as hawk's claw because it is long and slightly hooked. It is also ferociously hot and is used with caution.

SERVES 4
800 g (1¾ lb) skinned and boned mackerel fillets
Plain flour
Vegetable oil
250 ml (8 fl oz) first soup stock
3 tablespoons soy sauce
2 teaspoons sugar
1½ tablespoons rice vinegar
1 dried hot red pepper, seeded and chopped

Cut each mackerel fillet into 4 crossways slices and dust lightly with flour. Heat 5 to 7 cm (2 to 3 in) oil in a *tempura* pan or a heavy frying-pan to a temperature of 180°C (350°F) on a frying thermometer or until bubbles form on wooden chopsticks stirred in the oil. Fry the mackerel pieces, turning once, for 2 minutes, and drain on the rack of the *tempura* pan or on paper towels.

In a shallow saucepan or frying-pan large enough to hold the mackerel pieces in a single layer, combine the soup stock, soy sauce, sugar and vinegar. Bring to a boil. Add the mackerel and the hot chilli pepper and simmer, uncovered, over low heat for 5 minutes. Serve in bowls with the sauce poured over the fish.

VARIATION: For Mackerel with Grated White Radish (*Saba No Oroshini*), omit the hot chilli pepper. In the sauce, omit the rice vinegar and substitute 3 tablespoons *mirin*. Increase the soy sauce to 4 tablespoons. Finely grate and lightly squeeze out 125 g (4 oz) white radish (*daikon*). Cut 1 medium-sized spring onion, trimmed, into 4 diagonal slices. Cook the mackerel as in the main recipe, add to the hot soup stock mixture with the radish and spring onion. Bring back to the boil, uncovered, remove from the heat and serve in bowls with the sauce poured over the fish. SERVES 4.

GRILLED MARINATED SALMON

SAKE NO ISOBEYAKI

This dish has a very poetic name conveying the Japanese desire to please the eye and the mind as well as the palate. The dish is garnished with dried laver seaweed (*nori*) so that salmon and seaweed combine to remind of a scene at the beach (*isobe*).

SERVES 4
**375 g (12 oz) fresh salmon fillet with skin on
4 tablespoons *mirin*
4 tablespoons soy sauce
½ sheet dried laver seaweed (*nori*)
4 sprouts of pickled ginger, *or* sliced pickled ginger**

Cut the salmon fillet into 4 diagonal slices. In a bowl, mix together the *mirin* and soy sauce, add the salmon and marinate for 30 minutes, turning two or three times.

Lift out the salmon on to a plate and pour the marinade into a small saucepan. Simmer to reduce to half over moderate heat. Dip the fish in the marinade and grill over or under moderate heat for 2 minutes. Turn the pieces and, using a pastry brush, coat with the marinade. Grill for 1 minute, then turn. Repeat the grilling and basting until fish is cooked and marinade used up.

Put the salmon on 4 platters, oblong if possible. Toast the seaweed for a few seconds on both sides over a gas flame or electric burner, crush, sprinkle over fish. Garnish with ginger.

VARIATION: For a simpler version, Glazed Salmon (*Sake No Teriyaki*), which can be prepared in minutes, halve two 175 g (6 oz) salmon steaks with skin on. Heat 2 tablespoons vegetable oil in a frying-pan large enough to hold the fish comfortably in a single layer and sauté the fish over moderately high heat, turning once or twice, until the fish is lightly browned on both sides, about 4 minutes. Mix 2 tablespoons of soy sauce with 1 tablespoon of *mirin* and pour over the fish. Reduce the heat to low and cook, turning frequently, until the fish is glazed, about 2 to 3 minutes. Serve on 4 small plates, garnished with pickled ginger or cucumber. SERVES 4.

GLAZED SALMON

SAKE NO TERIYAKI

The technique of glazing while frying or grilling is one of the most attractive in the Japanese kitchen, providing a rich flavour while using little oil, so that all the healthful qualities of the fish are kept.

SERVES 4
**2 × 175 g (6 oz) salmon steaks with skin on
2 tablespoons vegetable oil
2 tablespoons soy sauce
1 tablespoon *mirin***

GARNISH:
Pickled ginger or pickled cucumber

Halve the salmon steaks. In a frying-pan large enough to hold the salmon pieces comfortably in a single layer, heat the oil and sauté the salmon until the fish is browned all over, turning once during cooking, about 4 minutes. Mix the soy sauce with the *mirin* and pour over the fish. Reduce the heat and cook, turning frequently, until the fish is glazed, 1 or 2 minutes.

Put the fish on 4 small platters or plates and garnish with pickled ginger or cucumber.

SALMON STEAMED WITH BEAN CURD

SAKE NO KENCHIN-MUSHI

This is an elegant and satisfying dish combining salmon, bean curd, mushrooms and prawns, the flavours of the unusual medley subtly complementing each other.

SERVES 4
**375 g (12 oz) fresh salmon fillet with
skin left on**
Salt
3 tablespoons *mirin*
2 jelly mushrooms (*kikurage*)
**1 bean curd (*momen tofu*), weighing about 250 g
(8 oz)**
1 large egg
**50 g (2 oz) cooked, peeled prawns, if frozen
thoroughly defrosted**
1 tablespoon cooked green peas
2 tablespoons light soy sauce (*usukuchi shoyu*)
350 ml (12 fl oz) first soup stock
1 teaspoon cornflour *or* arrowroot
**2.5 cm (1 in) slice fresh ginger root, cut into
julienne strips**

Cut the salmon into 4 diagonal slices. Sprinkle with a little salt, then with 1 tablespoon of the *mirin*, on both sides and set aside.

Soak the jelly mushrooms in warm water for 15 minutes. Squeeze out and cut into julienne strips. Rinse the bean curd and wrap in a piece of cheesecloth or a kitchen towel, weight down with a plate and let it stand for 10 minutes to press out the excess moisture. Put into a bowl and mash with a fork. Break the egg into a small bowl, stir with chopsticks until well-blended and stir into the bean curd. Add the mushrooms, prawns, peas, 1 tablespoon light soy sauce, ½ teaspoon salt, or to taste, and 1 tablespoon of *mirin*, mixing well.

Rinse off the salmon and pat it dry. Have ready 4 pieces of cheesecloth. Put a slice of salmon in the centre of a piece of cheesecloth and spread it with ¼ of the bean curd mixture. Fold it into a neat package and repeat with the rest of the salmon and bean curd to make 4 packages. Put the packages into a steamer, bean curd-side up, over boiling water, lower the heat to moderate and steam for 12 to 13 minutes.

In a small saucepan, combine the soup stock, salt to taste, 1 tablespoon light soy sauce, the remaining tablespoon *mirin*, and the cornflour or arrowroot mixed with a little cold water and simmer over low heat until the mixture is lightly thickened and smooth, a few minutes.

Unwrap the salmon and put into 4 bowls, bean curd-side down. Put a little heap of ginger in the centre of each slice of salmon and pour on the hot sauce. Serve hot.

GLAZED KING MACKEREL

SAWARA NO TERIYAKI

The preferred fish in Japan for this is the King mackerel which, as the name implies, grows to a great length up to 1.5 metres (about 5 feet) but any fresh mackerel will do just as well. This is a popular New Year dish.

SERVES 8
250 g (8 oz) mackerel fillets
3 tablespoons *mirin*
2 tablespoons soy sauce
2 teaspoons *sake*

Cut the fish into 8 slices. In a small bowl combine the *mirin*, soy sauce and *sake*. Add the fish and marinate for 20 minutes. Lift the fish out of the marinade and set it aside on a plate. Pour the marinade into a small saucepan, bring to a simmer over moderate heat and reduce to about one-quarter.

Thread the fish pieces on 2 or 3 metal skewers and grill over high heat about 15 cm (6 in) from the heat, or grill under high heat, until the fish is lightly browned. Using a pastry brush, coat with the marinade 3 or 4 times to glaze, still with high heat, turning often. When the fish is glazed, remove from the heat and let it cool before taking it off the skewers. Arrange on 8 small plates. Serve at room temperature.

SOLE WITH BEANCURD AND MUSHROOMS

HIRAME NO AGENI

SERVES 4
375 g (12 oz) skinned and boned fillet of sole
Plain flour
1 bean curd (*momen tofu*) weighing about 250 g (8 oz)
8 medium-sized flat fresh mushrooms
300 ml (½ pint) first soup stock
3 tablespoons soy sauce
2 teaspoons sugar
1 tablespoon *mirin*

Halve the fish lengthways, then cut into diagonal bite-size pieces. Coat with the flour, shaking to remove the excess. Roll the cake of bean curd in a bamboo mat (*sudare*) or in a kitchen towel and weight it with a plate. Let it stand for 10 minutes to press out excess moisture. Pat dry and cut into 2.5 cm (1 in) cubes. Coat with the flour. Wipe the mushroom caps with a damp cloth, remove the stems and coat with flour. Set aside.

In a medium-sized saucepan, combine the soup stock, soy sauce, sugar and *mirin*. Stir to dissolve the sugar and set aside.

Heat 5 to 7 cm (2 to 3 in) oil in a *tempura* pan or heavy frying-pan to 180°C (350°F) on a frying thermometer or until bubbles form on wooden chopsticks stirred in the oil. Add the pieces of sole, one at a time to prevent them sticking together, then add the mushrooms and cubes of bean curd in the same way and fry until lightly browned, 2 to 3 minutes. Do this in batches, if necessary, to avoid crowding the pan. Drain on the rack of the *tempura* pan or on paper towels.

Bring the soup stock mixture to a boil, add the fish, mushrooms and bean curd, bring back to a boil, then remove immediately from the heat. Serve in bowls with the sauce poured over.

GREEN PEPPERS STUFFED WITH FISH

TSUMAMONO-AGE

Stuffed peppers are very popular in traditional Mexican cooking and, though they did not reach Japan from Mexico until the middle of the 16th century, the culinary response is very similar. A slightly different pepper, the *poblano*, is used in Mexico but this has not migrated, so the sweet green pepper is the one most used. The Japanese have made this dish deliciously different from any other stuffed peppers.

SERVES 4

6 medium-sized green peppers
375 g (12 oz) skinned and boned fillets of any
white fish such as sole, plaice, flounder
1½ tablespoons *sake*
3½ tablespoons *katakuriko* starch *or* cornflour
Salt
⅛ teaspoon MSG
1 tablespoon finely chopped parsley
Vegetable oil for deep frying
2 teaspoons rice vinegar
1½ tablespoons soy sauce
1 tablespoon dry Japanese or English mustard

Rinse the peppers, carefully cut out the stem and remove the seeds and fibres, leaving the peppers intact. Rinse out to remove any remaining seeds and set, cut side down, to drain. Rinse the fish, pat it dry and grind in a Japanese serrated earthenware mortar (*suribachi*), or purée in a blender or food processor. Mix the *sake*, 2½ tablespoons of *katakuriko* or cornflour, salt to taste, MSG and parsley with the fish, mixing well. Put ½ teaspoon of the *katakuriko* or cornflour into each of the peppers and shake to coat the inside. Shake out any excess. Stuff the peppers with the fish mixture, pushing it in firmly but taking care not to break the peppers.

In a large shallow saucepan that will hold the peppers comfortably in a single layer, or in a fairly deep frying-pan heat enough oil to cover the peppers to a temperature of 150°C (300°F) on a frying thermometer, a little lower than moderate. Fry the peppers until they are tender, about 10 minutes, turning them several times during the cooking. Lift out and drain on paper towels. When they are cool enough to handle, cut the peppers into 4 to 6 slices according to size. Arrange a sliced pepper on each of 4 platters or plates. Mix the vinegar and soy sauce together and put into 4 small bowls. Mix the mustard with hot water in a small dish then put a small heap of it next to the peppers. Eat at room temperature, dipping the pepper slices into the sauce and adding a dab of mustard.

DEEP-FRIED RAINBOW TROUT

NIJIMASU NO KARAAGE

Rainbow trout are now available all year round, making this dish practical as well as delicious. It is cooked in the same way as *tempura*, but is not batter-coated. Cucumbers in Japan are smaller than those here and can be bitter. It is useful to know the Japanese technique for eliminating the bitterness but not necessary for our type of cucumber.

SERVES 4

**4 rainbow trout, each weighing about 175 g
(6 oz), cleaned, with head and tail left on
1 tablespoon *sake*
Salt
½ cucumber
25 g (1 oz) white radish (*daikon*)
4 fresh hot green chilli peppers
Pickled red ginger (*beni-shoga*)
Katakuriko starch *or* cornflour
Vegetable oil
3 tablespoons rice vinegar
2 teaspoons sugar
1 teaspoon fresh ginger juice**

Rinse the trout and pat dry with paper towels. Using a sharp knife, make 2 equally spaced shallow diagonal cuts on each side of the fish. Sprinkle with the *sake* and a little salt. Set aside.

To take the bitterness out of the cucumber, Japanese cooks cut a slice from each end and rub the cut surfaces with the ends. Discard the slices, then roll the cucumber in salt for a minute or two. Rinse and pat dry. This removes any bitter taste. Peel the cucumber in alternate lengthways strips, scrape out the seeds with a vegetable peeler or chopsticks and grate finely. Squeeze out the moisture and put onto a plate. Squeeze the moisture out of the finely grated radish and add it to the plate. Cut the stems off the peppers and scrape out the seeds with chopsticks. Set aside on a small plate with the pickled ginger which should be very finely sliced.

Drain the trout and pat dry. Coat lightly inside and out with the *katakuriko* starch or cornflour. Heat 7 cm (3 in) oil in a *tempura* pan or saucepan to 180°C (350°F) on a frying thermometer, or until bubbles form on wooden chopsticks stirred in the oil. Fry the peppers very briefly, for about 30 seconds. Lift out and drain on the rack of the *tempura* pan or on paper towels. Add the trout and cook, one at a time, unless the pan will hold more, for 5 minutes, turning twice. Serve on 4 oblong platters, or any suitable-sized plate, and garnish with the peppers and pickled ginger.

Combine the vinegar, sugar, salt to taste, ginger juice, cucumber and radish, in a bowl. Stir until the sugar in dissolved and pour over the trout.

DEEP-FRIED CRISPY FLOUNDER

KAREI NO KARAAGE

It is important to have small, whole fish weighing about 250 g (8 oz) for this. If the flounder are too large, use small plaice or dab or whole small whiting or smelt. Unskinned mackerel fillets can also be used but will not be as attractive as the whole fish.

SERVES 4

**4 small flounder, each weighing about
250 g (8 oz), cleaned with heads and tails left on
Plain flour
2 medium spring onions, trimmed, using white
and green parts
75 g (3 oz) slice white radish (*daikon*)
1 dried, hot red chilli pepper, seeded
1 tablespoon citrus vinegar (*ponzu*)
1 tablespoon soy sauce
2 tablespoons first or second soup stock
Vegetable oil**

Wash and dry the fish. Using a very sharp knife score the fish, on both sides, making diagonal cuts at about 5 cm (2 in) intervals. Score again, diagonally, in the opposite direction, making a diamond pattern. Dust the fish all over with flour and set aside for 2 or 3 minutes.

Cut the spring onions crossways into 2.5 cm (1 in) slices, then cut these finely lengthways. Put into a bowl of cold water to crisp for a few minutes, drain, pat dry and set aside for the garnish.

Peel the radish and using chopsticks, poke a hole in the centre. Stuff it with the chilli pepper. Finely grate the radish and chilli, lightly squeezing out the excess moisture. Set aside with the spring onions.

Make a dipping sauce. Mix together the citrus vinegar, soy sauce and soup stock and pour into 4 small bowls. Put a bowl at each place setting.

Heat 5 to 7 cm (2 to 3 in) vegetable oil in a *tempura* pan or heavy skillet to 180°C (350°F) on a frying thermometer, or until bubbles form on wooden chopsticks stirred in the oil. Fry the fish, as many at a time as the pan will hold comfortably, for 8 minutes, or until golden, turning once. Lift out and drain on the rack of the *tempura* pan, or on paper towels.

To serve, put the fish, dark–skinned–side up on 4 platters or plates, with the head facing left. Garnish the front of each platter with a pile each of radish and spring onion. To eat, stir the garnishes into the sauce, cut the fish into bite-size pieces with chopsticks and dip into the sauce.

GLAZED SMELT WITH GINGER

WAKASAGI NO AGENI

Smelt are a fish very much liked in Japan and are especially suitable for frying in a *tempura* pan. These are glazed, borrowing from the cooking technique not just of *tempura* but also of *teriyaki* where foods are grilled and glazed.

SERVES 4
**12 small smelt, cleaned and scaled with heads
and tails left on
Salt
Katakuriko starch *or* cornflour
Vegetable oil
2 tablespoons *sake*
3 teaspoons sugar
3 tablespoons soy sauce
2.5 cm (1 in) cube fresh ginger, grated**

Sprinkle the fish all over lightly with the salt and let it stand for 5 minutes. Pat it dry then roll in *katakuriko* starch or cornflour, shaking to remove the excess. Heat 5 to 7 cm (2 to 3 in) vegetable oil in a *tempura* pan or a heavy frying-pan to a temperature of 180°C (350°F) on a frying thermometer or until bubbles form on wooden chopsticks stirred in the oil. Fry the smelt in batches for 8 minutes, turning once or twice.

In a frying-pan or shallow saucepan large enough to hold all the fish comfortably, combine the *sake*, sugar and soy sauce, stir to mix and bring to a boil. Add the fish and cook, uncovered, over fairly high heat for 1 or 2 minutes, turning the fish once so that they are glazed on both sides. Arrange the smelt on 4 platters and garnish with a small mound of grated ginger.

GOLDEN-BROWN FRIED OYSTERS

KAKI NO KOGANEYAKI

The Japanese have lovely ways with oysters, and this is a splendid though very simple dish.

SERVES 4
**250 g (8 oz) spinach
16 large fresh oysters, shucked
Salt
1 tablespoon *sake*
Plain flour
2 large eggs
2 tablespoons vegetable oil**

Thoroughly wash the spinach, drain and drop into a saucepan of briskly boiling salted water. Bring back to a boil over high heat and boil for 2 minutes. Drain, rinse thoroughly in cold water and drain again. Put on to a bamboo mat (*sudare*) or on a kitchen towel. Roll up and squeeze out the moisture. Form the spinach into a roll, and cut into 1 cm (½ in) slices. Set aside.

Rinse the oysters quickly in salted water and drain. Put into a bowl and mix with the *sake* and a pinch of salt. Leave for 5 minutes. Lift out and pat dry with paper towels then dredge with flour, shaking to remove the excess. Break the eggs into a bowl and stir with chopsticks until they are well-blended but not foamy.

Heat the oil in a large heavy frying-pan that will hold the oysters comfortably, otherwise do them in two batches. Dip the oysters in the egg and fry for 1 or 2 minutes until golden-brown on both sides. Do not overcook. Drain quickly on paper towels. Arrange 4 oysters on each of 4 small plates or platters and garnish with the spinach rolls.

DEEP-FRIED OYSTERS

KAKI NO ISO-AGE

This is a more elaborate dish than Golden-Brown Fried Oysters (page 87). The oysters are dipped in batter made with a mixture of water and *sake*. The *sake* makes the batter very light and crisp.

SERVES 4
16 large, fresh oysters shucked
Salt
3 tablespoons *sake*
Flour to coat oysters
12 medium-sized green beans
75 g (3 oz) slice white radish (*daikon*)
2 dried hot red chilli peppers, seeded
1 large egg
¼ teaspoon sugar
65 g (2 oz) plain flour, sifted
1 sheet dried laver seaweed (*nori*)
Vegetable oil for deep frying
4 tablespoons soy sauce

Rinse the oysters in cold salted water, drain and put into a bowl with 1 tablespoon of the *sake*, and a little salt and marinate for about 5 minutes. Drain, coat lightly with the flour and set aside to dry.

Rinse and trim the beans, cut in half crossways and arrange in 4 bundles.

Peel the radish and using chopsticks, poke a hole in the centre. Stuff it with the chilli peppers. Finely grate the radish and chillies, lightly squeezing out the excess moisture. Set aside.

Make the batter. Break the egg into a bowl and stir with chopsticks until it is well-blended but not foamy. Add 75 ml (3 fl oz) water, the sugar and ¼ teaspoon salt. Stir in the remaining 2 tablespoons of *sake*. Add the flour stirring with chopsticks to mix lightly. It does not matter if it is slightly lumpy.

Cut the seaweed into 4 squares, then cut the squares into 16 strips and wrap a strip round each oyster. Or, toast the seaweed for a few seconds on both sides over a gas flame or electric burner, crush in a kitchen towel and add it to the batter. It is a matter of choice.

Heat 5 to 7 cm (2 to 3 in) vegetable oil in a *tempura* pan or large, heavy frying-pan and heat to 180°C (350°F) on a frying thermometer or until bubbles form on wooden chopsticks stirred in the oil. Dip the beans in the batter and fry for 2 minutes. Lift out and drain on the rack of the *tempura* pan, or on paper towels. Dip the oysters in the batter and fry, a few at a time, until light gold, about 2 minutes. Drain on the rack of the *tempura* pan, or on paper towels.

Pour a tablespoon of soy sauce into each of 4 small saucers. Put a little pile of grated radish and chilli in the centre of each one. Serve the oysters and green beans on bamboo plates (*zaru*) lined with paper napkins, or serve on ordinary plates. Serve immediately while the beans and oysters are hot.

OYSTERS IN VINEGARED BEAN PASTE

KAKI NO SUMISO-KAKE

This dish is another example of the imaginative way the Japanese have with oysters. The sauce is extremely subtle though quite strongly flavoured, but it does not mask the natural taste of the oysters.

SERVES 4
20 shucked oysters, about 375 g (12 oz)
1 tablespoon *sake*
Salt
8 medium-sized spring onions, trimmed, using white and green parts
1 teaspoon dry Japanese or English mustard
4 tablespoons white *miso* (bean paste)
1 teaspoon sugar
2 tablespoons *mirin*
2 tablespoons rice vinegar

Rinse and drain the oysters. In a medium-sized saucepan, combine the *sake* with 250 ml (8 fl oz) salted water and bring to a boil, add the oysters and cook just long enough to plump them, about 30 seconds. Drain the oysters and discard the liquid. Drop the spring onions into a saucepan of boiling water for 30 seconds, drain and pat dry. Cut them into 2.5 cm (1 in) slices.

In a bowl, mix the mustard to a paste with hot water. Add the bean paste, sugar, *mirin* and vinegar and stir until it is well-blended and smooth.

Divide the oysters among 4 small bowls, and garnish with the spring onions. Pour the sauce over the oysters and eat with chopsticks.

CLAMS IN BEAN PASTE, MUSTARD AND VINEGAR

HAMAGURI NO KARASHISUMISO-AE

This is a very traditional dish using clams which are considered food for special occasions. The dish is so carefully balanced that no one flavour predominates and all the flavours come through independently.

SERVES 4
8 large, or 16 small, clams, shucked
Salt
Rice vinegar
2 × 20 cm (8 in) fronds lobe-leaf seaweed (*wakame*)
6 medium-sized spring onions, trimmed, using white and green parts
6 tablespoons red *miso* (bean paste)
1 tablespoon sugar
1 tablespoon *sake*
2 tablespoons rice vinegar
1 teaspoon dry Japanese or English mustard
1 tablespoon fresh ginger root, cut into julienne strips

Rinse the clams in cold salted water, drain and drop into a saucepan of briskly boiling water and cook for 1 minute. Drain, chop coarsely and sprinkle with a little rice vinegar. Set aside.

In a bowl, soak the seaweed in cold water for 15 minutes. Drain, squeeze out, cut away the hard ribs and chop coarsely. Return the seaweed to the bowl and pour boiling water over it, drain and cool. Set aside.

Drop the spring onions into boiling water and cook for 2 minutes. Drain and arrange lengthways on a chopping board. Press with the back of a large knife to remove the excess liquid. Chop coarsely or cut into 1 cm (½ in) pieces. Set aside.

In a small saucepan, combine the bean paste, sugar, *sake* and rice vinegar. Stir over low heat until the mixture is smooth and well-blended. Do not let it boil. Mix the mustard with a little hot water and stir it into the sauce. Cool.

Add the clams, seaweed and spring onions to the sauce, mixing lightly. Serve in small, deep bowls, garnished with the ginger.

TEAPOT-STEAMED PRAWNS, CHICKEN AND FISH

DOBIN-MUSHI

A *dobin* is a small earthenware teapot, 1-cup size, so 4 are needed for this traditional, flavourful and amusing dish. *Mushi* refers to the cooking method of steaming so if no *dobin* are available, the ingredients may be steamed in bowls. In Japan *matsutake* mushrooms, which grow only in pine forests and are highly esteemed, would be used for this dish. *Tori-sasami*, known as the bamboo leaf chicken breast, is the small fillet of the skinned and boned chicken breast. The whole breast of a 1.4 kg (3 lb) chicken yields two 25 g (1 oz) 'bamboo leaves'. The rest of the breast can be reserved for another use, or can be cut into lengthways slices, each weighing about 25 g (1 oz), using just one skinned and boned chicken breast.

SERVES 4

**8 large uncooked, unshelled prawns, if frozen
then thoroughly defrosted**
50 g (2 oz) bamboo leaf chicken breast
**(*tori-sasami*) *or* use 1 small skinned and boned
chicken breast halved lengthways**
Salt
Sake
**125 g (4 oz) fillet of sole, sea bass, or similar
white fish**
4 medium-sized flat fresh mushrooms
12 cooked gingko nuts, tinned or bottled
700 ml (1¼ pints) first soup stock
1 teaspoon light soy sauce (*usukuchi shoyu*)
8 leaves trefoil (*mitsuba*), optional

Shell and devein the prawns, leaving the last segment of shell and the tail intact. Slice the chicken breast diagonally into bite-size pieces, sprinkle with a little salt and 1 teaspoon *sake*. Cut the fish into 4 pieces, sprinkle with a little salt and 1 teaspoon of *sake*. Trim the mushroom stems and cut the mushrooms into quarters. Cut the trefoil leaves, if available, into 2.5 cm (1 in) pieces. Drain the gingko nuts.

In a jug, combine the soup stock, 1 teaspoon salt, 1 tablespoon of *sake* and the light soy sauce and pour the mixture into 4 1-cup Japanese earthenware teapots, or into *donabe* (lidded earthenware bowls). Divide all the ingredients into 4 equal parts and add, except the trefoil, to each pot. Cover the teapots and place over very low heat on top of the stove, or on heat diffusing mats on moderate heat and bring to a boil. Remove from the heat, garnish with the trefoil, if using, and serve. Eat with chopsticks out of the teapot and pour the soup into small, matching tea bowls.

GRILLED CLAMS

YAKI HAMAGURI

Grilling with salt (*shio-yaki*) is a favourite method in Japan and is used for a number of fish, as well as shellfish. It works particularly well in this dish which is of the utmost simplicity and takes only minutes to prepare and cook. The clams should be bought and soaked ahead of time.

SERVES 4
8 large, or 16 small, clams, in the shell
Salt
Pine needle sprigs for garnish, if available

Soak the clams overnight in cold salted water. Scrub, if necessary, rinse and drain. Roll the clams in salt and arrange on the rack of a grill. When the grill is hot, cook the clams under moderate heat 10 to 12 cm (4 to 5 in) from the source of the heat for about 2 minutes, or until the clams open.

Have ready 4 small plates coated with a layer of salt, preferably sea salt, and arrange the clams on top. Garnish with a pine needle sprig, if available. Lift out the clams with chopsticks to eat and drink the liquid out of the shell.

VARIATION: For Clams Steamed with *Sake* (*Hamaguri No Sakamushi*), prepare the clams as above and put into a large shallow saucepan that will hold them, if possible, in a single layer. Pour 2 tablespoons *sake* over the clams, cover and cook over moderate heat for about 5 minutes, or until the clams open. Have ready 4 small plates coated with a layer of salt, preferably sea salt. Lift the clams carefully out of the saucepan and arrange on the plates. Decorate, as before, with a pine needle sprig, if available. The *sake* will have completely evaporated during the cooking, but will have flavoured the clams. SERVES 4.

SLICED RAW FISH

SASHIMI

SERVES 4

Choose 375 g (12 oz) of the freshest possible fish, including any of the following: sole, flounder, bream, red snapper, mackerel, sea bass, turbot, halibut, tuna and squid.

Have the fishmonger fillet the fish. It should be skinned and all bones removed. The squid should be cleaned. Refrigerate the fish until ready to use, then cut the fillets, except for the tuna, into very thin diagonal slices, about 0.5 × 2.5 cm ($\frac{1}{2}$ × 1 in). For the tuna, which should be a deep rose-red, cut into straight 5 mm ($\frac{1}{4}$ in) slices. Cut the squid open, so that there are 2 pieces, then halve each piece to make 4. Cut with a very sharp knife crossways into very thin slices. Arrange decoratively on 4 plates.

Have ready the following garnishes: white radish (*daikon*), carrot, cucumber, and celery cut into fine julienne strips and crisped in cold water. Use 1 or more of the garnishes on the plates to be dipped in the sauce and eaten alternately with the fish. For the simplest sauce, mix green horseradish powder (*wasabi*) to a paste and put a little mound of it on each plate. Pour soy sauce into 4 small bowls, one at each place. Stir the horseradish into the soy sauce according to taste and use as a dipping sauce, or if preferred put a tiny bit of horseradish on a piece of fish, fold it over and dip it in the soy sauce.

Choose any of the following dipping sauces:

125 ml (4 fl oz) soy sauce mixed with 2 tablespoons *Ponzu* vinegar, or use 1 tablespoon each lemon juice and rice vinegar.

125 ml (4 fl oz) soy sauce mixed with 1 tablespoon fresh grated ginger.

125 ml (4 fl oz) soy sauce mixed with 1 tablespoon dry Japanese or English mustard.

Mix 75 ml (3 fl oz) soy sauce with 1 tablespoon *sake* and 2 tablespoons dried bonito flakes (*hana-katsuo*) in a small saucepan and simmer for 1 minute. Strain, cool and pour into 4 small individual bowls.

ONE-POT DISHES

ÑABEMONO

The one-pot dishes which are cooked at the table, the *nabemono*, were introduced into Japan during the Meiji period in the 19th century when strict Buddhist vegetarianism was modified. These attractive dishes are especially popular for family dining, and for entertaining guests. Cooking *nabemono* presents few difficulties, though some pieces of cooking equipment are essential. They are a *donabe*, a fireproof, lidded earthenware casserole, a *sukiyaki-nabe*, a round cast-iron pan, and an on-the-table heater, or an electric frying-pan. Beautiful *donabe*, elegantly decorated, are available in Japanese shops, and are worth acquiring for the added grace they lend to the table for any meal.

The ingredients for the dishes are prepared ahead of time and set out attractively on platters. Sauces, chopsticks, and a bowl are set at each place. The garnishes are placed at the centre of the table near the cooking pot. As these dishes need little cooking time, cooking begins only after the diners are seated.

The presentation varies according to the dish. Sometimes, as with Simmered Beef and Vegetables (*Shabu Shabu*), each diner selects the piece of food to be cooked and holds it with chopsticks in the simmering stock to cook it. Or the ingredients can be added to the pot by the host or hostess, with fresh ingredients added from time to time to replenish the pot.

The dishes are versatile, allowing for substitution of ingredients such as chicken or pork for beef, watercress for spinach, and so on. Though the recipes given here are for four people, they can be doubled successfully. The one-pot dishes are ideal for parties. Guests can be seated at tables for four and all that is needed is an adequate number of table heaters, or electric frying-pans and casseroles. For outdoor dining, a charcoal-burning *hibachi* is fine. Rice and pickles are all that is needed to complete the meal.

SIMMERED BEEF AND VEGETABLES

SHABU SHABU

This is a favourite winter dish in which paper-thin slices of beef and fresh vegetables are cooked at table, held in chopsticks by the diners and swished back and forth in the cooking liquid making a noise that sounds like '*shabu shabu*'. Two dipping sauces are served, and when all the ingredients have been eaten the stock, enriched by the flavours of the beef and vegetables, is served as soup, sometimes with cooked rice, rice cakes or noodles, or just with a little soy sauce.

SERVES 4

500 g (1 lb) very thinly sliced fillet, *or* topside, *or* sirloin of beef
1 bean curd (*momen tofu*) weighing about 250 g (8 oz)
175 g (6 oz) about, drained-weight package devil's-tongue-root noodles (*shirataki*)
8 medium-sized flat fresh mushrooms
3 stalks trefoil (*mitsuba*), *or* 125 g (4 oz) trimmed spinach
6 leaves Chinese Leaves (*hakusai*), sometimes called Chinese cabbage

FOR THE SAUCES:
2 medium-sized spring onions, using white and green parts
10 cm (4 in) slice white radish (*daikon*)
4 tablespoons soy sauce
4 tablespoons citrus vinegar (*ponzu*)
125 ml (4 fl oz) second soup stock
4 tablespoons white sesame seeds
3 tablespoons rice vinegar
3 tablespoons light soy sauce (*usukuchi shoyu*)
1 tablespoon *mirin*
Piece kelp (*kombu*) about 10 × 15 cm (4 × 6 in)

Cut the thinly sliced steak into bite-size pieces, about 2.5 × 5 cm (1 × 2 in). Halve the bean curd lengthways, then cut into 2.5 cm (1 in) slices. Drop the noodles into boiling water for 1 minute, drain and cut in half. Wipe the mushroom caps and trim the stems. If trefoil is available, cut into 5 cm (2 in) slices. Wash and drain the spinach. Wash and drain the Chinese leaves, stack and cut into 2.5 cm (1 in) slices. Arrange all these ingredients on a large platter.

Make the dipping sauces. Finely chop the spring onions. Finely grate the radish and squeeze it out lightly. Put the radish and spring onions in separate piles in 4 small bowls. Mix the soy sauce, citrus vinegar and 4 tablespoons of the soup stock together and pour into the bowls over the radish and spring onions. Set a bowl at each serving place.

In a small frying-pan, toast the sesame seeds until they begin to jump. Put them into a Japanese mortar (*suribachi*) and grind them finely, or grind in a nut grinder or small coffee mill. Scrape the seeds out into a bowl, add the vinegar, light soy sauce, 4 tablespoons of the soup stock and the *mirin*, stirring to mix well. Pour into 4 small bowls and set at each place beside the other dipping sauce.

Clean the seaweed with a damp cloth and cut a 1 cm (½ in) fringe along one side. Put it on the bottom of a *sukiyaki* (round iron) pot, a cast-iron frying-pan, or a *donabe* (fireproof earthenware casserole) on a table heater. Or use an electric frying-pan. Pour in 1 litre (1¾ pints) water and bring to a boil over moderate heat, removing the seaweed just before the water comes to a boil.

Each diner selects a piece of food from the platter, using chopsticks, and swishes it back and forth in the simmering liquid until it is cooked. It will make a sound like '*shabu shabu*'. Care should be taken not to overcook the beef as this will toughen it. The food is dipped in one or other of the dipping sauces according to taste. Skim the surface of the pot from time to time.

When all the food has been eaten, cooked rice, cooked noodles or rice cakes may be added to the stock, and when warmed through ladled out into bowls to be eaten. Or add a little soy sauce and MSG to the pot, stir and ladle the soup into bowls. Drink the soup from the bowls.

SAUTÉED BEEF AND VEGETABLES

SUKIYAKI, TOKYO-STYLE

This is probably the best-known of all Japanese dishes. It is the classic one-pot dish. The beef, which must be of very good quality, sirloin or topside, is sliced paper-thin. Either have the butcher do this or stiffen the beef in the freezer to make it easier to slice.

SERVES 4
500 g (1 lb) boneless sirloin *or* topside steak
8 medium-sized spring onions, trimmed, using white and green parts
2 grilled bean curd (*yakidofu*), each weighing about 300 g (10 oz)
2 × 175 g (6 oz) drained weight devil's-tongue-root noodles (*shirataki*)
125 g (4 oz) edible chrysanthemum leaves (*shungiku*) *or* 250 g (8 oz) trimmed spinach

FOR THE SAUCE
125 ml (4 fl oz) soy sauce
125 ml (4 fl oz) *mirin*
250 ml (8 fl oz) second soup stock
⅛ teaspoon MSG
2 tablespoons sugar
Beef suet *or* vegetable oil
4 large eggs

Have the butcher cut the beef into slices about 5 × 3.5 cm (2 × 1½ in), or chill the beef briefly in the freezer to stiffen it and slice it thinly with a sharp knife.

Cut the spring onions into 5 cm (2 in) diagonal slices. Halve the bean curd lengthways, then cut into 4 crossways slices. Drop the noodles into boiling water for 1 minute, drain and cut in half. Strip the chrysanthemum leaves from the stems. Arrange all the ingredients on a platter.

Make the sauce. In a small saucepan, combine the soy sauce, *mirin*, soup stock, MSG and sugar. Bring to a simmer and stir to dissolve the sugar. Remove from the heat and pour into a small jug.

Put a *sukiyaki* pan or heavy iron frying-pan on a table heater in the middle of the dining table. Rub the pan with a small piece of beef suet to grease the cooking surface, or film with vegetable oil. If using suet, leave it in the pan. An electric frying-pan may also be used, in which case heat it to 200°C (400°F), then reduce it to 150°C (300°F) as soon as the meat and vegetables are cooked. Add the beef strips and cook for a minute or two without turning. Add the spring onions, then pour half the sauce over the contents of the pan. Add the noodles, bean curd, chrysanthemum or spinach, stirring with chopsticks. Cook for 3 or 4 minutes. Do not add all of an ingredient at once. Use a little of everything and add more from time to time as needed.

Break an egg into each of 4 small bowls and stir with chopsticks until well-blended. When eating the *sukiyaki*, lift out pieces of beef, vegetable or noodles and dip in the egg. Add the remaining ingredients to the pan and cook as before, using the rest of the sauce.

When the dish is finished, boiled rice, rice cake or noodles may be added to the pan and heated through with any of the sauce that is left.

Though this is a traditional dish it is also a flexible one. Thinly sliced onions, carrots thinly sliced and cooked until almost tender, and sliced bamboo shoots may all be used. Serve with plain boiled rice and pickles.

CHICKEN AND VEGETABLE CASSEROLE

TORI NO MIZUTAKI

This is a family dish and needs only plain boiled rice and pickles as an accompaniment.

SERVES 4

**1.4 kg (3 lb) chicken, cut into serving pieces
6 leaves Chinese cabbage (Chinese leaves)
(*hakusai*)
8 dried Japanese mushrooms (*shiitake*) *or* 8
medium-sized flat fresh mushrooms
½ × 150 g (5 oz) packet bean gelatine noodles
(*harusame*)
1 bean curd (*momen tofu*), weighing about 250 g
(8 oz), *or* silky bean curd (*kinugoshi tofu*)
125 g (4 oz) chrysanthemum leaves (*shungiku*), *or*
spinach, *or* watercress
6 medium-sized spring onions, trimmed, using
white and green parts
125 g (4 oz) white radish
2 dried red chilli peppers, seeded
2.5 cm (1 in) slice fresh ginger root
125 ml (4 fl oz) rice vinegar
125 ml (4 fl oz) soy sauce
1 tablespoon citrus vinegar (*ponzu*)**

Using a cleaver or poultry shears, cut the chicken pieces, skin, bones and all into approximately 5 cm (2 in) pieces. Put the chicken into a colander and pour boiling water over it. Transfer to a large, heavy saucepan and pour in 1.4 litre (2½ pints) cold water. Bring to a boil over high heat, reduce the heat to moderate and simmer, covered, for 10 minutes. Skim from time to time. Reduce the heat to low and cook until the chicken is tender, 30 to 40 minutes. Set aside.

Wash and drain the cabbage leaves, stack and cut into 2.5 cm (1 in) crossways slices. Soak the dried mushrooms for 30 minutes, drain and cut away the hard stems. Squeeze out, and cut a shallow cross in the tops. If using fresh mushrooms, wipe the caps with a damp cloth, trim the stems and cut a shallow cross in the tops. Soak the noodles in warm water for 10 minutes. Drain. Cut the bean curd into 8 cubes. Strip the chrysanthemum leaves from the stems. If using spinach or watercress, trim the stems. Cut 4 of the spring onions into 5 cm (2 in) diagonal slices. Set all of these ingredients on a large platter.

For the garnish, finely chop the remaining spring onions and place in a small bowl. Peel the radish, poke a hole in the centre with chopsticks and stuff with the chilli peppers. Finely grate the radish, squeeze out the excess moisture and put into a small bowl. Grate the ginger finely and place on a small saucer. For the sauce, combine the rice vinegar, soy sauce and citrus vinegar and stir to mix. Pour into 4 small bowls, one at each place setting with a bowl and chopsticks.

Put the chicken and about ½ the liquid in which it was cooked into a heatproof earthenware casserole (*donabe*) on a table heater over low heat. Gradually increase the heat to moderate. Or use an electric frying-pan on moderate heat. Add the cabbage, then the mushrooms, noodles, bean curd, chrysanthemum or spinach or watercress, and the spring onions. Simmer until the vegetables are tender, adding more of the chicken stock as needed.

To eat, put the garnishes into the sauce. Using chopsticks lift out pieces of chicken or vegetable and dip in the sauce. Drink any leftover stock as soup from the bowls.

CHICKEN, SEAFOOD AND VEGETABLE CASSEROLE

YOSENABE

This means, literally, many things cooked together in one pot, and is a very popular dish at the coldest time of the year as it is hearty enough for any winter appetite. It is also very flexible. Oysters, clams and prawns are interchangeable. Either fish, or fish sausage can be used and pork can be added as well as chicken.

SERVES 4
8 clams
8 large uncooked, unpeeled prawns, if frozen thoroughly defrosted
8 oysters, *or* scallops, opened, if frozen then thoroughly defrosted
125 g (4 oz) fillet of cod, *or* mackerel, *or* sole
125 g (4 oz) boned, but not skinned, chicken breast
1 medium carrot
125 g (4 oz) bamboo shoot
4 medium-sized spring onions, trimmed, using white and green parts
1 bean curd (*momen tofu*) weighing about 250 g (8 oz)
125 g (4 oz) bean gelatine noodles (*harusame*)
4 medium-sized flat mushrooms
250 g (8 oz) Chinese cabbage (Chinese leaves) (*hakusai*)
15 cm (6 in) piece fish sausage (*kamaboko*), optional

FOR THE STOCK
1 litre (1¾ pints) second soup stock
½ teaspoon salt
4 tablespoons *sake*
2 tablespoons *mirin*
2 tablespoons soy sauce

FOR THE DIPPING SAUCE
1 tablespoon soy sauce
1 tablespoon rice vinegar

FOR THE GARNISH
50 g (2 oz) slice white radish (*daikon*)
1 medium-sized spring onion, trimmed, using white and green parts

Soak the clams in cold, salted water overnight and scrub clean. Devein the prawns and peel, leaving the tail and the last segment of shell intact. Arrange on a large platter with the oysters or scallops removed from their shells. Cut the fish into bite-size diagonal slices, slice the chicken and add with the fish to the platter. Scrape the carrot and flute it making 5 lengthways grooves so that when it is sliced it is flower shaped, (*hana-giri*). Cook in salted water for 3 minutes. Thinly slice the bamboo shoot. Cut the spring onions into 2.5 cm (1 in) pieces. Cut the bean curd into 2.5 cm (1 in) cubes. Soak the noodles in warm water for a few minutes to soften then cut into 7 cm (3 in) pieces. Wipe the mushroom caps with a damp cloth, remove the stems and cut a shallow cross in the tops. Stack the cabbage leaves and cut into 2.5 cm (1 in) slices. Cut the fish sausage into 1 cm (½ in) slices. Arrange all these ingredients on the platter; use another platter if necessary.

Pour the soup stock, salt, *sake*, *mirin* and soy sauce into a large flameproof earthenware casserole (*donabe*) on a table heater, or into an electric frying-pan. Mix the soy sauce and rice vinegar together and pour into 4 small bowls, one at each place setting. Grate the radish finely and squeeze out the moisture. Put it into a small bowl. Finely chop the spring onion and put it into a small saucer. Place these at the centre of the table. Bring the stock to a simmer and add some of each of the ingredients. When the food is cooked, in about 8 minutes, diner help themselves with chopsticks to the cooked food, and dip it into the sauce, mixed with a little radish and spring onion. Replenish the pot with the remaining ingredients as needed. When all the solids are eaten, ladle the stock into the bowls, mix with any remaining sauce and drink as soup.

SALMON AND VEGETABLE CASSEROLE

ISHIKARI-NABE

This is a Hokkaido dish from the far north of Japan and is a great family favourite in that region, which is famous for its salmon.

SERVES 4

500 g (1 lb) salmon fillet, with skin left on
Salt
250 g (8 oz) Chinese cabbage (Chinese leaves)
(*hakusai*)
1 medium-sized carrot
1 medium-sized potato
1 devil's-tongue-root cake (*konnyaku*)
50 g (2 oz) butter
2 medium-sized onions
1 litre (1¾ pints) first soup stock
6 tablespoons white *miso* (bean paste) or more to
taste
Japanese pepper (*kona sansho*)

Halve the salmon lengthways, and check for any small bones. Cut the fish into 2.5 cm (1 in) diagonal slices. Sprinkle lightly with salt and set aside.

Separate the cabbage leaves and drop them into a large saucepan of briskly boiling salted water and cook for 2 minutes. Drain and cut the leaves into pieces about 5 × 10 cm (2 × 4 in) and roll each one up to make it easier to pick up with chopsticks. Scrape the carrot, cut it into 5 mm (¼ in) slices and cook in a small saucepan of boiling water, covered, for 5 minutes. Add the potato, peeled and cut into 5 mm (¼ in) slices and simmer for 10 minutes longer. Wash the devil's-tongue-root cake, and use a teaspoon to cut it into pieces, add to the saucepan and cook for 1 minute longer. Drain and arrange the vegetables on a platter with the cabbage rolls.

Put the butter into a heatproof earthenware casserole (*donabe*) and place on a table heater over moderate heat. Or use an electric frying-pan. Halve the onions and cut into 5 mm (¼ in) slices and add to the casserole. Sauté until tender but not browned. Pour in the soup stock. Mix the bean paste with a little stock until smooth and stir into the casserole over low heat. Do not let the mixture boil. Taste and add 2 more table-spoons if liked. Add the salmon and all the vegetables and the noodles and cook at just under a simmer until the salmon loses its translucent look, about 3 minutes.

Diners help themselves with chopsticks into bowls and season the dish to taste with Japanese pepper. When the solids are eaten the broth is poured into the bowls as soup. This is a main course usually served with rice, pickles and a salad or vegetable dish.

RED SNAPPER AND VEGETABLE CASSEROLE

TAICHIRI NABE

This is another very popular winter dish, making more use of vegetables. Cabbage and spinach are combined to make neat, pretty rolls. A whole fish may be used, the head and bones added to enrich the cooking liquid.

SERVES 4

700 g (1½ lb) whole red snapper, cleaned and scaled, with head and tail left on
500 g (1 lb) Chinese leaves (Chinese cabbage) (*hakusai*)
Salt
300 g (10 oz) trimmed spinach
6 medium-sized spring onions, trimmed, using white and green parts
8 medium-sized fresh mushrooms, *or* 8 small dried Japanese mushrooms (*shiitake*)
125 g (4 oz) bean gelatine noodles (*harusame*)
1 bean curd (*momen tofu*) weighing about 250 g (8 oz)
10 cm (4 in) square kelp seaweed (*kombu*)
125 g (4 oz) slice white radish (*daikon*)
2 dried hot red chilli peppers
4 tablespoons citrus vinegar (*ponzu*)
6 tablespoons soy sauce
6 tablespoons second soup stock
⅛ teaspoon MSG

Have the fishmonger remove the head from the snapper and cut it in half, then fillet the fish, leaving the skin on. Cut the fish into 2.5 cm (1 in) diagonal slices. Chop the bones. Pour boiling water over the fish, fish head and bones. Drain, rinse in cold water and drain again.

Separate the cabbage leaves and cook in boiling salted water, covered, for 2 minutes. Drain. Cook the trimmed spinach in boiling salted water for 1 minute. Drain and squeeze out. Arrange an overlapping layer of the cabbage leaves on a bamboo mat (*sudare*) or on a kitchen towel. Top with the spinach, roll up and squeeze out any remaining moisture and make a firm roll.

Unroll and cut into 2.5 cm (1 in) slices. Arrange on a platter with the fish.

Cut 4 of the spring onions into 5 cm (2 in) slices. Add to the platter. Finely chop the remaining 2 spring onions and set aside for the garnish. Trim the stems of the fresh mushrooms. If using dried mushrooms, soak in warm water for 30 minutes, cut away the hard stems. Add to the platter. Soak the bean gelatine noodles in warm water to soften for a few minutes, drain and add to the platter. Cut the bean curd into 8 slices and add.

Peel the radish, poke a hole with chopsticks in the centre and stuff with the chilli peppers. Grate finely, squeeze out the moisture and put into a small bowl. Mix the citrus vinegar, soy sauce, soup stock and MSG together and pour into 4 small bowls. Set one bowl at each place setting. Put the chopped spring onion and grated radish at the centre of the table.

Wipe the seaweed with a damp cloth and cut into a 1 cm (½ in) fringe on one side. Place on the bottom of an earthenware casserole (*donabe*) on a table heater, or in an electric frying-pan. Pour in 1 litre (1¾ pints) water and bring to a boil over moderate heat, removing the seaweed just before the water boils. Add the fish, fish head and bones, the cabbage rolls, noodles, spring onions, mushrooms and bean curd. Skim as necessary. Cook for about 6 minutes, on moderate heat, or until fish and vegetables are done.

To eat, put the garnishes, scallion and radish into the sauce and use it as a dipping sauce, lifting food out of the pot with chopsticks. When all the solids are finished, add cooked rice with 1 or 2 eggs stirred and poured over the rice to the pot, or add rice cakes, 1 per person, cut in half and cooked in the soup just until heated through, about 5 minutes. Or pour the soup into the bowls and drink.

CASSEROLED COD

TARACHIRI NABE

This is a very popular winter dish, robust and rich-flavoured. Any firm-fleshed, non-oily, white fish can be used instead of cod. Bream, haddock, plaice or sea bass are all suitable.

SERVES 4

1 piece kelp seaweed (*kombu*) 10 cm (4 in) square
500 g (1 lb) cod fillet with the skin left on, *or* 4 cod steaks
200 g (7 oz) Chinese leaves (Chinese cabbage) (*hakusai*)
4 large, flat fresh mushrooms
4 medium-sized spring onions, trimmed, using white and green parts
1 bean curd (*momen tofu*), weighing about 250 g (8 oz) *or* silky bean curd (*kinugoshi tofu*)
150 g (5 oz) chrysanthemum leaves (*shungiku*), *or* spinach, trimmed
200 g (7 oz) slice white radish (*daikon*)
2 dried hot red chilli peppers, seeded
4 teaspoons soy sauce
4 teaspoons citrus vinegar (*ponzu*), *or* lemon or lime juice

Wipe the seaweed with a damp cloth and cut a 1 cm (½ in) fringe along one side. Cut the cod fillet into pieces about 2.5 × 5 cm (1 × 2 in). If using cod steaks, cut into chunks. Put the fish into a colander and pour boiling water over it. Cut the cabbage into 5 cm (2 in) slices. Wipe the caps of the mushrooms with a damp cloth and cut into 1 cm (½ in) slices. Cut 4 of the spring onions into 5 cm (2 in) diagonal slices. Finely chop the remaining spring onion and put it to crisp in cold water for a few minutes, drain and squeeze out the moisture in a cloth. Put it into a small bowl for use as a garnish. Cut the bean curd into 8 slices. Wash and dry the chrysanthemum leaves or spinach. Remove any tough stems. Arrange all the ingredients on a large platter.

Peel the radish and poke a hole in the centre with chopsticks. Stuff the peppers into the hole then finely grate the radish, squeeze out the excess moisture and put into a bowl. Pour 1 teaspoon of the soy sauce into each of 4 small bowls and add 1 teaspoon of the citrus vinegar or lemon or lime juice, and stir to mix. Put the bowls, with chopsticks, at each place setting. Put the radish and finely chopped spring onion at the centre of the table near the casserole.

Put the seaweed into a large fireproof earthenware casserole (*donabe*) on a table heater, or use an electric frying-pan. Pour in 1 litre (1¾ pints) cold water and bring to a boil over moderate heat. Remove the seaweed just before the water comes to a boil. Add the fish, cabbage, mushrooms, bean curd, spring onions and chrysanthemum leaves or spinach, skim as necessary and cook for about 6 minutes, or until fish and vegetables are both tender.

To eat, put a little spring onion and radish into the soy sauce mixture and use as a dipping sauce, lifting out fish and vegetables from the pot with chopsticks. Add more sauce if needed.

SIMMERED BEAN CURD

YUDOFU

This is a vegetarian dish which originated in a Buddhist monastery in Kyoto. It is a winter dish and though the flavours are delicate it is satisfyingly rich in protein because of the bean curd, yet with the pure and delicate flavours characteristic of Kyoto cooking. Its summer counterpart is *Hiya-Yakko* (Garnished Fresh Bean Curd) (see Bean Curd Dishes, page 156).

SERVES 4

3 bean curd (*momen tofu*) each weighing about 250 g (8 oz)
2 × 15 cm (6 in) squares of kelp seaweed (*kombu*)
15 g (½ oz) dried bonito flakes (*hana-katsuo*)
6 tablespoons soy sauce
4 tablespoons *mirin*
2.5 cm (1 in) slice fresh ginger root
2 medium spring onions, trimmed, using white and green parts
2 sheets dried laver seaweed (*nori*)

Cut each piece of bean curd into quarters and put into a bowl of cold water until ready to use. Clean the seaweed with a damp cloth and cut both pieces into a 1 cm (½ in) fringe along one side. Put 1 square into the bottom of a heatproof earthenware casserole (*donabe*) and place on a turned-off table heater until ready to use. Or use an electric frying-pan.

To make the sauce, put the other square of seaweed into a small saucepan with 50 ml (2 fl oz) cold water and bring to a boil over moderate heat. Just before the water boils, remove the seaweed and add half the dried bonito flakes (*hana-katsuo*). Simmer for 2 minutes, then add the soy sauce and *mirin*. Remove from the heat and strain into a bowl. Discard the seaweed and bonito flakes.

To assemble the garnishes, peel the ginger, grate it finely and put it into a small bowl. Slice the spring onions finely and put into another small bowl. Toast the dried laver seaweed on both sides for a few seconds over a gas flame or electric burner, fold into small squares and cut with scissors into julienne strips. Put into a small bowl, and put the remaining dried bonito flakes into a fourth little bowl. Put these garnishes in the centre of the table.

Pour enough water into the casserole to cover the bean curd when it is added. Bring the water to a boil over moderate heat, removing the seaweed just before the water boils. Add the bean curd and reduce the heat to low. Put the bowl with the sauce in the centre of the casserole to heat it through and cook the bean curd just long enough to heat it through. The sauce can be poured into a small saucepan and heated on the stove if preferred.

To eat, have small bowls at each place setting. Lift out the bean curd into the bowls with chopsticks and pour on some of the sauce. Garnish to taste.

OYSTERS WITH BEAN PASTE

KAKI NO DOTENABE

This is a winter dish as oysters, harvested from the Inland Sea, are available all winter. Oysters are not as much of a luxury in Japan as they are here, so that there are very many imaginative ways of presenting them. They are especially delicious with *miso* (bean paste), and the name of the dish is as imaginative as the cooking method. *Dotenabe* is the retaining wall built to protect a river bank and the casserole is 'protected' with a thick layer of *miso* surrounding the oysters in the river. The retaining wall of *miso* goes, little by little, into the simmering broth.

SERVES 4
4 tablespoons red *miso* (bean paste)
8 tablespoons white *miso* (bean paste)
3 tablespoons *mirin*
24 freshly shucked oysters, about 500 g (1 lb), *or*
if frozen thoroughly defrosted
Salt
2 grilled bean curd (*yakidofu*)
4 medium-sized spring onions, trimmed, using
white and green parts
125 g (4 oz) chrysanthemum leaves (*shungiku*)) *or*
250 g (8 oz) trimmed spinach
600 ml (1 pint) second soup stock
Seven-flavour spice (*shichimi-togarashi*), *or*
ground hot red pepper, *or* Japanese pepper (*kona*
***sansho*)**

Mix the red and white *miso* with the *mirin* to a smooth paste. Using the fingers make a layer of the paste on the bottom and sides of an earthenware casserole (*donabe*).

Rinse the oysters in salted water and drain. Rinse and drain the bean curd and cut each into 8 squares. Cut the spring onions into 1 cm (½ in) diagonal slices. Wash the chrysanthemum leaves (*shungiku*) and drain. If using spinach, drop into briskly boiling salted water for 1 minute. Rinse in cold water and drain. Squeeze lightly to get rid of the excess moisture. Arrange all the ingredients in the casserole ending with the *shungiku* or spinach. Put the casserole on the table heater over low heat and pour in the soup stock little by little. Raise the heat to moderate and cook, uncovered for 2 or 3 minutes.

Have ready a small bowl at each place setting. The diners help themselves from the casserole, eating with chopsticks. The bean paste gradually mixes with the soup stock which is poured into the bowls to drink. Season the dish with any of the ground peppers.

If liked, an egg may be beaten into 4 bowls and the contents of the pot dipped into the egg before eating. If liked, bean curd (*momen tofu*) may be used instead of grilled *tofu*. Eight dried Japanese mushrooms (*shiitake*) soaked 30 minutes in warm water, hard stems removed and sliced may be added so may devil's-tongue-root noodles (*konnyaku*), sliced.

VARIATION: For Oysters with Chinese Cabbage (*Kaki No Mizutake*), omit the bean paste. Separate the leaves from a Chinese cabbage (Chinese leaves) (*hakusai*), wash and drain them and stack to cut into 2.5 cm (1 in) crossways slices. If the leaves are very large, halve them lengthways, then crossways. Pour 1 litre (1¾ pints) second soup stock into an earthenware casserole (*donabe*) on a table heater over low heat so as not to crack it. An electric frying-pan can also be used. Raise the heat to moderate and bring to a boil.

Have ready a bowl of grated, squeezed out white radish (*daikon*), a small jug of soy sauce, a bowl of finely chopped spring onions and a lemon cut into 4 wedges. Group these round the casserole and put a bowl with chopsticks at each place setting. Have seven-flavour spice (*shichimi-togarashi*) on the table. When the soup stock comes to a boil, add the cabbage and 12 medium-sized fresh mushrooms, left whole but with stems trimmed, and simmer until the cabbage is tender, about 10 to 15 minutes. Add the oysters, a few at a time, and cook just long enough to plump them, about 1 minute. To eat, put the garnishes into the small bowl at the place setting and use as a dipping sauce for the contents of the casserole. Squeeze on lemon juice as liked. Season the soup stock with a little soy sauce and drink as a soup when the cabbage, oysters and mushrooms have been eaten. SERVES 4.

It was only with the Meiji period, little more than a century ago when Japan was opened to the West, that the Japanese kitchen really welcomed poultry and meat, though some chicken had always been eaten. Because of the influence of Zen Buddhism, there had been a long, virtually meatless era, although before the introduction of Zen these foods had been regularly eaten. All the dishes in this section are therefore relatively new and bear the influence of the kitchens of the Western world.

All meats and poultry are cut into bite-size pieces so that they can be easily handled with chopsticks. It seems bizarre to the Japanese that food should be cut up at table, so in Japan all cutting is done in the kitchen, not only for convenience in eating but also to reduce cooking time as Japan is fuel-short. Japanese cooking methods and culinary style changed the imported dishes beyond recognition. The result is a number of original and very attractive dishes to choose from in this untraditional field.

Paradoxically, many adapt well to the framework of Western meals. *Sukiyaki* (Sautéed Beef and Vegetables), in the One-Pot section, page 95, is an example, as this can quite appropriately be the main course of a Western meal, though we lack the pampered cattle of the region that provides Kobe beef, famous for its excellence.

CHICKEN, PORK AND BEEF DISHES

GRILLED SPICED CHICKEN

WAKADORI NO NANBANYAKI

This is an interesting, as well as appetizing, dish. Chilli peppers were introduced into Japan only in the 16th century, probably by the Portuguese following the discovery of the New World, as all peppers, sweet or hot, originated in Mexico. The use of both dried red chillies and fresh green chillies in the same dish is both original and sophisticated.

SERVES 4

**500 g (1 lb) boned chicken thighs, with skin left on
3 tablespoons soy sauce
1 tablespoon *mirin*
1 tablespoon *sake*
2 medium-sized spring onions, using green and white parts
2 dried hot red chilli peppers
1 large egg yolk
12 small fresh hot green peppers
Vegetable oil
Salt**

Prick the skin of the chicken thighs all over with a fork and put into a bowl. Add the soy sauce, *mirin* and *sake* and marinate for 20 minutes, turning 2 or 3 times. Thread the thighs on a skewer. Reserve the marinade.

Chop the spring onions. Seed and chop the dried red peppers. Grind the spring onions and peppers in a Japanese earthenware mortar (*suribachi*) or in a food processor, until smooth. Add the reserved marinade and mix, then beat in the egg yolk. Put into a bowl and set aside.

Using a *hibachi* or an electric or other grill, grill the chicken on both sides until about half done, about 4 minutes on each side. Using a pastry brush paint the chicken with the spring onion sauce, return to the grill and cook for 1 minute on each side. Repeat until the sauce is used up and the chicken is done.

Cut the stems from the fresh green peppers and remove the seeds by scraping them out with chopsticks or use a small serrated spoon. Rinse, dry and paint with oil. Grill, turning once, for about 1 minute. Sprinkle lightly with salt.

Slice the chicken diagonally and arrange on 4 individual platters. Garnish with the peppers.

DEEP-FRIED MARINATED CHICKEN

TORINIKU NO TATSUTA-AGE

This beautifully simple dish is great for picnics, as a first course, or as an accompaniment to drinks.

SERVES 4
375 g (12 oz) skinned and boned chicken breast
2.5 cm (1 in) slice fresh ginger root
125 ml (4 fl oz) soy sauce
50 ml (2 fl oz) *sake*
***Katakuriko* starch, *or* cornflour**
Vegetable oil for deep frying
2 medium-sized spring onions, using white and green parts

Cut the chicken into bite-size pieces and put into a bowl. Grate the ginger and mix with the chicken. Pour in the soy sauce and *sake* and mix. Leave to marinate for 30 minutes, stirring once or twice. Lift out the chicken pieces and roll in *katakuriko* starch or cornflour, shaking to remove the excess.

Heat 5 to 7 cm (2 to 3 in) vegetable oil in a *tempura* pan or heavy frying-pan or wok and heat to 180°C (350°F) on a frying thermometer, or until bubbles form on wooden chopsticks stirred in the oil. Fry the chicken pieces, a few at a time, until golden brown. Drain on the rack of the *tempura* pan or on paper towels. Lift out on to a platter.

Cut the spring onions into 2.5 cm (1 in) crossways pieces, then cut into fine lengthways strips. Crisp for a few minutes in cold water, then squeeze dry on a kitchen cloth. Add to the platter with the chicken as a garnish.

DEEP-FRIED SESAME-COATED CHICKEN

TORINIKU NO GOMA-GOROMO-AGE

This is a *tempura* dish using a batter made with sesame seeds, which are deliciously crunchy. Black sesame seeds are the ones used.

SERVES 4
375 g (12 oz) skinned and boned chicken breast
1 teaspoon fresh ginger juice
2 tablespoons soy sauce
1 tablespoon *mirin*
4 fresh hot green chilli peppers
1 large egg
1 tablespoon *sake*
⅛ teaspoon MSG
1 tablespoon black sesame seeds
50 g (2 oz) plain flour, sifted
Vegetable oil for deep frying

Slice the chicken diagonally into bite-size pieces and put into a bowl with the ginger juice, soy sauce and *mirin*. Marinate for 20 minutes.

Cut the stems ends off the chillies and, using chopsticks, scrape out the seeds. Rinse and pat dry. If they are large, halve them crossways.

Break the egg into a bowl and stir with chopsticks until it is well-blended but not foamy. Stir in the *sake*, 2 tablespoons water, MSG and sesame seeds. Sift in the flour, mixing lightly with chopsticks.

Heat 5 to 7 cm (2 to 3 in) vegetable oil in a *tempura* pan or a heavy frying-pan, to 180°C (350°F) or until bubbles form on wooden chopsticks stirred in the oil. Add the chillies and fry for 1 minute. Lift onto the rack of the *tempura* pan or drain on paper towels. Lift the chicken pieces out of the marinade, dip in the batter, and add to the pan in batches, taking care not to overcrowd the pan. Cook, turning, for about 2 minutes. Drain with the chillies.

Line an oblong platter with a paper napkin, arrange the chicken pieces on the platter, and garnish with the chillies.

CHICKEN STEAMED WITH *SAKE*

TORI NO SAKAMUSHI

This is one of the steamed dishes called *Mushi-mono* in Japanese. They are among the most visually beautiful of the dishes in the cuisine, as the steaming method not only preserves the flavour of foods but heightens the colour of vegetables. The cooked ingredients are arranged to show them to their best advantage. The foods, often steamed unseasoned, are served with sauces and garnishes. Steamed chicken, a simple dish, is a great hot-weather favourite.

SERVES 4
**375 g (12 oz) boned chicken breast, skin left on
4 tablespoons *sake*
2 teaspoons soy sauce
¼ teaspoon salt
1 medium-sized spring onion, trimmed, using white and green part
2.5 cm (1 in) slice fresh ginger root
½ medium-sized cucumber
2 teaspoons dry mustard, Japanese *or* English**

Pierce the chicken skin all over with a fork and put the chicken into a bowl. Mix the *sake*, soy sauce and salt together and pour over the chicken. Marinate for 20 minutes.

Finely chop the spring onion, then crush with the blade of a knife. Peel the ginger, grate finely and crush with the back of the knife. Put the spring onion and ginger on top of the chicken, then put the bowl in a steamer over boiling water and steam, uncovered for 10 to 15 minutes, or until cooked. Lift out of the steamer and cool. Cut the chicken into 1 cm (½ in) diagonal slices and put into 4 small bowls with the cooking liquid, unstrained, poured over them.

Trim the cucumber and cut in half lengthways. Scrape out the seeds and cut into 5 cm (2 in) crossways slices. Put into cold, lightly salted water to crisp for 5 minutes, drain, pat dry and divide among the bowls with the chicken.

Mix the mustard to a paste with boiling water and place a small mound beside the chicken slices.

VARIATION: Omit the soy sauce from the marinade. Steam as above without the ginger or spring onion. Arrange the sliced chicken on 4 small oblong platters, or on plates. Garnish with the cucumber and a wedge of lemon. Serve with a separate garnish of a small mound of green horseradish (*wasabi*) and a small mound of finely grated, squeezed out white radish (*daikon*) in tiny bowls at each place setting. Pour a little soy sauce over the radish, or serve the soy sauce separately in a little jug. SERVES 4.

SIMMERED CHICKEN AND VEGETABLES

TORINIKU NO JIBUNI

This *nimono* (simmered) dish is very pretty with the brown of mushrooms, orange of carrot cut into flower shapes, pale yellow of gingko nuts, green of spring onions and gold of chicken. It is also delicious with its mixture of harmonizing flavours.

SERVES 4

250 g (8 oz) boned chicken thighs, skin left on
3 tablespoons soy sauce
1 tablespoon *sake*
2.5 cm (1 in) slice fresh ginger root
4 small dried Japanese mushrooms (*shiitake*)
½ teaspoon sugar
2 large spring onions, trimmed, using white and green parts *or* 2 small leeks, thoroughly washed
1 medium carrot
Second soup stock
½ teaspoon salt
Plain flour
2 tablespoons *mirin*
12 cooked gingko nuts, tinned or bottled
Lime peel

Slice the chicken diagonally into bite-size pieces. Combine 1 tablespoon of the soy sauce and the *sake*. Peel and grate the ginger finely and squeeze the juice into the bowl. Add the chicken pieces and marinate at room temperature for 20 minutes, or until ready to cook, turning the chicken once or twice.

Soak the mushrooms in warm water for 30 minutes. Squeeze out and remove the hard stems. Put on a plate. Cut the spring onions or leeks into 2.5 cm (1 in) crossways slices and grill until lightly browned, about 1 minute. Put on the plate. Scrape and trim the carrot, then cut it *nana giri*, plum-blossom shape. Make 5 evenly spaced, small, shallow, wedge-shaped cuts the length of the carrot by placing a sharp knife at an oblique angle when cutting. Cut into 8 crossways slices. The slices look like conventionalized plum blossoms. If necessary trim to smooth the 'petal' edges. The carrot can be sliced and cut into flower shapes with a very small biscuit cutter, if this is easier. Add to the plate.

In a medium-sized saucepan combine the mushrooms, spring onions or leeks and carrot slices with enough soup stock to cover. Add the salt and sugar and cook, covered, over moderate heat until the liquid has evaporated and the carrot is tender.

Lift the chicken pieces out of the marinade and coat with flour, shaking to remove the excess. In a saucepan large enough to hold the chicken pieces in a single layer, bring the *mirin* to a boil and immediately add 350 ml (12 fl oz) soup stock, the remaining 2 tablespoons soy sauce and bring to a simmer over moderate heat. Add the chicken pieces, one at a time so that they do not stick together. Simmer, uncovered, until the chicken is tender, 3 to 4 minutes.

Arrange the chicken pieces in 4 bowls. Add the vegetables and gingko nuts in a decorative pattern round the chicken placing the mushrooms dark side up. Pour the stock from the chicken over the bowls and garnish each bowl with a thin strip of lime peel tied in a knot, or cut into a tiny V-shape to represent a pine needle.

GLAZED CHICKEN

TORI NO TERIYAKI

The fresh taste of Cucumber Salad (*Jabara Kyuri*) complements the delicate mildness of chicken in *teriyaki* sauce in this simple dish. Japanese cucumber, smaller than ours, can be bitter and cooks have devised a method for removing any bitter taste. Our cucumbers do not need this, but the technique is an interesting one. The cutting method for the cucumber salad is also interesting and is the same as the method used for cutting chrysanthemum turnips, *kikukagiri*.

SERVES 4
1 medium, or 2 small, cucumbers
Salt
2 tablespoons rice vinegar
Soy sauce
Sugar
375 g (12 oz) chicken breast, boned with skin left on
2 tablespoons vegetable oil
50 ml (2 fl oz) *mirin*
⅛ teaspoon MSG

If using small Japanese-type cucumbers, cut a thin slice from each end and rub the cut surfaces with the peel side of the slices for a minute or two. Sprinkle a chopping board with salt and roll the cucumber back and forth in the salt for several minutes. This process removes any bitterness from this type of cucumber. Rinse and pat dry. For whatever type of cucumber, peel in alternate strips, then place between 2 chopsticks and slice finely. The chopsticks will prevent the knife cutting right through the cucumber which will be held together along its length. Sprinkle the cucumber lightly with salt, let it stand for 10 minutes, then rinse carefully so as not to break. Drain. Mix together the vinegar, 1 tablespoon soy sauce and ½ teaspoon salt and pour over the cucumber. Marinate for 20 minutes.

Meanwhile, halve the chicken breast lengthways and score the skin very lightly at 1 cm (½ in) intervals, or prick with a fork. Heat the oil in a frying-pan and sauté the chicken until it is lightly browned on both sides. Lift it out of the pan. Wipe the pan with paper towels and return the chicken to it, off the heat. In a small saucepan, combine 50 ml (2 fl oz) soy sauce, the *mirin*, 2 tablespoons sugar and the MSG and heat, stirring, until the sugar has dissolved. Pour the mixture over the chicken and cook over moderate heat, turning so that the chicken is well-coated, until the sauce is glossy and thick. Cut the chicken into 1 cm (½ in) slices and arrange on individual plates.

Lift cucumber out of marinade, cut into 4 slices and arrange on the plates beside the chicken.

Boned chicken thigh or leg can also be used.

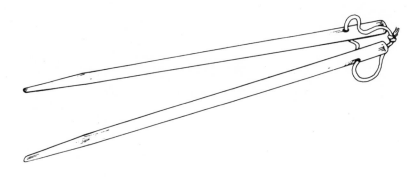

CHICKEN SASHIMI

TORISHASHI

Tori-sasimi, which the Japanese call bamboo-leaf chicken breasts, are the small fillets found partly attached to the main fillet of a boned and skinned chicken breast. They are the same shape as a bamboo leaf and are regarded as the best and most delicate part of the breast. Save the larger fillets for another use.

SERVES 4
8 bamboo leaf chicken breasts (*tori-sasami*)
Salt
½ medium-sized cucumber
1 large tomato
5 tablespoons white *miso* (bean paste)
1 teaspoon sugar, or to taste
75 ml (3 fl oz) second soup stock
½ teaspoon dry Japanese or English mustard
2 tablespoons rice vinegar

Sprinkle the chicken fillets lightly with salt and let them stand for a few minutes. Drop into boiling water, then transfer quickly to a bowl of iced water and cool for a minute or two. Lift out of the water, pat dry and put into the refrigerator to chill.

Do not peel the cucumber. Cut it into 4 lengthways slices, then slice thinly crossways.

Drop the tomato into boiling water for 30 seconds, lift out and peel then cut it into 8 wedges. Put the cucumber and tomato on a plate and refrigerate.

Make the sauce. Combine the bean paste, sugar and soup stock in a small saucepan and mix well with the egg yolk. Cook over low heat, stirring, until heated through but do not let the mixture boil. Cool. Mix the mustard with a little boiling water and the vinegar and stir into the sauce. Divide among 4 small dishes and put one at each place setting.

Cut the chicken into 1 cm (½ in) diagonal slices and arrange at one end of 4 individual oblong dishes, or use plates. Put the cucumber in the middle and the tomato at the other end. Using chopsticks, dip the chicken and vegetables into the sauce.

Another popular sauce is Green Horseradish Sauce (*Wasabi-Joyu*) made by mixing 2 teaspoons green horseradish (*wasabi*) to a paste with a little water, then mixing it with 4 tablespoons soy sauce and 6 tablespoons soup stock. For Ginger Sauce (*Shoga-Joyu*), mix 2 tablespoons finely grated fresh ginger root with 4 tablespoons soy sauce and 6 tablespoons soup stock.

SIMMERED CHICKEN CHIKUZEN-STYLE

CHIKUZEN-NI

This dish comes from Fukuoka in northern Kyushu, the southernmost island of Japan. The town was called Chikuzen in the Edo period and the dish is in its special cooking style. Ferries from Chikuzen went over to Korea and the Chinese mainland and brought back many new culinary ideas, creating a regional kitchen. It is a popular dish for lunch boxes and for New Year.

SERVES 4

300 g (10 oz) boned chicken thighs, with skin on
2 medium-sized carrots
Salt
½ devil's-tongue-root cake (*konnyaku*)
125 g (4 oz) bamboo shoot
4 small potatoes
2 tablespoons vegetable oil
200 ml (7 fl oz) second soup stock
2 tablespoons *mirin*
1 tablespoon sugar
3 tablespoons soy sauce
50 g (2 oz) mangetout

Cut the chicken into 2 cm (¾ in) slices. Scrape the carrots and cut into diagonal chunks (*rangiri*). Put the carrot chunks into a small saucepan with salted water to cover, bring to a boil, reduce the heat and simmer for 8 minutes.

Rub the devil's-tongue-root cake with salt on both sides, rinse well, then tear into 4 pieces with the fingers. Drop into a saucepan of boiling salted water and cook for 3 minutes. Cut the bamboo shoot into diagonal chunks (*rangiri*) and parboil for 3 minutes in boiling salted water. Peel the potatoes and cut them into chunks (*rangiri*). Parboil in salted water for 3 minutes. Drain all the vegetables and the devil's-tongue-root cake and arrange on a plate.

In a saucepan large enough to hold all the ingredients comfortably, heat the oil. Add the chicken pieces and stir-fry turning, to coat with oil. Add the carrots, devil's-tongue-root cake pieces, the bamboo shoot and potatoes and cook over moderate heat, turning the pieces frequently with chopsticks for about 5 minutes. Pour in the soup stock, sugar and soy sauce, cover and simmer for 5 minutes. Add the *mirin* and cook, uncovered, until the stock has reduced to about half its volume, about 5 minutes longer. Trim the mangetout and drop into boiling salted water, blanch for 2 minutes, drain and add to the saucepan just before serving. Serve in 4 individual bowls.

FRIED AND SIMMERED CHICKEN AND VEGETABLES

IRIDORI

This is a popular dish for lunch boxes and for New Year, indeed with its tender chicken and variety of crisp-cooked vegetables it is popular at any time.

SERVES 4

250 g (8 oz) boned chicken thighs, skin left on
4 dried Japanese mushrooms (*shiitake*)
1 medium carrot
125 g (4 oz) burdock root (*gobo*) fresh or tinned,
***or* salsify, *or* scorzonera**
½ devil's-tongue-root cake (*konnyaku*)
Salt
Sugar
12 mangetout, trimmed
125 g (4 oz) slice lotus root (*renkon*), tinned
125 g (4 oz) whole tinned bamboo shoot
(*takenoko*)
Rice vinegar
2½ tablespoons vegetable oil
1 tablespoon *mirin*
3½ tablespoons soy sauce
1 tablespoon *sake*
350 ml (12 fl oz) second soup stock

Cut the chicken into diagonal bite-size pieces. Put the mushrooms in to soak in warm water for 30 minutes. Squeeze out, remove hard stems and quarter. Trim and scrape the carrot then cut in wedges (*rangiri*), cutting on a diagonal then giving the carrot a half turn and cutting on the opposite diagonal into pieces about 2.5 cm (1 in) long. Scrape the burdock root under cold running water (if fresh), then cut in the same way as the carrot. Rub the devil's-tongue-root cake on both sides with salt, rinse and tear with the fingers into 8 pieces. Drop into a saucepan of boiling water, bring back to a boil on high heat and drain. Drop the mangetout into boiling salted water, bring back to a boil on high heat and cook for 2 minutes. Drain. Cut the lotus root into 1 cm (½ in) slices, then into quarters. Soak in cold water with 1 tablespoon of vinegar. Cut the bamboo shoot into diagonal 1 cm (½ in) slices.

To cook, assemble all the ingredients, drained where necessary, on a large platter. Pour 1 tablespoon oil into a wok or a heavy frying-pan and stir-fry the chicken pieces on high heat for 2 minutes, or until they change colour, using chopsticks to stir. Lift the chicken out into a bowl and sprinkle with 1 teaspoon of sugar, the *mirin*, and 1 tablespoon of the soy sauce. Mix well and set aside.

Pour the rest of the oil into the wok or frying-pan and stir-fry the burdock root over high heat for 1 minute, add the carrot and stir-fry 1 minute longer, then the lotus root and bamboo shoot, again for 1 minute. Add the devil's-tongue-root cake and the mushrooms, lower the heat to moderate and cook for 2 minutes, stirring with chopsticks. Add the soup stock, bring to a simmer, cover and cook for 5 minutes, then add 1 teaspoon of sugar and the remaining 2½ tablespoons of soy sauce and the *sake* and cook until the vegetables are tender, about 10 minutes. Add the chicken and the marinade and cook uncovered, over fairly high heat for about 3 minutes or until almost all the liquid has evaporated. Add the mangetout and cook for about ½ minute longer to heat through. Serve in bowls.

CHICKEN, SQUID
AND VEGETABLE PLATTER

MUSHIDORI TO IKA NO GOMAZU

This is a very attractive dish in hot weather for either lunch or dinner.

SERVES 4

4 small chicken breasts, boned with skin on
1 tablespoon *sake*
Salt
1 squid, body sac only
Rice vinegar
4 × 20 cm (8 in) fronds lobe-leaf lettuce (*wakame*)
2 spring onions, trimmed, using white and green parts
½ medium-sized cucumber
1 medium-sized carrot
4 tablespoons white sesame seeds
1 large clove garlic
1 tablespoon soy sauce
1 tablespoon *mirin*
1 tablespoon mayonnaise, preferably homemade
Ground hot red chilli pepper (*togarashi*)

Prick the skin of the chicken breasts all over with a fork. Put them into a shallow dish, sprinkle with *sake* and salt and put into a steamer over boiling water. Steam over moderate heat for 15 minutes. Remove from the steamer, cut into 2.5 cm (1 in) diagonal slices, return to the dish and leave to cool in the cooking liquid.

Cut the squid sac open and score all over with a sharp knife in a diamond pattern. Cut into 2.5 cm (1 in) squares, drop into a saucepan of briskly boiling water for a few seconds, lift out, rinse in cold water and drain. Put into a shallow bowl and sprinkle with a little rice vinegar and salt.

Soak the seaweed in cold water for 15 minutes. Drain, drop into a saucepan of boiling water for a few seconds, rinse in cold water and drain. Cut away the hard ribs, squeeze out and cut into 2.5 cm (1 in) slices.

Cut the spring onions into 5 cm (2 in) slices, then cut these very thinly lengthways and crisp for a few minutes in cold water. Drain and squeeze dry in a cloth.

Peel the cucumber in alternate strips, cut into thin lengthways slices, then cut into thin crossways slices. Rinse in cold water and drain.

Scrape the carrot, cut into thin lengthways slices, then cut in half, crossways, cut the pieces into thin lengthways strips. Rinse in cold water and drain.

Toast the sesame seeds in a small saucepan over moderate heat until they begin to pop. Transfer to a Japanese earthenware mortar (*suribachi*), or nut or coffee grinder and grind until smooth. Crush the clove of garlic and grind with the sesame seeds. Add 1 teaspoon salt, the soy sauce, *mirin*, mayonnaise, 5 tablespoons rice vinegar and the liquid in which the chicken has been cooling. Add a little hot chilli pepper and mix. Pour into a bowl.

On a large platter arrange the chicken slices, the squid, seaweed, carrot, cucumber and spring onions. Place in the centre of the table with the bowl of sauce. Diners serve themselves from the platter with chopsticks into small bowls, taking a little of everything as the meal proceeds, and some of the sauce, poured on with a spoon.

GLAZED CHICKEN BALLS

TORINIKU DANGO NO TERINI

This is a spring dish and served as part of a dinner menu. It also makes a very attractive accompaniment to drinks.

SERVES 4
250 g (8 oz) minced raw chicken
2 tablespoons plain flour
Soy sauce
1 small egg, stirred
1 teaspoon sugar, or more to taste
1½ tablespoons *mirin*
2 teaspoons poppy seeds

Put the chicken into a Japanese earthenware mortar (*suribachi*) and pound with the pestle until it is smooth and light, or put into a food processor or blender and process until smooth and light. Add the flour, 1 teaspoon soy sauce and egg and mix thoroughly. Form into 2.5 cm (1 in) balls and drop into a saucepan with 300 ml (½ pint) boiling water and bring back to a boil over high heat, reduce the heat to moderate and cook for about 3 minutes. Add the sugar, *mirin* and 3 tablespoons soy sauce to the pan, shake to mix and cook for about 5 minutes longer, covered. Remove the lid, raise the heat and cook until all the liquid has evaporated and the chicken balls are glazed. Thread the balls, 3 at a time, on bamboo skewers, sprinkle with the poppy seeds and serve.

CHICKEN LIVERS, CHILLIES AND EGG

TORIKIMO NO TAMAGO-TOJI

This dish is another example of the Japanese using a non-traditional ingredient – chillies – in an imaginative way. Chillies vary a great deal in heat. Nibble a tiny bit of chilli and if it is very hot, soak it in cold, salted water for 30 minutes, then rinse and drain. This will take out the excess heat. It is always wise to wash the hands with warm soapy water after handling hot chillies.

SERVES 4
375 g (12 oz) chicken livers
8 medium-sized hot green chillies
2 tablespoons vegetable oil
175 ml (6 fl oz) second soup stock
1 teaspoon sugar
4 tablespoons soy sauce
2 tablespoons *mirin*
1 large egg

Rinse the chicken livers in cold water, drain and halve, then slice in half again, diagonally. Pat dry. Cut the stem end of the chillies and, using chopsticks, scrape out the seeds. Cut the chillies into 1 cm (½ in) diagonal slices.

Heat the oil in a shallow saucepan and sauté the chicken livers over high heat, turning constantly until lightly browned, about 4 minutes. Reduce the heat to moderate and sauté for 1 minute longer. Add the soup stock, sugar, soy sauce and *mirin* and simmer for 2 minutes. Skim, add the chillies and bring back to a simmer. Reduce the heat to low and cover with an inner wooden lid (*otoshibuta*), or a plate and cook for another 2 minutes. Remove the inner wooden lid or the plate and skim the surface. Break the egg into a small bowl and stir with chopsticks until it is well-blended but not foamy then pour over the chicken liver mixture in a thin stream to cover the whole surface of the pan. Cover with the saucepan lid and cook until the egg is set, about 1 minute. Serve in small bowls with the pan juices poured over the livers.

CHICKEN LIVERS WITH GINGER AND SOY SAUCE

TORIKIMO NO SHOGAJOYU

This is a more traditional dish than Chicken Livers, Chillies and Egg (page 115). For a spicier garnish the white radish may be grated *momijioroshi*, red maple radish, that is stuffed with dried red chillies before it is grated. This is a popular accompaniment to a number of dishes and is typical of the subtleties of the Japanese palate as well as their poetic use of language in the kitchen.

SERVES 4
375 g (12 oz) chicken livers
Salt
2.5 cm (1 in) slice fresh ginger root
50 g (2 oz) slice white radish (*daikon*)
2 or 3 dried hot red chillies (optional), seeded
Soy sauce

Rinse and drain the livers and drop into a saucepan of boiling salted water. Simmer for 3 minutes, drain and cool. Slice diagonally and divide among 4 small plates.

Peel and grate the ginger finely and add to the plates in little heaps. If using red maple radish, peel the radish, poke a hole in the centre with chopsticks, stuff with the chillies and grate finely. Squeeze out the excess moisture and put small mounds of radish beside the ginger. If not using the chillies, simply peel, grate, squeeze out and put on the plates. Pour a little soy sauce over both ginger and radish.

SIMMERED PORK WITH MUSTARD SAUCE

YUDEBUTA

Another simmered (*nimono*) pork dish that owes a good deal to foreign influences in Nagasaki is this very simple and tasty dish.

SERVES 4
500 g (1 lb) lean boneless pork, loin or other cut
1 medium-sized onion
2.5 cm (1 in) slice fresh ginger root
50 ml (2 fl oz) rice vinegar
2 teaspoons dry mustard, Japanese *or* English
4 tablespoons soy sauce
⅛ teaspoon MSG

Choose a saucepan or heavy casserole just large enough to hold the pork comfortably. Cut the peeled onion into thin lengthways slices. Peel and thinly slice the ginger. Add the onion, ginger and rice vinegar to the saucepan with 350 ml (12 fl oz) water and bring to a simmer over moderate heat. Add the pork and cover with an inner wooden lid (*otoshibuta*) or a plate and the saucepan lid. Cook over moderate heat until the pork is tender, about 50 minutes. Let the pork cool in the liquid then lift it out of the pan and slice thinly. Arrange on a platter.

Make the mustard sauce (*karashi-joyu*). Mix the mustard to a paste with boiling water. Add the soy sauce and MSG and pour into 4 tiny bowls, one at each place setting. Put the platter at the centre of the table. Using chopsticks, dip the pork slices into the sauce to eat. The pork may be served on individual platters or plates if preferred.

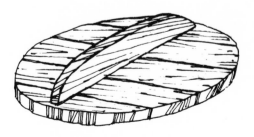

PORK SIMMERED WITH RICE WINE

BUTA NO SAKENI-NABE

This rich pork dish is a good example of what happened in the Japanese kitchen as a result of the mingling, over the centuries, of foreigners from the rest of the world, with the Japanese in Nagasaki. A flavourful blending of diverse culinary traditions.

SERVES 4

**500 g (1 lb) lean, boneless pork, loin or other cut
1 teaspoon fresh ginger juice
Salt
4 medium-sized fresh mushrooms, *or* 4 Japanese
dried mushrooms (*shiitake*)
2 devil's-tongue-root cakes (*konnyaku*)
2.5 cm (1 in) slice fresh ginger root
5 medium-sized spring onions, trimmed, using
white and green parts
250 g (8 oz) white radish (*daikon*)
175 ml (6 fl oz) *sake*
2 tablespoons light soy sauce (*usukuchi shoyu*)
500 g (1 lb) chrysanthemum leaves (*shungiku*) or
spinach
Soy sauce**

Thinly slice the pork and mix it with the ginger juice and 1 teaspoon salt in a bowl. Set aside.

Trim the stems of the fresh mushrooms and cut the mushrooms in halves. If using dried mushrooms, soak for 30 minutes in warm water, cut away the hard stems, and halve the mushrooms.

Drop the devil's-tongue-root cakes into boiling water, simmer for about 3 minutes, drain and halve, then cut into 5 mm (¼ in) slices and continue to drain in a sieve or colander.

Peel the slice of ginger and cut it in half, crossways. Thinly slice one half, grate the other. Cut the spring onions into 2.5 cm (1 in) slices. Peel and finely grate the radish, squeeze out lightly, put into a dish and reserve the juice.

Put the *sake*, radish juice and sliced ginger into a *sukiyaki* pan or heavy frying-pan, cast iron if possible, and heat the *sake* mixture through over moderate heat. Add the devil's-tongue-root cake slices, light soy sauce, ½ teaspoon salt, mushrooms and pork slices. Cook over moderate heat turning the pork from time to time until it is done, about 10 minutes. Add the spring onions and cook for 1 or 2 minutes longer, then add the chrysanthemum leaves or the spinach and cook for about 3 minutes longer. If the mixture seems too dry add a little more *sake* and ginger juice.

Divide the radish among 4 small bowls and top with the grated ginger. Pour over a little soy sauce, about 1 teaspoon. Put the sukiyaki pan in the centre of the table, or if using a frying-pan transfer the contents to a warmed platter. Eat with the radish and ginger sauce.

BREADED PORK CUTLETS

TONKATSU

This is one of the most popular luncheon dishes in Japan. An *agemono* (deep-fried) dish, always on the menu in restaurants, the cutlets can be bought ready-cooked to take away. Served with rice and a salad they make a satisfying meal.

SERVES 4

**4 slices boneless pork loin weighing about 150 g (5 oz) or 4 pork chops, boned and trimmed of fat
Salt and pepper
Plain flour
1 large egg, lightly beaten
125 g (4 oz) freshly made breadcrumbs
Vegetable oil for deep frying**

FOR THE GARNISH:
Lettuce leaves, lemon wedges, freshly made mustard from dry Japanese or English mustard

FOR THE DIPPING SAUCE:
**2 tablespoons Worcestershire sauce
1 tablespoon tomato ketchup
2 tablespoons soy sauce
1 tablespoon *sake*
1 teaspoon freshly made mustard from dry Japanese or English mustard**

If using boneless pork loin, flatten the slices between 2 sheets of greaseproof paper with a wooden mallet. Season loin slices or chops with salt and pepper, coat with flour, dip in the beaten egg and coat on both sides with breadcrumbs.

Heat 7 cm (3 in) vegetable oil in a heavy frying-pan to 180°C (350°F), or until bubbles form on wooden chopsticks stirred in the oil. Deep-fry the cutlets, 2 at a time for about 7 minutes, turning once or twice until the meat is thoroughly cooked and golden brown. Drain on paper towels. Serve on 4 small individual plates and garnish with lettuce leaves, lemon wedges and a small mound of mustard.

To make the dipping sauce, if liked, combine all the ingredients, taste and adjust the amounts as liked. In Japan instead of the dipping sauce, Worcestershire sauce is often served by itself.

PORK WITH SESAME SEEDS

BUTA NO GOMAYAKI

A dressing made with black sesame seeds, soy sauce and *sake* give this pork dish a rich and unusual flavour balanced by the cool crispness of the cucumber salad.

SERVES 4

**375 g (12 oz) lean boneless pork, loin or other cut
3 tablespoons soy sauce
1 teaspoon fresh ginger juice
2 tablespoons vegetable oil
2 tablespoons black sesame seeds
2 tablespoons *sake*
½ tablespoon sugar
1 teaspoon *katakuriko* starch or cornflour
Cucumber Salad (see recipe for *Jabara Kyuri* in recipe for Glazed Chicken, page 110)**

Thinly slice the pork then cut into 2.5 × 5 cm (1 × 2 in) diagonal slices. Put into a bowl and mix with 1 tablespoon of the soy sauce and the ginger juice. Let stand for a few minutes. Heat the oil in a heavy frying-pan and sauté the pork until lightly browned on both sides. Do not over-crowd the pan. The pork should be in a single layer so that it cooks thoroughly. Set aside.

Toast the sesame seeds in a small frying-pan over moderate heat until they begin to jump. Transfer to a Japanese earthenware mortar (*suribachi*) and grind finely or use a nut grinder or small coffee grinder. Combine the remaining 2 tablespoons of soy sauce with the *sake*, sugar and *katakuriko* starch or cornflour mixed with 1 teaspoon of water in a small saucepan and add the ground sesame seeds. Cook, stirring, over low heat until the mixture is smooth. Spread the sesame paste on the pork slices and arrange on 4 plates. Garnish with the cucumber salad.

GLAZED PORK

BUTANIKU NO TERIYAKI

This is one of the *Yakimono* (grilled) dishes using sweet *teriyaki* sauce. The *teriyaki* dishes whether using pork, beef, chicken or fish are all extremely popular and lend themselves to a wide variety of garnishes.

SERVES 4
2 teaspoons fresh ginger juice
2 teaspoons *sake*
4 tablespoons soy sauce
500 g (1 lb) boneless pork loin, cut into 4 slices
Vegetable oil
2 tablespoons *mirin*
2 teaspoons sugar

FOR THE GARNISH:
Pickled cucumber slices, pickled ginger, tomato wedges

Mix together the ginger juice, *sake* and 2 tablespoons of the soy sauce and pour it over the pork slices, coating both sides. Marinate for 30 minutes.

Heat a heavy frying-pan large enough to hold the pork slices comfortably and film it with oil. Sauté the pork over high heat for 3 to 4 minutes, or until browned on both sides. Reduce the heat to low and cook for 5 minutes longer. Transfer the pork to a plate.

Add the *mirin*, the remaining 2 tablespoons of soy sauce, the sugar and a tablespoon of water to the pan, mix well and bring to a simmer. Return the pork to the pan and cook over high heat, turning the pieces frequently until the liquid has evaporated and the pork is glazed, about 2 minutes. Cut the pork into 1 cm (½ in) diagonal slices and arrange on individual plates or platters. Garnish with pickled cucumber slices, pickled ginger and tomato wedges.

VARIATION: For Glazed Beef (*Gyuniku No Teriyaki*), marinate 250 g (8 oz) sirloin or other tender steak, trimmed of fat, in 2 tablespoons each of *mirin* and soy sauce for 10 minutes, turning 2 or 3 times. Drain and reserve the marinade. Lightly oil a frying-pan and sauté the beef for 1 minute on each side. Lift out and wipe the pan with paper towels. Add the reserved marinade to the pan and glaze the steak on both sides cooking for only a minute or two longer for rare meat. Cut the steak into 1 cm (½ in) slices, arrange on an oblong platter, or use a plate, and pour any pan juices over the meat. Garnish with pickled ginger and lettuce leaves. SERVES 1 OR 2.

GINGER GLAZED PORK WITH VEGETABLES

BUTANIKU NO SHOGAZUKEYAKI

Ginger juice squeezed from fresh grated ginger root gives this glazed (*teriyaki*) pork dish its special flavour.

SERVES 4
375 g (12 oz) boneless pork loin
1 tablespoon fresh ginger juice
1 tablespoon *sake*
4 tablespoons soy sauce
75 g (3 oz) green beans
½ teaspoon dry mustard, Japanese *or* English
8 small radishes
1 dried hot red chilli pepper
2 teaspoons rice vinegar
1 teaspoon sugar
½ teaspoon salt
Plain flour
Vegetable oil
2 tablespoons *mirin*

Thinly slice the pork then cut into bite-size pieces. Put into a bowl with 1 teaspoon of the ginger juice, *sake* and 2 tablespoons of the soy sauce. Marinate for 20 minutes.

Wash and trim the beans and drop into boiling water. Cook for 3 minutes. Drain and cut into 2.5 cm (1 in) pieces. Mix the mustard with a little boiling water to a paste and stir into 1 tablespoon of the soy sauce. Pour over the beans and mix.

Trim and thinly slice the radishes and put into a bowl. Seed and chop the chilli pepper and mix with the radish slices, vinegar, sugar and salt.

Lift the pork pieces out of the marinade and reserve it. Coat the pork lightly with the flour. Heat 2 tablespoons of oil in a large, heavy frying-pan and sauté the pork pieces until they are browned on both sides. Do not overcrowd the pan. Do in batches if necessary, adding more oil to the pan. When all the pork pieces are browned, wipe the pan with paper towels, add the remaining 2 teaspoons of ginger juice, 1 tablespoon of soy sauce, *mirin* and the reserved marinade. Bring to a simmer, add the pork and cook, stirring, over fairly high heat turning frequently, until the pork is glazed. Arrange the pork on a platter. Drain the beans and radishes and put onto the platter in a decorative way. It looks very pretty with the pink and white radish, brown pork and green beans. Serve as a main course with rice.

MEATBALLS

HIKINIKU-DANGO

The plain word meatballs does not convey the attractiveness of this dish with its garnish of radish cut to look like a chrysanthemum flower coloured to a pretty pink with a little red wine. The cutting technique for the radish, *kikuka-daikon* is interesting and not at all difficult.

SERVES 4

5 cm (2 in) slice white radish (*daikon*)
Salt
2 tablespoons rice vinegar
2 tablespoons dry red wine
Sugar
1 dried hot red chilli pepper
2 dried Japanese mushrooms (*shiitake*)
375 g (12 oz) minced beef
1 teaspoon finely chopped fresh ginger root
1 large egg, stirred
4 tablespoons freshly made breadcrumbs
2 tablespoons plus 1 teaspoon soy sauce
1 tablespoon *sake*
Cornflour
Vegetable oil for deep frying
2 tablespoons *mirin*

First make the radish garnish, *Kikuka-Daikon* (Chrysanthemum-Looking Radish Flowers). Peel the radish. Place on a chopping board with a chopstick on each side. (See *kikukagiri* on page 9.) The chopsticks prevent the knife cutting right through the radish, leaving about 5 mm (¼ in) holding it together. Turn the radish round and cut across again, making tiny squares. Sprinkle with salt. Place 1 or 2 plates on top of the radish and let it stand for 30 minutes to get rid of some of the moisture. Drain the radish, rinse in cold water and squeeze very carefully in a cloth so as not to break it. Cut the radish into quarters. Mix the rice vinegar, red wine, 1 tablespoon sugar

and ¼ teaspoon salt together and pour over the radish. Marinate for 15 minutes. Take the radish, quarters out of the marinade carefully. Gently separate the 'petals' to form a flower, pushing a finger down in the centre. Shake the seeds out of the dried chilli and chop it finely. Put the chopped pepper into the centres of the 4 radish flowers. Set aside.

To make the meatballs soak the mushrooms in warm water for 30 minutes. Drain, squeeze out and cut away the hard stems, chop the mushrooms finely. In a bowl, combine the mushrooms, beef, ginger, egg, breadcrumbs, ½ teaspoon salt, the teaspoon of soy sauce and the *sake* and mix well. Shape into 16 small balls and roll them in the cornflour. Heat 5 to 7 cm (2 to 3 in) oil in a *tempura* pan or heavy frying-pan to a temperature of 180°C (350°F) on a frying thermometer or until bubbles form on wooden chopsticks stirred in the oil. Add the meatballs and cook, turning once, for about 3 minutes. Drain on the rack of the *tempura* pan or on paper towels.

In a frying-pan combine 2 tablespoons sugar, the 2 tablespoons soy sauce and the *mirin*, bring to a simmer, add the meatballs and cook over moderate heat turning them so that they are coated all over with the sauce. Simmer until all the liquid has evaporated or been absorbed. Shake the pan from time to time to prevent the meatballs from sticking. Remove and thread the meatballs 2 at a time on small bamboo skewers (*takegushi*). Lay 2 skewers diagonally across each of 4 platters.

Put a radish flower on each of the platters. Eat the radish with chopsticks and eat the meatballs off the skewers.

BEEF AND SPRING ONION ROLLS

GYUNIKU NO NEGIMAKI

These attractive and delicious beef rolls can be varied by changing the stuffing and the cooking method to take advantage of the freshest and best vegetables in the market. Asparagus is a favourite stuffing during its short season.

SERVES 4
375 g (12 oz) beef topside *or* any top quality cut
2 tablespoons soy sauce
1 tablespoon *mirin*
1 teaspoon finely grated fresh ginger root
4 medium-sized spring onions, trimmed, using
white and green parts
Plain flour
Vegetable oil
1 lemon, cut into 4 wedges

Cut the beef into paper-thin slices about 12 × 7 cm (5 × 3 in). This is easier to do if the beef has been stiffened in the freezer. Or have the butcher do it. Combine the soy sauce, *mirin* and ginger and pour over the beef in a bowl. Marinate for 30 minutes, turning the beef slices once or twice.

Cut the spring onions into pieces as long as the beef is wide. Divide the spring onions so that there will be some white and some green to stuff each roll.

Lift the beef slices out of the marinade and arrange on a flat surface. Lay the spring onions crossways on the beef leaving a small margin at each end and roll up. Dab a little flour on the end of each beef strip to hold the rolls together. Coat the rolls with flour, shaking to remove the excess. Heat 5 to 7 cm (2 to 3 in) oil in a *tempura* pan or heavy frying-pan to 180°C (350°F) on a frying thermometer, or until bubbles form on wooden chopsticks stirred in the oil. Cook the rolls, a few at a time so as not to overcrowd the pan, for about 3 minutes, turning once or twice. Drain on the rack of the *tempura* pan or on paper towels. Garnish with lemon wedges, squeezing some lemon juice over the rolls. Serve hot and as freshly cooked as possible.

VARIATION 1: Instead of being deep-fried (*agemono*), the rolls may be sautéed, in which case do not coat them with flour. Heat 2 tablespoons oil in a heavy frying-pan and sauté the rolls over moderately high heat, turning to brown them all over, about 4 minutes. The flavour is surprisingly different.

VARIATION 2: For *Butaniku No Negimaki* (Pork and Spring Onion Rolls), make in the same way as the beef rolls but substitute *sake* for the *mirin* in the marinade and use boneless pork, preferably loin. Sauté the rolls. Do not deep-fry them. When the rolls are cooked mix 2 tablespoons each *sake*, soy sauce and sugar with 1 tablespoon *mirin*, pour it over the rolls and cook, turning frequently, over fairly high heat until they are glazed. To serve, cut in half diagonally, showing the spring onion. SERVES 4.

MIXED GRILL

TEPPAN-YAKI

The literal meaning of *teppan-yaki* is iron-plate grilling and there are restaurants which specialize in this type of cooking. Tables have a heated rectangular cast-iron insert on which food is cooked in front of the customers. At home a large, heavy cast-iron frying-pan on a table heater can be used, or the dish can be cooked in the kitchen and brought to the table.

SERVES 4
4 × 125 g (4 oz) sirloin *or* fillet steaks
Salt and pepper
4 large uncooked prawns, if frozen, thoroughly defrosted
4 large scallops, if frozen, thoroughly defrosted
2 medium-sized onions
1 large sweet green pepper
4 medium-sized mushrooms
50 g (2 oz) mangetout

FOR THE DIPPING SAUCE:
250 ml (8 fl oz) soy sauce
125 ml (4 fl oz) *mirin*
150 ml (¼ pint) *sake*
1 tablespoon fresh ginger juice
½ tablespoon sesame oil (optional)

GARNISHES:
4 tablespoons finely chopped spring onions, using white and green parts
125 g (4 oz) finely grated white radish (*daikon*)
Citrus vinegar (*ponzu*)
1 tablespoon mustard, made from dry Japanese or English mustard

Trim the steaks, and season on both sides with salt and pepper. Shell and devein the prawns. Rinse the scallops and pat dry. Thinly slice the onions lengthways. Slice off the stem end and remove the seeds from the pepper. Cut it into 8 lengthways slices. Trim the stems of the mushrooms and cut a shallow cross in the tops. Trim the mangetout. Set the ingredients on a large platter.

Make the dipping sauce. In a bowl, mix together all the ingredients and the sesame oil if liked. Pour into 4 small individual bowls and put one at each place setting. Put the garnishes in separate bowls at the centre of the table.

Heat the frying-pan and film with oil. Cook the ingredients, some of each over moderate heat. Diners help themselves with chopsticks to the food according to their choice, seasoning the food with the dipping sauce and garnishes.

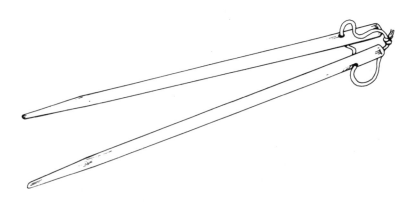

The Japanese were not always vegetarians. They became vegetarian during the Zen Buddhist era, but for the last century or so they have reverted to a diet which includes fish, fowl and meat. All the same, the Japanese have an unsurpassed appreciation of vegetables and include more of them in their daily diet than do most people.

A wide variety of vegetables is cultivated in Japan, both indigenous and introduced, and all of superb quality. These are never served plain but are always in combination with other foods, giving a delicious mixture of flavours, all discernable, a characteristic feature of Japanese cooking. Soy sauce and vinegar are used to make a salad dressing without oil. The equivalent of our mayonnaise, Golden Dressing, made with eggs but without oil, is light and delicate. Even simple root vegetables like turnips and onions are transformed, and more exotic vegetables like bamboo shoots and aubergines make delectable small dishes.

The distinction between vegetables and salads is not very clearly defined. Many dishes that would be served hot in Western kitchens as vegetables, are served at room temperature as salads in Japan. It does not really matter what a vegetable dish is called since it will be part of a meal with a main course of fish, poultry or meat, soup, rice and so on. Vegetable and salad dishes can be complicated or very simple, but all have the same aim, a fresh, natural taste with the cooking method used only to enhance, never to mask, nature's flavours, though many flavours may be harmoniously present in a single dish. Vegetable and salad dishes, like almost all dishes in the Japanese kitchen, are eaten with chopsticks.

VEGETABLES AND SALADS ĀEMONO

PUMPKIN IN THICK SAUCE

KABOCHA NO ANKAKE

Pumpkin, one of the squash family, which originated in Mexico, was introduced into Japan by the Portuguese. The name is a corruption of the Mexican name of the vegetable, *calabaza*. The best variety to use is West Indian pumpkin available in autumn and winter.

SERVES 4
750 g (1½ lb) pumpkin
1 tablespoon sugar
1 teaspoon soy sauce
1 teaspoon salt
⅛ teaspoon MSG
125 g (4 oz) ground chicken
1 teaspoon ginger juice
2 teaspoons *katakuriko* starch *or* potato flour

Cut the unpeeled pumpkin into 2.5 cm (1 in) pieces. Using a small, sharp knife, carefully trim a thin strip of peel round the edge of each piece to prevent it breaking up during cooking. Put the pumpkin pieces into a saucepan with the sugar, soy sauce, salt, MSG and enough water to cover and bring to a boil over high heat. Reduce the heat to low and simmer gently, uncovered, until the pumpkin is tender and the liquid reduced to half, about 15 minutes. Lift out the pumpkin onto a platter and keep warm.

To the liquid in the saucepan, add the ground chicken and ginger juice and cook, stirring for about 3 minutes. Mix the *katakuriko* starch or potato flour with a little water and stir it into the liquid. Cook, stirring, until the sauce is lightly thickened. Taste for seasoning adding a little more salt or sugar to taste. Arrange the pumpkin pieces on 4 small oblong platters, or plates and pour the sauce over them.

VARIATION 1: For Fried and Boiled Pumpkin (*Kabocha No Itameni*), cut and prepare the pumpkin as above. Choose a frying-pan large enough to hold all the pieces in a single layer. Heat 4 tablespoons of vegetable oil in the pan and sauté the pumpkin over moderate heat on both sides. Add water to cover, 7 g (¼ oz) dried bonito flakes (*hana katsuo*), 4 tablespoons sugar, or to taste, and 2 tablespoons of *mirin*. Bring to a boil, cover with an inner wooden lid (*otoshibuta*) or a plate, reduce the heat and simmer for 10 minutes. Add 4 tablespoons soy sauce and cook, uncovered, over low heat until the squash is tender, basting once or twice with the cooking liquid. Serve in 4 small bowls with the sauce poured over. SERVES 4.

VARIATION 2: For Pumpkin with Chicken or Meat Sauce (*Kabocha No Soboroni*), cut and prepare the pumpkin as in the main recipe. Heat 2 tablespoons vegetable oil in a frying-pan and add 250 g (8 oz) ground chicken, pork or beef and 2 teaspoons finely chopped fresh ginger root and cook, stirring, over high heat for about 3 minutes. Add the pumpkin pieces and cook, stirring, for 2 minutes longer. Add enough water just to cover, bring to a simmer, cover, reduce the heat and cook until the pumpkin is tender, about 10 minutes. Skim, if necessary. Add 1 tablespoon sugar, 2 tablespoons *mirin* and cook 5 minutes longer. Stir in 3 tablespoons soy sauce and cook, uncovered, over low heat until the liquid is reduced to about a third. Serve with sauce in small bowls. SERVES 4.

AUBERGINES WITH BEAN PASTE

NASU NO MISONI

Aubergines are a summer favourite in Japan where their beautiful purple colour is greatly esteemed. As in the Middle East, they are either soaked in salted water, or blanched to remove the bitterness. This is a *nimono* (simmered) dish.

SERVES 4
8 small aubergines, about 7 × 3.5 cm (3 × 1½ in)
Salt
3 tablespoons red or white *miso* (bean paste)
3 tablespoons second soup stock, *or* water
1 tablespoon sugar
5 tablespoons vegetable oil
1 teaspoon finely chopped fresh ginger root
2 tablespoons *sake*
1 teaspoon white sesame seeds

Cut the aubergines, unpeeled, into 1 cm (½ in) slices and soak in cold, salted water for 20 minutes. Drain and pat dry.

In a small bowl mix together the bean paste, soup stock and sugar until smooth and set aside.

Heat the oil in a large frying-pan, add the aubergines and ginger and sauté, turning the aubergine slices from time to time until they are lightly browned, 10 to 15 minutes. Add the bean paste mixture and the *sake* and continue cooking until the liquid has evaporated. Arrange the aubergines on 4 small platters or dishes.

Toast the sesame seeds in a small frying-pan over moderate heat until they begin to jump. Sprinkle them over the aubergines.

GRILLED AUBERGINE

NASU NO SHIGIYAKI

This is a *yakimono* (grilled) dish and is a favourite cooking method for aubergines.

SERVES 4
375 g (12 oz) aubergine
Vegetable oil
4 tablespoons red *miso* (bean paste)
3 tablespoons sugar, or to taste
4 tablespoons second soup stock
1 teaspoon white sesame seeds

Wash the aubergine and cut it in half crossways, then cut it into 2.5 cm (1 in) lengthways slices. Thread the aubergine slices on metal skewers and brush the cut surfaces with oil. Grill 7 to 10 cm (3 to 4 in) from the source of heat until the aubergine is tender and browned all over, about 5 minutes. Slide off the skewers and arrange on 4 small oblong platters, or plates.

In a small saucepan combine the *miso*, sugar and soup stock and cook, stirring, over low heat until the mixture is smooth and hot. Do not let it boil. Pour the sauce over the aubergine. In a small frying-pan toast the sesame seeds until they jump and sprinkle them over the aubergine.

VARIATION: For Whole Grilled Aubergine (*Yakinasu*), grill the vegetable under moderate heat, turning frequently, until it is tender and the peel is blackened and blistered, about 15 minutes. As soon as the aubergine is cool enough to handle, cut off the stem and peel away the blackened skin. Pull away the aubergine into lengthways strips and divide among 4 small dishes. Sprinkle with MSG. Sprinkle each dish with 1 teaspoon of dried bonito flakes (*hana-katsuo*) and about ½ teaspoon of soy sauce. Eat at room temperature. SERVES 4.

STUFFED CHINESE CABBAGE (LEAVES)

MUSHI HAKUSAI

Chinese cabbage, or Chinese leaves as it is sometimes called, (*hakusai*), is a favourite vegetable in Japan and is used in many dishes as well as for pickles. It has a very delicate flavour and texture. This is a steamed (*mushimono*) dish and, like all these dishes, is very attractive to look at as well as to eat.

SERVES 4

9 large leaves Chinese cabbage (*hakusai*)
Vegetable oil
Salt
1 small onion, finely chopped
125 g (4 oz) minced beef
125 g (4 oz) minced pork
1 teaspoon grated ginger
3 tablespoons breadcrumbs
1 large egg
Soy sauce
***Katakuriko* starch *or* potato flour**
175 ml (6 fl oz) first soup stock
4 tablespoons *mirin*
Grated lime peel

Cut away and discard the stalk end of the cabbage leaves. Rinse the leaves and drain. Put ½ teaspoon vegetable oil into a saucepan of boiling salted water, add the cabbage leaves, bring back to a boil on high heat and cook for 1 minute. Lift out the cabbage and drain in a colander.

In a small frying-pan, heat 1 tablespoon vegetable oil and sauté the onion until it is tender and lightly browned. Let it cool. Combine the onion, beef, pork, ginger, breadcrumbs and the egg, stir in 1 teaspoon soy sauce and ½ teaspoon salt. Divide the mixture into 4 patties.

Lightly squeeze out any excess moisture. Have ready a small bowl about 10 cm (4 in) wide and 5 cm (2 in) deep. Place a cabbage leaf in the bowl and sprinkle it lightly with *katakuriko* or potato flour. Top with another leaf, then a patty and sprinkle with starch. Continue until all the ingredients are used up, ending with a cabbage leaf. Fold the leaves over into a neat package. Put the stuffed cabbage, in the bowl, into a steamer and steam, over high heat, for 20 to 25 minutes.

Make the sauce. In a small saucepan, combine the soup stock, *mirin*, and 3 tablespoons of soy sauce. Mix 2 teaspoons *katakuriko* or potato flour with cold water and stir into the sauce. Cook over moderate heat, stirring, until the sauce is lightly thickened.

Turn the stuffed cabbage out of the bowl onto a platter or plate. This will be the smooth side. Using a small, sharp knife cut a cross in the top and pour the sauce over the cabbage. Sprinkle with the lime peel. To serve, cut into quarters with chopsticks and place in small, individual bowls, with the sauce.

CHINESE CABBAGE (LEAVES) WITH BONITO FLAKES

HAKUSAI NO OHITASHI

This is a winter vegetable dish and, with similar vegetable dishes, is very popular because of its simple, natural flavour doubly welcome at a time when so few fresh things are available.

SERVES 4
8 large leaves Chinese cabbage (*hakusai*)
Salt
1 tablespoon rice vinegar
1 tablespoon soy sauce
4 tablespoons first soup stock
2 tablespoons dried bonito flakes (*hana-katsuo*)

Put the cabbage leaves into a large saucepan full of boiling salted water, bring back to a boil over high heat, lower the heat and simmer until the cabbage is tender, about 5 minutes. Drain the cabbage and arrange the leaves on a bamboo mat (*sudare*) or a kitchen cloth, cool and roll up the mat to squeeze out the excess moisture. Unroll and cut the cabbage into 4 slices. Put into 4 small shallow bowls.

Combine the rice vinegar, soy sauce, soup stock and a little salt to taste in a small bowl, stir to mix and pour over the cabbage. Garnish with the bonito flakes.

GREEN BEANS WITH WHITE SESAME SEEDS

SAYA-INGEN NO GOMA-AE

Japanese cooks have created a number of original recipes for green beans. Here are some of them.

SERVES 4
375 g (12 oz) green beans
Salt
3 tablespoons white sesame seeds
1 tablespoon sugar
2 tablespoons soy sauce
Dried bonito flakes (*hana-katsuo*)

Rinse the beans then drop them into a saucepan of briskly boiling salted water. Bring back to a boil over high heat, reduce the heat and simmer, uncovered, for about 4 minutes, or according to the degree of crispness liked. Rinse the beans in cold water, drain and cut into 2 or 3 diagonal slices according to the size of the beans.

In a small frying-pan, toast the sesame seeds until they begin to jump. Put them into an earthenware mortar (*suribachi*) and crush them coarsely with a pestle, or put them into a nut grinder or small coffee mill and crush coarsely. Scrape them into a bowl. Add the sugar and soy sauce and stir to mix. Toss the beans in the sesame seed mixture and divide among 4 small bowls. Sprinkle with bonito flakes. Serve at room temperature.

VARIATION 1: For Green Beans with Walnuts (*Saya-ingen No Kurumi-ae*), use 4 tablespoons coarsely crushed walnut meats, about 8 whole walnuts, instead of the sesame seeds.

VARIATION 2: For Green Beans with Peanuts (*Saya-ingen No Peanuts-ae*), replace sesame seeds with 4 tablespoons coarsely crushed peanuts.

VARIATION 3: For Green Beans with Black Sesame Seeds (*Saya-ingen No Kuro Goma-ae*), cook the beans as above and put them into a bowl with 1 tablespoon of black sesame seeds instead of white ones then mix with 2 tablespoons soy sauce, 2 teaspoons *mirin*, and ⅛ teaspoon MSG. Pour over the beans, mixing lightly. Serve at room temperature in 4 small bowls. SERVES 4.

GREEN BEANS WITH BEAN PASTE

SAYA-INGEN NO MISO-AE

Green beans originated in Mexico and were introduced into Japan only in the 16th century. The Japanese poetic eye helped in the naming of the new vegetable. *Saya* refers to the outside of the bean, not to the immature beans inside. It means the scabbard of the sword, hence the scabbard of the bean covering the beans (*ingen*) inside.

SERVES 4
375 g (12 oz) green beans
Salt
4 tablespoons either red or white *miso* (bean paste)
3 tablespoons sugar
3 tablespoons *mirin*

Rinse the beans then drop them into a large saucepan of boiling salted water. Bring back to a boil over high heat, reduce the heat and cook uncovered, for 6 minutes. Drain, cool a little, then trim the ends of the beans. Slice diagonally into 2 or 3 pieces according to the size of the beans. Put into a bowl.

In a small saucepan, combine the bean paste with the sugar and *mirin* and cook, stirring, over very low heat until the mixture is smooth. Do not let it boil. Cool. Mix the sauce with the beans and divide among 4 small bowls or dishes.

GREEN BEANS WITH SOY SAUCE

SAYA-INGEN NO SHOYUNI

This is a simple, very flavourful way of cooking green beans.

SERVES 4
375 g (12 oz) green beans
250 ml (8 fl oz) second soup stock
2 tablespoons soy sauce
2 tablespoons *mirin*
⅛ teaspoon MSG

Rinse the beans and cut them into 5 cm (2 in) pieces. Put them into a medium-sized saucepan with the soup stock, soy sauce, *mirin* and MSG. Simmer, uncovered, over moderate heat until the liquid has evaporated and the beans are tender, 15 to 20 minutes. Divide among 4 small bowls.

TARO WITH CHICKEN AND VEGETABLES

SATO-IMO TO TORINIKU NO UMANI

Taro is a term covering an ancient group of mostly tropical root vegetables of the Arum Family that have been cultivated for thousands of years. The many varieties have a number of local names but in Japan are called *Sato-imo*, and are often available tinned in Japanese shops. They are often to be found in West Indian markets where they may be called coco, yautia, dasheen, tannia, or eddo. They look a little like very rough skinned potatoes.

SERVES 4
750 g (1½ lb) taro, about 8 small ones
350 ml (12 fl oz) second soup stock
3 tablespoons *sake*
1 tablespoon sugar
½ teaspoon salt
1 tablespoon, plus 1 teaspoon, soy sauce
1 tablespoon, plus 1 teaspoon, *mirin*
1 teaspoon ginger juice
150 g (5 oz) skinned and boned chicken breast,
cut into diagonal bite-size pieces
1 medium carrot, scraped
6 large green beans, trimmed and cut into thin
lengthways slices
2 teaspoons grated lime peel

Rinse the taro and peel, then rub with salt and rinse in cold water. If small taro are not available, cut larger ones into 8 equal-sized pieces. In a saucepan large enough to hold the taro in a single layer, combine the soup stock, 2 tablespoons of the *sake*, the sugar and salt. Add the taro, cover with a double layer of cheese-cloth wrung out in cold water. Bring to a boil, reduce the heat to low and simmer, uncovered, until the liquid is reduced to about one third and the taro is tender, about 30 minutes. Remove the cheesecloth, add 1 teaspoon of soy sauce and the tablespoon of *mirin*. Simmer for a few minutes to blend the flavours, remove from the heat and set aside.

In a saucepan combine the ginger juice, the remaining tablespoon of *sake* and the tablespoon of soy sauce. Bring to a boil, add the chicken pieces, reduce the heat to very low and cook, stirring, until the liquid has evaporated and the chicken is tender, 3 or 4 minutes. Set aside.

Flute the carrot, cutting 5 small wedges at even intervals down its length, then cut into 12 slices which will be flower shaped (*hana giri*). Cook with a pinch of sugar in salted water to cover the carrot by about 2.5 cm (1 in). Simmer until the water has evaporated and the carrot is tender, about 15 minutes. Set aside.

Drop the beans into salted water and cook for 8 minutes. Drain, sprinkle with a little salt and the teaspoon of *mirin* and set aside.

Arrange the taro on a serving platter or dish and top with the chicken and any sauce from both the taro and chicken. Garnish with the carrots and beans and sprinkle with the lime peel and eat at room temperature. If liked, divide among 4 small dishes.

WHITE RADISH WITH *MISO* SAUCE

FUROFUKI

This is a simmered (*nimono*) winter dish and is eaten hot. The radish holds the heat so that when it is cut with chopsticks steam rises from it, which is why it is called a 'blow-on-it-to-cool-it' dish. It is extremely pretty with the white radish, red-brown *miso* and vivid green lime. In Japan *yuzu*, a type of lime with a fragrant skin, would be used. Ordinarily lime is a good substitute and if limes are not available, then use lemon peel, though it will lack the lovely green colour, and not look much like a pine needle, which the lime peel represents.

SERVES 4
375 g (12 oz) Japanese white radish (*daikon*)
1 teaspoon salt
10 cm (4 in) square kelp seaweed (*kombu*)
4 tablespoons black sesame seeds
3 tablespoons red *miso* (bean paste)
4 tablespoons second soup stock
4 tablespoons sugar, or to taste
1 tablespoon *mirin*
Lime peel cut into 4 V-shapes

Peel the radish and cut it into 4 equal-sized slices. Peel a very thin strip from the top and bottom edge of each slice. This will prevent it breaking up in cooking. Cut a shallow cross in one side of each slice and arrange, cut-side down in a saucepan large enough to hold all the radish slices in a single layer. Cover with cold water. Add the salt. Cut the seaweed along one side into a 1 cm (½ in) fringe and add to the pan. Cover with an inner wooden lid (*otoshibuta*) or use a plate. Just before the water comes to a boil over moderate heat remove the seaweed. Do not replace the inner wooden lid, or the plate. Cover with the saucepan's own lid, reduce the heat to low and cook until the radish is tender, about 45 minutes.

In a small frying-pan, lightly toast the sesame seeds until they jump. Put them into an earthenware mortar (*suribachi*) and grind them to a paste, or use a nut grinder or small coffee grinder. Scrape them into a bowl and set aside.

In a small saucepan, combine the red *miso* (bean paste) with the soup stock, sugar to taste and *mirin* and heat gently, stirring until smooth and well-blended. Stir in the sesame paste off the heat. Keep the sauce warm until ready to use. Do not let it boil.

Arrange the radish slices in 4 warmed dishes and pour any cooking liquid over them. Spread the bean paste sauce over each slice so that a little runs down the sides. Garnish with the lime peel.

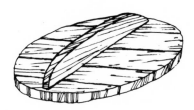

GRATED STEAMED TURNIPS

KABU NO OROSHIMUSHI

Small white turnips are transformed into a
delicate medley of textures and flavours in this
mushimono (steamed) dish.

SERVES 4
**125 g (4 oz) uncooked, shelled prawns, if frozen
thoroughly defrosted, and coarsely chopped
125 g (4 oz) skinned and boned chicken breast,
coarsely chopped
2 teaspoons light soy sauce (*usukuchi shoyu*)
2 teaspoons *sake*
2 large eggs
3 medium-sized white turnips, *or* 4 small ones
4 small dried Japanese mushrooms (*shiitake*)
1 tablespoon uncooked green peas
Salt
1 teaspoon sugar
4 teaspoons *mirin*
350 ml (12 fl oz) second soup stock
4 teaspoons soy sauce
2 teaspoons arrowroot *or* cornflour
1 tablespoon finely grated fresh ginger root**

Sprinkle the prawns and chicken with the light
soy sauce and set aside for 5 minutes. Break the
eggs into a bowl and stir with chopsticks until
they are well-blended but not foamy. Peel and
finely grate the turnips. Squeeze lightly or drain
through a sieve to get rid of excess liquid. Add to
the eggs. Soak the mushrooms for 30 minutes in
warm water. Squeeze out, cut away the hard
stems and cut into quarters. Add to the eggs with
the chicken and prawns and any liquid, the peas,
½ teaspoon salt, the sugar, 2 teaspoons of the *mirin*
and mix well. Pour into 4 deep bowls, large
enough so that they are only ¾ full, leaving room
for the sauce. Place in a steamer over boiling
water and steam over high heat for about 12
minutes.

In a small saucepan, combine the soup stock, ¼
teaspoon salt, the soy sauce, the remaining 2
teaspoons *mirin* and the arrowroot or cornflour
mixed with a little water, and bring to a boil.
Simmer, stirring, over moderate heat until the
sauce is lightly thickened. Lift out the bowls
from the steamer and pour the sauce into each of
them. Garnish each bowl with a little mound of
grated ginger.

STEAMED STUFFED TURNIPS

KABU NO TSUMEMUSHI

This is another *mushimono* (steamed) winter
turnip dish. It has been said that the *mushimono*
dishes give the cook the greatest chance to create
'the picture on the plate'. Certainly this is a very
attractive dish.

SERVES 4
**4 medium-sized white turnips, peeled
2 jelly mushrooms (*kikurage*)
12 cooked tinned or bottled gingko nuts
125 g (4 oz) fillet of sole, red snapper *or* sea bass,
thinly sliced on the diagonal
Salt
175 ml (6 fl oz) second soup stock
½ teaspoon light soy sauce (*usukuchi shoyu*)
2 teaspoons arrowroot *or* cornflour**

Cut a small slice from the top of the turnips to
make a lid. Using a sharp spoon (a grapefruit
spoon is ideal), hollow them out leaving a shell
about 1 cm (½ in) thick. Slightly hollow out the
slices for the lids.

Soak the mushrooms in warm water for 10
minutes. Drain and slice thinly. Put the mushrooms into a bowl with the gingko nuts and fish,
season with salt, mix thoroughly and stuff into
the turnips. Cover the turnips with their lids and
put into a steamer over boiling water. Steam
over high heat for 20 minutes.

In a small saucepan, combine the soup stock,
light soy sauce and ½ teaspoon salt. Mix the
arrowroot or cornflour with a little cold water
and add to the saucepan. Bring to a boil over
moderate heat, stirring constantly, lower the
heat and simmer, stirring, until the sauce is
lightly thickened. Put the turnips on small plates
or into shallow bowls. Remove the turnip lids
and balance them at the side of the vegetables.
Pour the sauce over the turnips.

OKRA WITH VINEGAR DRESSING

OKURA NO SANBAIZU

This is very like the cabbage recipe on page 129. It is easy to make with a simple, natural taste.

SERVES 4
20 small okra pods
2 tablespoons rice vinegar
4 tablespoons first soup stock
½ teaspoon salt
1 tablespoon soy sauce
2 teaspoons sugar

Drop the okra into a large saucepan of boiling salted water, bring back to a boil over high heat, lower the heat and cook, uncovered for 3 to 4 minutes. Drain, rinse quickly in cold water and drain again. Cut off the stem ends of the pods and cut the okra into 1 cm (½ in) slices. Transfer to a bowl.

Mix the vinegar, soup stock, salt, soy sauce and sugar together, pour over the okra slices, tossing lightly to mix. Divide among 4 small bowls.

TURNIPS WITH BEAN PASTE AND CHICKEN SAUCE

KOKABU NO TORIMISOKAKE

This is an autumn or winter *nimono* (simmered) dish, with the turnips in a rich *miso*-based sauce.

SERVES 4
12 small white turnips, rinsed and peeled
350 ml (12 fl oz) second soup stock
1 teaspon salt
1 teaspoon soy sauce
175 g (6 oz) skinned and boned chicken breast
1 teaspoon finely chopped fresh ginger root
2 tablespoons *mirin*
4 tablespoons red *miso* (bean paste)
2 teaspoons arrowroot *or* cornflour
1 medium-sized spring onion, trimmed, using white and green parts

Cut a shallow cross in the bottom of each turnip. In a saucepan large enough to hold the turnips in a single layer, combine the soup stock, salt, soy sauce and turnips. Cover, bring to a boil, reduce the heat and simmer until the turnips are tender, 20 to 25 minutes. Drain, reserve the stock and set the turnips aside.

Put the chicken twice through the fine blade of a meat grinder or chop finely in a food processor. Put the chicken into a saucepan with the ginger and 1 tablespoon of the *mirin*, and cook, stirring constantly, over moderate heat until the chicken is cooked, 3 or 4 minutes. Stir in the *miso* (bean paste), add 175 ml (6 fl oz) of the reserved turnip stock. Mix the arrowroot or cornflour with a little water and stir into the sauce. Cook, stirring, over moderate heat until the sauce is lightly thickened. Put the turnips into 4 small bowls and cover with the sauce.

Finely chop the spring onion, crisp for a few minutes in cold water and squeeze dry in a cloth. Sprinkle it over the sauce.

AUBERGINES WITH RED AND WHITE BEAN PASTE

NASU NO DENGAKU

This is a popular vegetarian dish in Japan and, as well as being healthful, is delicious to eat and very attractive to look at with the purple aubergine topped with the contrasting sauces.

SERVES 4

RED *MISO* (BEAN PASTE) SAUCE:
2 tablespoons red *miso* (bean paste)
1 tablespoon *mirin*
1 tablespoon sugar
2 tablespoons first soup stock, about

WHITE *MISO* (BEAN PASTE) SAUCE:
2 tablespoons white *miso* (bean paste)
1 tablespoon *mirin*
2 teaspoons sugar
2 tablespoons first soup stock, about

2 medium aubergines
Vegetable oil
White sesame seeds
Black sesame seeds *or* poppy seeds
½ medium cucumber
Salt
2 tablespoons rice vinegar
1 tablespoon soy sauce

Make the red *miso* (bean paste) sauce. In a small, heavy saucepan, combine the bean paste with the *mirin*, sugar and soup stock. Mix to a smooth paste over very low heat and cook, stirring, until the sugar has dissolved. Do not let it boil. Make the white *miso* (bean paste) sauce in the same

way. Set the two sauces aside.

Trim the stem end of the aubergines and halve them lengthways. Score the flesh lightly with a sharp knife. In a frying-pan large enough to hold the aubergines comfortably (or use 2 pans), heat 2 tablespoons of vegetable oil. Add the aubergines, cut-side down and cook over moderate heat, turning from time to time until the aubergines are tender and cooked through, about 15 minutes. Lift out and drain on paper towels.

Spread the top half of each aubergine with the red *miso* (bean paste) sauce. Spread the other half with the white *miso* (bean paste) sauce.

In a small frying-pan toast the black sesame seeds until they pop and garnish the white *miso* with a little pile. Or use poppy seeds. Toast the white seeds and garnish the red *miso* with them. Arrange on 4 oblong platters, or plates.

Trim the cucumber and peel lengthways in alternate strips. Scrape out the seeds with chopsticks. Cut into 1 cm (½ in) slices and sprinkle lightly with salt. In a bowl, combine the vinegar, soy sauce, 1 teaspoon of sugar and add the cucumber slices, mixing well. Let stand for about 5 minutes then use to garnish the platters with the aubergines.

PEAS IN
SOUP STOCK

ENDO NO AONI

The cooking method gives the peas an intense fresh colour, hence the name of the recipe as *ao* means blue-green, and *ni* means boiled. The peas are also very well-flavoured as they absorb the delicate taste of the soup stock enhanced with a little light soy sauce. This is a summer dish.

SERVES 4
250 g (8 oz) fresh green peas
Salt
350 ml (12 fl oz) second soup stock
1 teaspoon light soy sauce (*usukuchi shoyu*)
2 teaspoons *mirin*

Put the peas into a saucepan of briskly boiling salted water and cook, uncovered, over moderate heat until the peas are tender, about 10 minutes. Drain and set aside.

In another saucepan combine the soup stock, ¼ teaspoon salt, the light soy sauce and *mirin* and bring to a boil. Add the peas, bring back to a boil, then remove from the heat. Stand the saucepan in a larger pan, or bowl of cold water with ice cubes, pouring off the water and adding more ice cubes from time to time to keep it very cold. Let stand for 2 to 3 hours. To serve pour the soup and peas into 4 small bowls.

GREEN PEAS WITH
CHICKEN AND EGGS

ENDO NO NATANENI

This dish means literally 'peas looking like the seeds of rape greens'. It gets its name from the green of the peas and the yellow of the eggs, a combination which, to the poetic Japanese eye, looks like rape greens when the yellow flowers are running to seed.

SERVES 4
250 g (8 oz) fresh green peas
Salt
150 g (5 oz) skinned and boned chicken, coarsely chopped
350 ml (12 fl oz) second soup stock
1 teaspoon sugar
1 tablespoon light soy sauce (*usukuchi shoyu*)
1 tablespoon *mirin*
3 large eggs

Drop the peas into a saucepan of briskly boiling salted water and cook, uncovered, over moderate heat for 8 minutes. Drain and let stand in cold water until ready to use.

Put the chicken into a small saucepan with the soup stock and simmer for 5 minutes over moderate heat. Add the sugar, ½ teaspoon salt, the light soy sauce and *mirin*, skimming the surface if necessary. Drain the peas and add them to the chicken mixture. Break the eggs into a bowl and stir until they are well-blended but not foamy. Bring the chicken mixture to a boil then pour the eggs in a thin stream to cover the whole surface of the pan. Cover, remove from the heat and let stand for 1 or 2 minutes or until the eggs are set. Serve hot in 4 small bowls.

BURDOCK AND CARROT WITH SESAME SEEDS

KINPIRA

This is a New Year dish and is also very popular for lunch boxes. Because of its fresh and natural taste it is one of those dishes that is popular at any time, even though it is special to a holiday. Burdock (*gobo*) is very seldom available fresh. It can be bought tinned from shops specializing in Japanese foods, or use salsify or scorzonera – like burdock, members of the Daisy Family.

SERVES 4

375 g (12 oz) burdock, fresh or tinned, *or* salsify, *or* scorzonera
1 medium-sized carrot
1 or 2 dried hot red chilli peppers, to taste
1 tablespoon vegetable oil
1 tablespoon sugar, or to taste
2½ tablespoons soy sauce
1 tablespoon white sesame seeds

Scrape the burdock root, salsify or scorzonera, if using fresh, with the back of a knife under cold running water. Cut into 5 cm (2 in) pieces, then slice each piece thinly lengthways. Drop into cold water until ready to use. Scrape and cut the carrot in the same way. Cut the ends from the chillies and shake out the seeds. If they are very dry soak for 2 to 3 minutes in cold water to soften. Lift out, pat dry and cut into diagonal strips.

Heat the oil in a large saucepan, add the chillies and sauté for a few minutes. Drain and add the burdock root, and sauté over moderate heat, stirring from time to time, for about 10 minutes. Add the carrot and sauté for 5 minutes longer. Add 2 tablespoons water, cover and cook for about 3 minutes, or until the carrot is tender. Add the sugar and soy sauce and stir to mix. Bring to a boil over moderate heat and cook, stirring with chopsticks, until the liquid has evaporated, about 5 minutes. Toast the sesame seeds in a small frying-pan until they begin to jump. Set aside.

Serve the vegetable mixture in 4 small individual bowls and sprinkle with the sesame seeds.

RAPE BLOSSOMS WITH SESAME SEEDS

NA-NO-HANA NO GOMA-AE

Rape greens, also called broccoli di rapa, rapa or colza, are available quite widely in summer and autumn. The yellow blossoms (*Na-No-Hana*) are prized by the Japanese who use them in recipes, as a garnish, and sometimes pickled.

SERVES 4

300 g (10 oz) rape blossoms, tough stems removed
3 tablespoons white sesame seeds
2½ tablespoons soy sauce
1 tablespoon sugar

Rinse the blossoms and drop them into a saucepan of boiling water. Bring back to a boil over high heat and cook for 4 minutes. Drain and drop into a bowl of cold water. When cool, drain, squeeze out any excess moisture and cut in 1 cm (½ in) pieces.

Toast the sesame seeds in a small frying-pan until they begin to jump. Transfer them to an earthenware mortar (*suribachi*), and grind to a paste, or use a small coffee mill or nut grinder. Scrape the paste into a bowl and mix with the soy sauce and sugar. Use chopsticks to scrape the paste out of the mortar, which is serrated.

To serve toss the rape blossoms with the dressing and divide among 4 small bowls.

ONIONS IN SESAME SEED SAUCE

TAMANEGI NO GOMA ANKAKE

This is an attractive and unusual vegetable dish which transforms onions into something special. It is simple to make with quite a robust sauce.

SERVES 4

**4 medium onions, about 5 cm (2 in) across
350 ml (12 fl oz) second soup stock
1 tablespoon *mirin*
1½ tablespoons plus 2 teaspoons soy sauce
1 tablespoon vegetable oil
175 g (6 oz) ground chicken
⅛ teaspoon MSG
1 tablespoon potato flour *or* cornflour
2 tablespoons white sesame seeds**

Peel the onions and halve them crossways. Put them into a saucepan large enough to hold them in a single layer and pour in enough boiling water to cover. Bring back to a boil on moderate heat and simmer for 3 minutes, uncovered. Add the soup stock, *mirin*, and 1½ tablespoons soy sauce. Cover and simmer until tender, about 10 minutes. Lift out the onions and divide among 4 small individual bowls. Measure the liquid and make up the quantity to 350 ml (12 fl oz) with second soup stock, if necessary. Set aside.

In another saucepan, heat the vegetable oil, add the chicken and stir-fry for 2 minutes. Add the reserved stock, the 2 teaspoons soy sauce, MSG and potato flour or cornflour mixed with cold water. Cook, stirring, until the sauce is lightly thickened. In a small frying-pan, toast the sesame seeds until they jump. Crush coarsely and stir into the sauce. Pour the sauce over the onions.

SPINACH, PARSLEY AND BLACK SESAME SEED SALAD

SERI NO GOMA-AE

Seri, or water dropwort, originally from the Mediterranean area, can best be described as a kind of aquatic parsley. It has long been cultivated in China and Japan. The best substitute, since it is not usually available in our markets, is flat (Continental) parsley. It makes an unusual and refreshing salad.

SERVES 4

**175 g (6 oz) flat (Continental) parsley, stems removed
Salt
375 g (12 oz) spinach, stems removed
3 tablespoons black sesame seeds
2 tablespoons soy sauce
1 tablespoon sugar**

Rinse the parsley and drop it into a saucepan of boiling salted water. Boil for 2 minutes, drain and put into a bowl of cold water. Drain, squeeze lightly and form into a roll on a bamboo mat (*sudare*) or a kitchen cloth. Roll up to squeeze out the excess moisture and cut into 1 cm (½ in) slices. Set aside.

Rinse the spinach and drop into a saucepan of boiling salted water. Bring back to a boil over high heat and cook for 1 minute. Drain, rinse in cold water, drain, squeeze lightly and form into a roll on a bamboo mat (*sudare*) or a kitchen cloth. Roll up to squeeze out the excess moisture and cut into 2.5 cm (1 in) slices. Toss the spinach and parsley lightly together in a bowl.

In a small frying-pan, toast the sesame seeds until they begin to jump. Put into an earthenware mortar (*suribachi*) and grind to a paste or use a small coffee mill or nut grinder. Scrape the paste into a bowl and add the soy sauce and sugar. Mix well and toss with the spinach and parsley. Serve in 4 small bowls.

SIMMERED BAMBOO SHOOTS

WAKATAKENI

This is a spring dish when fresh young bamboo shoots are available. Whole tinned bamboo shoots can be used instead. In Japan the dish would be garnished with a leaf of Japanese pepper (*sansho*). *Kona sansho*, the ground leaf sold packaged as Japanese pepper, can be used instead.

SERVES 4
725 ml (24 fl oz) second soup stock
3 tablespoons light soy sauce (*usukuchi shoyu*)
2 tablespoons sugar, or to taste
⅛ teaspoon MSG
250 g (8 oz) skinned and boned chicken, cut into diagonal bite-size pieces
750 g (1½ lb) bamboo shoots cut into 5 mm (¼ in) slices
6 × 20 cm (8 in) fronds lobe-leaf seaweed (*wakame*)
2 tablespoons *mirin*

Combine the soup stock, light soy sauce, sugar to taste and MSG in a saucepan. Add the chicken, bring to a simmer and cook over low heat for 2 minutes. Lift out the chicken pieces and set aside. Add the bamboo shoots to the pan and simmer over low heat for 20 to 30 minutes, or until the bamboo shoots are tender.

Soak the seaweed in cold water for 10 to 15 minutes, drain, cut away the hard ribs and chop into 2.5 cm (1 in) pieces. Add to the saucepan with the reserved chicken pieces and the *mirin* and simmer, covered, for 5 minutes over low heat. Divide among 4 small deep bowls. Have Japanese pepper (*kona sansho*) on the table to be used if liked.

ONION SALAD

TAMANEGI NO SUNOMONO

This is a beautifully simple salad that takes little time to make.

SERVES 4
2 medium-sized onions, peeled and halved lengthways
4 tablespoons rice vinegar
4 tablespoons soy sauce
4 tablespoons dried bonito flakes (*hana-katsuo*)

Slice the onions very thinly lengthways and put to soak in iced water for 15 to 30 minutes, according to how strongly flavoured they are. Drain thoroughly and put into a bowl. Add the vinegar, soy sauce and 3 tablespoons of the dried bonito flakes. Stir to mix. Divide among 4 small individual bowls and sprinkle with the remaining tablespoon of bonito.

WHITE RADISH AND CARROT SALAD

KOHAKU-NAMASU

SERVES 4
375 g (12 oz) Japanese white radish (*daikon*)
1 medium-sized carrot
Salt
6 tablespoons rice vinegar
2 tablespoons sugar
⅛ teaspoon MSG

Peel the radish and cut it into 5 cm (2 in) julienne strips. Scrape the carrot and cut it into the same size julienne strips. Put both vegetables into a bowl with a little salt and mix gently with the fingers. Set aside for about 3 minutes, then squeeze lightly and put on a bamboo mat (*sudare*) or a kitchen cloth, roll up and squeeze out the excess moisture.

In a bowl, mix together the rice vinegar, sugar, MSG and salt to taste. Add the radish and carrot mixture and toss lightly. Cover and refrigerate until ready to use. Put into 4 small bowls.

CHICKEN AND VEGETABLE SALAD

TORINIKU NO OROSHI-AE

Vegetables in Japanese salads are not, traditionally, served raw and dressings have no oil. This mixture of chicken and vegetables with a light vinegar and soy sauce dressing is typical of the Japanese approach to salads where texture, flavour and colour are all of importance.

SERVES 4
250 g (8 oz) small fillets (bamboo leaf) chicken
breasts (*tori sasami*), *or* use skinned and boned
chicken breast
Salt
1 teaspoon *sake*
4 medium-sized fresh mushrooms
1 medium-sized stalk celery
1 large, *or* 2 small, sprigs flat (Continental)
parsley
250 g (8 oz) Japanese white radish (*daikon*)
2½ tablespoons rice vinegar
½ teaspoon light soy sauce (*usukuchi shoyu*)
⅛ teaspoon MSG

Sprinkle the chicken lightly with salt and the *sake* and grill until cooked, about 4 minutes, turning once. Cool slightly then shred into lengthways strips.

Wipe the mushroom caps and trim the stems. Sprinkle with salt and grill until cooked, about 5 minutes. Slice thinly.

Rinse the celery and remove any strings. Cut into julienne strips. Drop the parsley into boiling salted water and simmer for 2 minutes. Rinse in cold water, squeeze out and cut into 2.5 cm (1 in) pieces. Grate the radish finely and squeeze out the excess moisture.

Mix the rice vinegar with the light soy sauce, ½ teaspoon salt and the MSG. Combine all the ingredients in a bowl and mix lightly with the dressing. Divide among 4 individual bowls.

CUCUMBER SALAD WITH
LOBE-LEAF SEAWEED

KYURI TO WAKAME NO SUNOMONO

This is a classic of Japanese home cooking. The delicate fronds of lobe-leaf seaweed combine with crisp cucumber in a refreshing salad. The Japanese have a special technique for removing any bitterness from their type of cucumber. This is not necessary with our cucumbers.

SERVES 4
250 g (8 oz) cucumber
Salt
6 × 20 cm (8 in) fronds lobe-leaf seaweed
(*wakame*)
2 tablespoons rice vinegar
2 teaspoons sugar
1 teaspoon soy sauce
⅛ teaspoon MSG

Cut the cucumber, unpeeled, in half lengthways. Using a spoon, scrape out the seeds then put the cucumber, cut side down on a chopping board and slice as thinly as possible on the diagonal. Put the cucumber into a bowl with 1 teaspoon salt and 50 ml (2 fl oz) water and let stand for 10 minutes. Drain then squeeze gently to remove the excess moisture. Divide among 4 small platters or bowls.

Rinse the seaweed, and put it into a bowl with cold water to cover and soak for 15 minutes. Drain, squeeze out the excess moisture, remove any hard ribs and chop coarsely. Arrange on the platters or bowls at the side of the cucumber.

In a small bowl, combine the vinegar, sugar, soy sauce, MSG and ¼ teaspoon salt and stir to mix. Pour over the cucumber and seaweed.

VARIATION 1: For Cucumber Salad (*Kyuri-momi*), prepare the cucumber in the same way as in the main recipe. Put the sliced cucumber into a bowl. In a small bowl, mix 2 tablespoons rice vinegar, 2 teaspoons soy sauce, 1 teaspoon sugar and ⅛ teaspoon MSG together. In a small frying-pan, toast 1 teaspoon white sesame seeds until they begin to jump. Crush coarsely. Toss the cucumber with the dressing and divide among 4 small bowls. Sprinkle with the sesame seeds. SERVES 4.

VARIATION 2: For Seaweed and Cucumber Salad with Bean Paste Dressing (*Wakame To Kyuri No Sumiso-ae*), prepare lobe-leaf seaweed (*wakame*) and cucumber as in the main recipe. In a small saucepan, combine 4 tablespoons white *miso* (bean paste), 1 tablespoon *mirin*, 1 teaspoon sugar and heat through, stirring until smooth without letting the mixture boil. Cool. Mix 1 teaspoon dry Japanese or English mustard with hot water and add. Stir in 2 tablespoons rice vinegar, mixing well. Put the seaweed and cucumber into a bowl and toss with the dressing. Serve in 4 small bowls. SERVES 4.

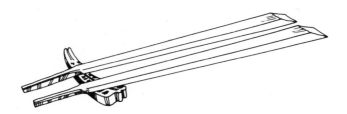

SPINACH SALAD

HORENSO NO OHITASHI

SERVES 4
500 g (1 lb) spinach, stems removed
1 teaspoon sugar
1 teaspoon plus 2 tablespoons soy sauce
⅛ teaspoon MSG
125 ml (4 fl oz) second soup stock
2 tablespoons dried bonito flakes (*hana-katsuo*)

Rinse and drain the spinach. Drop into a large saucepan of boiling water with the sugar, bring back to a boil over high heat and cook, uncovered, for 2 minutes. Drain in a colander, then rinse under cold running water. Drain and squeeze out. Put into a bowl and sprinkle with the teaspoon of soy sauce and the MSG and let stand for 2 to 3 minutes. Arrange in a roll on the bottom edge of a bamboo mat (*sudare*) or a kitchen cloth, roll up and squeeze out the excess moisture, while firming up the spinach roll. Unroll and cut into 2.5 cm (1 in) slices.

Divide the spinach among 4 small bowls. Mix together the soup stock and the 2 tablespoons of soy sauce and pour over the spinach. Sprinkle with the bonito flakes, crumbled with the fingers.

GREEN ASPARAGUS SALAD

GREEN ASPARAGUS NO KIMIJOYUKAKE

This is an unusual salad with its raw egg yolk and soy sauce dressing, refreshing and spring-like.

SERVES 4
300 g (10 oz) green asparagus, about 20 thin
stalks
Salt
1 tablespoon black sesame seeds
1 large egg yolk
2 tablespoons soy sauce

Wash and drain the asparagus and trim away the hard ends. Drop the asparagus into a large saucepan of briskly boiling salted water, bring back to a boil over high heat, reduce the heat and simmer for 5 minutes. Lift out onto a bamboo colander (*zaru*) or into a colander, plunge into cold water for 1 minute, then drain.

In a small frying-pan, toast the sesame seeds until they begin to jump. Put into a bowl and set aside.

Put the egg yolk into a small bowl and stir in the soy sauce, mixing thoroughly but not beating. Cut the asparagus stalks in half. Lay the end halves on 4 small oblong platters, then arrange the tips diagonally across them. Pour the egg yolk dressing over them and sprinkle with the sesame seeds. Serve at room temperature.

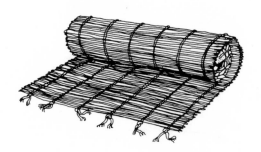

CRAB AND CUCUMBER WITH GOLDEN DRESSING

KANI TO KYURI NO KIMIZU-AE

This is one of the dressed salads (*aemono*) differing from the vinegared salads (*sunomono*) only in the dressing, not in the ingredients which in both types of salad may range from a simple vegetable or two to mixtures of vegetables with fish, shellfish, meat or poultry. Golden dressing (*kimizu*) has the consistency of mayonnaise but is much lighter as it contains no oil. It is particularly good with this crab and cucumber salad, but can be used with combination salads using scallops or chicken with celery and cucumber, or simpler salads like broccoli and Japanese white radish (*daikon*). The cook is encouraged to experiment.

SERVES 4

175 g (6 oz) white crab meat
½ medium-sized cucumber
Salt
Rice vinegar

FOR GOLDEN DRESSING:
2 large egg yolks
4 tablespoons second soup stock
2 tablespoons rice vinegar
1 tablespoon sugar
1 teaspoon cornflour
½ teaspoon salt

Pick over the crab meat to remove any shell and cartilage. Peel the cucumber in alternate lengthways strips, then halve lengthways. Scrape out the seeds with a spoon and slice thinly crossways. Soak for 20 minutes in salted water. Drain, squeeze gently to remove excess moisture and pat dry with paper towels. Sprinkle the crab meat and the cucumber lightly with rice vinegar and set aside.

Put the egg yolks into the top of a double boiler. Stir in the other ingredients including the cornflour mixed with a little water. Place over boiling water and cook, stirring constantly, until the mixture has thickened slightly. Remove from the heat and continue to stir until it is cool and has the consistency of mayonnaise.

Divide the crab meat and cucumber among 4 small bowls. Spoon the dressing over, about 1 tablespoon for each serving.

CURRIED BEAN SPROUT SALAD

MOYASHI NO KARESU-AE

The use of curry powder in this recipe is interesting as it shows the Japanese talent for adapting foreign foods into their own culinary traditions. It is a pleasant salad with a nice crunchy bite.

SERVES 4
500 g (1 lb) bean sprouts
Salt
75 ml (3 fl oz) rice vinegar
75 ml (3 fl oz) *mirin*
1 teaspoon salt
1½ teaspoons curry powder
2 teaspoons light soy sauce (*usukuchi shoyu*)
2 teaspoons sugar

Rinse and drain the bean sprouts. Drop into a large saucepan of boiling salted water and cook, uncovered, for 2 minutes. Drain and put into a bowl. Mix together all the remaining ingredients and pour over the bean sprouts. Toss lightly to mix. Let stand for 30 minutes. Divide among 4 small individual bowls.

CUCUMBER AND BEAN SPROUT SALAD WITH SESAME SEEDS

KYURI TO MOYASHI NO GOMA-AE

Crisp cucumber and crunchy bean sprouts combine to make this a very refreshing summer salad.

SERVES 4
250 g (8 oz) bean sprouts
½ medium-sized cucumber
Salt
1 tablespoon rice vinegar
1 tablespoon sesame oil
2 tablespoons soy sauce
1 tablespoon white sesame seeds
Seven-flavour spice (*shichimi-togarashi*)

Rinse and drain the bean sprouts and drop into a saucepan of boiling salted water. Cook for 2 minutes. Drain and cool. Cut the unpeeled cucumber in half lengthways and scrape out the seeds with a spoon. Slice thinly crossways. Put into a bowl of salted water and let stand for 20 minutes. Drain and squeeze gently to get rid of excess moisture.

In a bowl, combine the vinegar, sesame oil and soy sauce and mix well. Season to taste with salt. Add the bean sprouts and cucumber and mix lightly. In a small frying-pan, toast the sesame seeds until they begin to jump. Divide the bean sprout and cucumber mixture among 4 small individual bowls. Sprinkle with the sesame seeds then with the seven-flavour spice.

OYSTER SALAD

KAKI NO SUNOMONO

In Japan, in the winter, oysters from the Inland Sea come onto the market. They are not as much of a luxury as oysters are here. Lately, frozen Japanese oysters from the Inland Sea have been appearing in British fishmongers. Though nothing can compare with a freshly opened oyster, these are still very good. They should be completely defrosted in the refrigerator. Use for this lovely, luxurious salad.

SERVES 4
20 oysters
75 g (3 oz) Japanese white radish (*daikon*)
3 tablespoons rice vinegar
500 g (1 lb) spinach
Salt
1½ teaspoons sugar
1 tablespoon soy sauce
½ teaspoon MSG

Put the oysters into a bowl. Peel and finely grate the radish, add to the oysters and mix gently with the fingers for about 2 minutes. Pour in enough cold water to cover. Let stand for a minute or two, then lift out and rinse the oysters. Discard the radish and rinse out the bowl. Return the oysters to the bowl and pour 1 tablespoon of the rice vinegar over them.

Trim the stems of the spinach and drop it into a saucepan of briskly boiling salted water. Bring back to a boil over high heat and cook for 2 minutes. Drain, rinse in cold water, drain again and form into a roll at the end of a bamboo mat (*sudare*), or use a kitchen cloth. Roll up and squeeze lightly to get rid of the excess moisture. Unroll and cut into 2.5 cm (1 in) slices.

In a bowl, mix together the remaining 2 tablespoons rice vinegar, the sugar, soy sauce and MSG. Arrange the oysters and spinach rolls in 4 small individual bowls and pour the dressing over them.

In Japan edible chrysanthemum leaves (*shun-giku*) are very much liked for this salad. They are cooked exactly as the spinach.

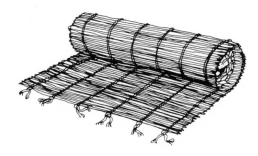

The soy bean is one of the most versatile foods that exists, far more versatile than any other bean. Apart from soy sauce and *miso* (bean paste), several types of bean curd are made from it. The most used is *momen tofu*, often called cotton bean curd to distinguish it from the more fragile and delicate *kinugoshi tofu*, silky bean curd. They are both widely available in health food shops as well as in Japanese shops. Other forms of bean curd such as *aburaage* (fried bean curd), *yakidofu* (grilled bean curd) and *koya-dofu* (freeze-dried bean curd) are less easy to find and are available usually only in Japanese shops.

Tofu was probably brought to Japan in the 8th century from China by Buddhist monks and it was soon adopted by the court nobility who were deeply interested in Chinese culture. In the early days there were *tofu* shops in temples and monasteries, run by Buddhist priests and the temple cooks and *tofu* became daily fare for the priesthood. Farmers began to grow more soy beans, and the Japanese invented new forms of the food including fried, freeze-dried, grilled and silken *tofu*. Its popularity has never diminished, and there are still restaurants that specialize in *tofu*.

The bean curd dishes belong to Japan's vegetarian period. They are varied, subtle in flavour, healthful and very high in protein as well as being delectable.

BEAN CURD DISHES

TOFU

TREASURE BAGS

TALARA BUKURO

This attractively named dish, popular in winter, is a special favourite with children who enjoy the fun of eating the 'string' tying the bags, and then the bags themselves.

SERVES 4
4 pieces fried bean curd (*aburaage*)
½ × 300 g (10 oz) package devil's-tongue-root noodles (*shirataki*)
1 dried Japanese mushroom (*shiitake*)
3 tablespoons *sake*
4 tablespoons soy sauce
1 tablespoon plus 2 teaspoons sugar
125 g (4 oz) ground chicken
1 teaspoon finely chopped fresh ginger root
8 gingko nuts, tinned or bottled
8 strips dried gourd shavings (*kanpyo*), about 15 cm (6 in) long
350 ml (12 fl oz) first soup stock
1½ tablespoons *mirin*
2 teaspoons cornflour

Rinse the bean curd pieces in hot water to remove the excess oil, pat dry and cut into halves, crossways. The bean curd can then be opened into 8 little bags.

Take out half the noodles from the package and close and refrigerate the other half. Cut the noodles into 3.5 cm (1½ in) pieces and drop into a saucepan of boiling water. Bring back to a boil over high heat and cook for 2 minutes. Drain. Soak the mushrooms for 30 minutes in warm water, squeeze out, cut away the hard stems and chop finely. Set aside with the noodles.

In a saucepan, combine 1 tablespoon of the *sake*, 1 tablespoon of the soy sauce and 2 teaspoons of sugar and bring to a boil. Lower the heat and add the chicken. Stir to mix and add the ginger, gingko nuts, mushroom and noodles and cook, stirring, over low heat for 3 minutes. Cool slightly then stuff the mixture into the bean curd bags.

Rub the dried gourd shavings with a little salt, wash and soak for a few minutes to soften. Gather up the tops of the bean curd bags, run the gourd strips twice round the bags and tie with a single knot. Prick each bag in 3 places with a toothpick.

In a medium-sized shallow saucepan, large enough to hold the bags upright in a single layer, combine the remaining 2 tablespoons of *sake*, 1 tablespoon of sugar, the *mirin* and remaining 3 tablespoons of soy sauce. Stir to mix. Bring to a simmer, place the bean curd bags upright in the pan, cover with an inner wooden lid (*otoshibuta*), or a plate, reduce the heat to moderate and cook for 15 minutes. Lift the bags out carefully and put 2 into each of 4 small bowls.

Mix the cornflour with a little water and stir into the sauce in the pan. Cook, stirring, until the sauce has thickened lightly, and pour it over the bean curd bags. To eat, untie the bags with chopsticks and eat the string. Then eat the contents of the bag and finally the bag itself.

SOLE WITH BEAN CURD

YUZENDOFU

Translated literally this means 'printed-silk-used-for-kimonos bean curd'. The sole and bean curd make a subtle off-white background which is flecked with the green of beans, the orange of carrot and the brown of mushrooms. The resulting pattern is as pretty as printed silk. In Japan fresh *shiitake* mushrooms would be used, but as these are not available it is better to use the dried *shiitake* rather than fresh local mushrooms, because of their pretty brown colour.

SERVES 4
250 g (8 oz) skinned fillet of sole
1 bean curd (*momen tofu*) weighing about 250 g (8 oz)
Sugar
Salt
3 teaspoons soy sauce
2½ tablespoons *katakuriko* starch, *or* potato flour
4 dried Japanese mushrooms (*shiitake*)
4 green beans
½ medium carrot, top end
First soup stock
1 tablespoon *mirin*
2.5 cm (1 in) slice fresh ginger root, finely grated

Chop the sole coarsely and put it into an earthenware mortar (*suribachi*) and grind it with a pestle until smooth, or reduce to a purée in a food processor. Drop the bean curd into a saucepan of boiling water, remove from the heat and let it stand for 3 minutes. Drain in a sieve lined with a kitchen cloth. Squeeze out all the moisture crushing the bean curd. Add it to the fish with 1 tablespoon of sugar, or to taste and 1 teaspoon each salt and soy sauce and mix well. Push the mixture through a sieve and mix in 2 tablespoons of the *katakuriko* starch or potato flour. Put into a bowl and set aside.

Soak the mushrooms for 30 minutes in warm water, squeeze out, cut away the hard stems and slice thinly. Drop the green beans into boiling salted water and cook, uncovered, for 3 minutes. Drain, trim the ends and cut into very thin diagonal slices. Scrape the carrot and cut it into thin julienne strips.

In a small saucepan, combine 125 ml (4 fl oz) first soup stock, 2 teaspoons sugar, or to taste, salt to taste, and a few drops of soy sauce. Add the carrot and mushrooms and simmer, uncovered, until the carrot is tender and the liquid almost evaporated, about 5 minutes. Add the green beans and cook until the mixture is quite dry, 2 or 3 minutes longer. Fold into the bean curd and sole mixture, lightly but thoroughly.

Pack the mixture into a *nagashikan*, about 7 × 12 cm (3 × 5 in). This is a stainless steel loaf pan with a removable tray that makes unmoulding delicate dishes very easy. Otherwise use a lightly oiled loaf pan. Put into a steamer and steam over moderate heat for 20 minutes, or until firm.

Make the sauce. Combine 250 ml (8 fl oz) soup stock, *mirin*, ¼ teaspoon salt, the remaining 2 teaspoons of soy sauce, and the remaining 1½ teaspoons *katakuriko* starch or potato flour mixed with a little water. Stir to mix, bring to a simmer, stirring, and remove from the heat.

To serve, cut the steamed sole and bean curd into slices and put into 4 individual bowls. Pour the sauce over each and top with a little ginger. Eat with chopsticks and drink any remaining sauce from the bowl.

CHRYSANTHEMUM-FLOWER BEAN CURD

KIKUKADOFU

This is a delightfully pretty dish as well as being good to eat. It is not difficult to make and adds a special touch for a dinner party. As quail eggs are hard to shell, it may be more convenient to buy them ready-cooked and shelled.

SERVES 4

**2 bean curd (*momen tofu*), each weighing about
250 g (8 oz)
Salt
2 tinned quail eggs, cooked and shelled
250 ml (8 fl oz) first soup stock
½ teaspoon light soy sauce (*usukuchi shoyu*)
2 teaspoons *mirin*
2 teaspoons arrowroot *or* cornflour
Few chrysanthemum leaves (*shungiku*), *or*
spinach (optional)
1 tablespoon finely grated fresh ginger root**

Wrap the bean curd in a kitchen cloth and weight with a light board or plate for 20 minutes to remove excess moisture. Slide the bean curd into a saucepan of boiling salted water, reduce the heat to low and simmer for 3 minutes. Lift the bean curd carefully out of the pan with a spatula and place on a chopping board. Cut each

bean curd in half and transfer to 4 shallow bowls large enough to hold the bean curd comfortably, but not much larger.

Slice the pieces of bean curd ¾ way through, at about 1 cm (½ in) intervals, then slice the opposite way, giving the look of a chrysanthemum flower. Cut the quail eggs in ½ and place, cut-side up, in the centre of each piece of bean curd chrysanthemum flower, separating the 'petals' very gently with the fingers to place the egg.

In a small saucepan, heat together the soup stock, light soy sauce, ¼ teaspoon salt, and *mirin*. Mix the arrowroot or cornflour with a little water and stir into the soup mixture. Cook, stirring, over low heat until the sauce is lightly thickened, a matter of minutes. Pour over the bean curd flowers.

Garnish, if liked, with the edible chrysanthemum leaves (*shungiku*), or spinach leaves placed at each side of the 'flower'. Eat with chopsticks, holding the bowl quite near the face to lessen the distance as the bean curd is a little hard to manoeuvre.

MIXED VEGETABLES WITH BEAN CURD

TOFU NO SHIRO-AE

This is a purely vegetable dish and also a very flavourful one, from Japan's vegetarian past.

SERVES 4
1 medium-sized carrot
½ devil's-tongue-root cake (konnyaku)
4 jelly mushrooms (kikurage)
125 ml (4 fl oz) first soup stock
2 teaspoons sugar
3 tablespoons light soy sauce (usukuchi shoyu)
1 bean curd (momen tofu), weighing about 250 g (8 oz)
¼ teaspoon salt
½ teaspoon soy sauce
1 teaspoon sake

Trim and scrape the carrot and cut it into thin julienne strips. Cut the devil's-tongue-root cake into julienne strips. Drop into boiling water and blanch for 10 seconds. Drain. Soak the jelly mushrooms in warm water for 20 minutes, blanch in boiling water for 10 seconds. Drain and slice thinly. In a saucepan combine the soup stock, 1 teaspoon of the sugar and the light soy sauce and bring to a simmer. Add the carrot, devil's-tongue-root cake and the mushrooms and cook, covered, over moderate heat for 5 minutes. Drain and set aside.

Rinse the bean curd and cut it into quarters. Drop it into a saucepan of boiling water and simmer for 3 minutes. Drain it through a sieve lined with a double layer of cheesecloth and squeeze to break it up. Turn it out of the cheesecloth and push it through the sieve. Transfer it to an earthenware mortar (suribachi) and add the remaining teaspoon of sugar, the salt, soy sauce and sake. Grind until smooth. Add the carrot mixture, and mix lightly with chopsticks, or put the drained bean curd into a food processor and process until it is smooth. Scrape it out into a bowl and fold in the carrot mixture. Serve in small bowls.

PORK WITH BEAN CURD

NIKU-DOFU

This is a light, delicate main course using silky bean curd (kinugoshi tofu) instead of the firmer and rather denser cotton bean curd (momen tofu) which is the bean curd of everyday use.

SERVES 4
2 silky bean curd (kinugoshi tofu) each weighing about 250 g (8 oz)
125 g (4 oz) boneless loin of pork, or any lean cut
3 medium-sized spring onions, trimmed, using white and green parts
1 cm (½ in) slice fresh ginger root
2 tablespoons vegetable oil
125 ml (4 fl oz) first soup stock
2 teaspoons red miso (bean paste)
3 tablespoons soy sauce
2 tablespoons sake
1 tablespoon sugar

Cut the pieces of bean curd in half and put into a shallow pan with just enough boiling water to cover. Let stand about a minute, drain and set aside.

Coarsely chop the pork. Thinly slice the spring onions diagonally. Peel and chop the ginger root. In a medium-sized saucepan, heat the oil and add the ginger, stir, then add the pork and spring onions and sauté, stirring, over moderate heat until the pork has lost all its pink colour, about 4 minutes.

In a bowl, mix together the soup stock, bean paste, soy sauce, sake and sugar to taste, and add to the saucepan with the pork mixture. Bring to a simmer, then reduce the heat to low and add the bean curd pieces, taking care not to break them, and cook, covered, for 15 to 20 minutes longer. Divide among 4 bowls and serve as a main course.

SIMMERED GRILLED BEAN CURD AND CHICKEN

YAKIDOFU TO TORINIKU NO NIMONO

Grilled bean curd (*yakidofu*), subtly different in taste and texture from the other kinds, is used in this simple and pleasant dish. It is a simmered dish (*nimono*) using the inner wooden lid (*otoshibuta*) to make sure the food is kept submerged in the liquid and so cooks evenly. A plate can be used instead of the lid.

SERVES 4
**250 g (8 oz) skinned and boned chicken thighs
2 grilled bean curd (*yakidofu*), each weighing about 300 g (10 oz)
350 ml (12 fl oz) first soup stock
½ teaspoon salt
1 tablespoon *mirin*
1 tablespoon light soy sauce (*usukuchi shoyu*)
2 medium-sized spring onions, trimmed, using white and green parts
Vegetable oil
1 tablespoon grated fresh ginger root**

Cut the chicken into bite-size pieces. Rinse the bean curd and cut each piece into 6 cubes. Put the bean curd into a bowl of cold water until ready to use.

Pour the soup stock into a medium-sized saucepan and bring to a simmer over moderate heat. Add the salt, *mirin*, light soy sauce, chicken and the drained bean curd. Cover with an inner wooden lid (*otoshibuta*) or a plate, and simmer over low heat for 20 minutes. Skim any froth that has risen to the surface.

Cut the spring onions into 2.5 cm (1 in) pieces and thread on 2 metal skewers. Brush lightly with oil and grill for 3 minutes, turning once or twice. Remove from the skewers.

Divide the chicken and bean curd mixture among 4 individual bowls together with the cooking liquid. Garnish with the spring onions and the ginger. Eat with chopsticks and drink the soup from the bowls.

SIMMERED BEAN CURD WITH DRIED BONITO FLAKES

NI-YAKKO

This is a very simple winter bean curd dish. It is important to serve it hot to appreciate its flavour.

SERVES 4
**1 medium-sized spring onion, trimmed, using white and green parts
4 × 5 cm (2 in) squares kelp seaweed (*kombu*)
2 bean curd (*momen tofu*), each weighing about 250 g (8 oz)
8 tablespoons dried bonito flakes (*hana-katsuo*)
1 tablespoon finely grated fresh ginger root
Soy sauce**

Finely chop the spring onion, put it into a bowl of cold water to crisp for a few minutes, squeeze out in a kitchen towel and set aside.

Wipe the seaweed with a damp cloth and put into the bottom of a medium-sized saucepan. Pour in water to a depth that will cover the bean curd and bring to a boil over moderate heat. Remove the seaweed just before the water boils, and put into 4 small, shallow bowls.

Cut the bean curd pieces in half and add to the saucepan. Simmer for 4 minutes over low heat, then lift carefully and place on top of the seaweed in the bowls. Sprinkle the spring onions on top, then the dried bonito flakes and the ginger. Pour soy sauce into 4 small saucers to use as a dipping sauce and have a small jug of soy sauce on the table to be used as liked.

BEAN CURD, CHICKEN AND VEGETABLE CUSTARD

KUYA-MUSHI

This delicate steamed (*mushimono*) dish is the creation of Buddhist monks of the Kuya sect during the Heian period from 794 to 1192. The monks were vegetarians, so the chicken may be a later addition.

SERVES 4
**1 bean curd (*momen tofu*), weighing about
250 g (8 oz)
Salt
4 dried Japanese mushrooms (*shiitake*)
125 g (4 oz) skinned and boned chicken breast
Light soy sauce (*usukuchi shoyu*)
4 small okra, *or* 4 sprigs trefoil (*mitsuba*) if
available
2 large eggs
First soup stock
1 teaspoon *mirin*
⅛ teaspoon MSG
½ teaspoon *katakuriko* starch *or* potato flour
4 small strips lime peel cut into V-shapes**

Slide the bean curd into a pan of boiling salted water, bring back to a boil over high heat and simmer just long enough to heat the bean curd through, 1 or 2 minutes. Lift the bean curd out of the water and pat dry with a cloth. Cut into quarters.

Soak the mushrooms in warm water for 30 minutes, squeeze out and cut away the hard stems. Cut the chicken breast into 1 cm (½ in)

diagonal slices and sprinkle with about 1 teaspoon of light soy sauce. Cook the okra in boiling salted water for 3 minutes. Drain, trim and cut into halves. If using trefoil, cut the sprigs into 2.5 cm (1 in) pieces.

Break the eggs into a bowl and stir with chopsticks until well-blended but not foamy. Measure the eggs and mix with 4 times the amount of soup stock. Stir in ½ teaspoon salt, 1 teaspoon light soy sauce, the *mirin* and MSG.

In 4 bowls, arrange the bean curd, mushrooms, chicken, okra or trefoil, and pour the egg mixture over them. If there are any bubbles on the surface, break them with chopsticks, otherwise the finished custard will have a pitted, instead of a smooth surface. Put the bowls into a steamer over boiling water, reduce the heat to moderate and steam for 20 minutes, or until the custard is set.

Make the sauce. In a small saucepan, combine 175 ml (6 fl oz) soup stock, and ¼ teaspoon each of salt and light soy sauce. Mix the *katakuriko* or potato flour with a little cold water and stir into the stock. Simmer, stirring, until lightly thickened.

Lift the custard out of the steamer, pour the sauce over it, garnish with the lime peel and eat with chopsticks and a spoon.

FREEZE-DRIED BEAN CURD WITH VEGETABLES

KOYADOFU TO SHIITAKE NO TAKIAWASE

This is a popular dish for lunch boxes, for New Year, or at any time. The bean curd gets its name from Koya where it was first made. It is sometimes called *koridofu*, a self-explanatory title as *kori* is the Japanese for ice.

SERVES 4
2 cakes dried bean curd (*koyadofu*)
700 ml (¼ pints) first soup stock
3 tablespoons sugar
1 teaspoon salt
1½ tablespoons *sake*
2 teaspoons light soy sauce (*usukuchi shoyu*)
8 dried Japanese mushrooms (*shiitake*)
1 tablespoon *mirin*
2 tablespoons soy sauce
8 green beans

Put the bean curd into a bowl with hot water to cover and weight so that they are kept under the water. Soak for 3 minutes or until they are soft with a spongy texture, turning once or twice, for about 3 minutes. Lightly squeeze them out in cold water, changing the water until it is clear. This may be up to 6 times. Squeeze out. Put into a saucepan large enough to hold them in a single layer. Combine the soup stock, 2 tablespoons of the sugar, or to taste, the salt, *sake* and light soy sauce, and pour over the bean curd. Cover with an inner wooden lid (*otoshibuta*), or use a plate, and cook over low heat for 1 hour. Remove from the heat and let stand for 2 hours.

Soak the mushrooms in warm water for 30 minutes, drain, squeeze out and cut away the hard stems. Put into a saucepan with enough of the water in which they were soaked to cover, cover with an inner wooden lid (*otoshibuta*) or a plate and cook over moderate heat for 3 minutes. Add the remaining tablespoon of sugar and the *mirin* and cook, uncovered, for 3 minutes. Add the soy sauce and cook for 1 minute longer. Lift out the mushrooms on to a bamboo plate (*zaru*) or a chopping board and fan briskly to make the mushrooms glisten.

Trim the beans and boil in salted water for 3 to 5 minutes, or until they are tender. Drain and halve diagonally.

When the bean curd has stood for 2 hours, squeeze out the liquid and cut each into quarters. Reserve the liquid. Arrange the bean curd on 4 plates with the mushrooms and beans and pour 2 tablespoons of the liquid over each serving.

DEEP-FRIED BEAN CURD WITH BONITO FLAKES

KATSUOMABUSHI AGE-DOFU

This winter dish is another of the delicious vegetarian dishes that were developed during Japan's vegetarian era. It has a satisfying yet subtle flavour.

SERVES 4
**2 bean curd (*momen tofu*), each weighing about
250 g (8 oz)**
15 g (½ oz) dried bonito flakes (hana-katsuo)
Plain flour
1 large egg
Vegetable oil for deep frying
1 tablespoon *mirin*
75 ml (3 fl oz) soy sauce
⅛ teaspoon MSG
125 ml (4 fl oz) first soup stock
2.5 cm (1 in) slice fresh ginger root

Rinse the bean curd and wrap in a cloth. Weight the bean curd with a board or plate for about 30 minutes to press out the excess liquid. Cut the bean curd into quarters. Set aside. Heat a heavy frying-pan, remove from the heat, add the bonito flakes and shake the pan several times. Put the flakes into a bowl.

Coat the bean curd pieces in flour, shaking to remove the excess. Break the egg into a bowl and stir with chopsticks until it is well-blended but not foamy. Dip the bean curd pieces in the egg, then coat with the bonito flakes.

Heat 5 to 7 cm (2 to 3 in) vegetable oil in a *tempura* pan or heavy frying-pan to 180°C (350°F)

or until bubbles form on wooden chopsticks stirred in the oil, add the bean curd pieces in batches so as not to overcrowd the pan and fry for 2 minutes. The oil should completely cover the bean curd. Lift out, drain on paper towels and put onto 4 individual plates.

Mix together the *mirin*, soy sauce, MSG and soup stock and pour into 4 small, deep bowls. Peel the ginger, cut it into julienne strips and put it in small mounds beside the bean curd. To eat, mix the ginger into the sauce, cut the bean curd into pieces with chopsticks and dip into the sauce, or pick up the pieces of bean curd, dip in the sauce, take a bite and dip in the sauce again. However, this requires great skill with chopsticks.

VARIATION: For Deep-Fried Bean Curd in Broth (*Agedashi-dofu*), coat the bean curd with cornflour, or arrowroot instead of plain flour. Do not coat in bonito flakes. Have ready small bowls of garnishes, dried bonito flakes, finely chopped spring onions, finely grated fresh ginger root and finely grated, squeezed out white radish (*daikon*) which are put on top of the bean curd. Make a warm dipping sauce with 250 ml (8 fl oz) second soup stock and 3 tablespoons each light soy sauce (*usukuchi shoyu*) and *mirin*. Put the bean curd into 4 bowls and pour the dipping sauce over it. SERVES 4.

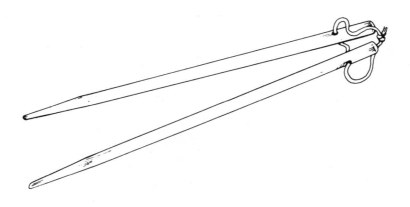

GARNISHED FRESH BEAN CURD

HIYA-YAKKO

This light and refreshing bean curd dish is ideal for hot summer weather. Serve it lightly chilled with a variety of garnishes and soy sauce.

SERVES 4

2 bean curd (*momen tofu*), each weighing about 250 g (8 oz)
5 × 10 cm (2 × 4 in) kelp seaweed (*kombu*) (optional)

FOR THE GARNISHES:
2 medium-sized spring onions, trimmed, using white and green parts
2 tablespoons finely grated ginger
2 teaspoons grated lime peel (optional)
1 tablespoon dried bonito flakes (*hana-katsuo*)
1 teaspoon green horseradish powder (*wasabi*)
Soy sauce

Rinse the bean curd and cut each piece into quarters. Put the seaweed into a saucepan large enough to hold the bean curd in a single layer and pour in enough water to cover it. Bring the water to a boil over moderate heat, removing the seaweed just before the water boils. The kelp will flavour the bean curd lightly. If preferred, omit this step and bring the water to a boil without the seaweed. Reduce heat to low, add bean curd and poach at just under a simmer for 3 minutes. Drain and put the bean curd into a bowl of cold water with ice cubes to chill it quickly, about 5 minutes. Transfer to a glass bowl with water to cover and 6 or 8 ice cubes.

Finely chop the spring onions and put them into a small bowl. Put the ginger, lime peel if using, and dried bonito flakes into small bowls. Mix the horseradish powder to a paste with a little cold water and put it into a small dish. Arrange around the bowl of bean curd.

Pour a little soy sauce into each of 4 bowls. To eat, add the garnishes to the soy sauce and, using chopsticks, dip the pieces of bean curd into the sauce.

If preferred, put the bean curd into 4 individual bowls, sprinkle with spring onion, a little ginger and the bonito flakes and pour a tablespoon of soy sauce over each serving. Or put the bean curd into individual bowls and serve the garnishes separately.

Silky bean curd (*kinugoshi tofu*) may also be used.

FRIED BEAN CURD WITH SEAWEED FLAKES

HIJIKI TO ABURAAGE NO NIMONO

Aburaage are deep-fried cakes of bean curd that can be bought in Japanese shops. *Hijiki* is a member of the order *Fucales* related to *fucus*, the rockweed kelp. It has fine little blades on long stalks and the Japanese believe it is not only good for the hair, but will bring wealth and beauty to the eater. It is sold dried and packaged in both Chinese and Japanese shops and, though it may not live up to all its claims, makes this a very refreshing and attractive dish.

SERVES 4
4 tablespoons *hijiki* flakes
2 pieces fried bean curd (*aburaage*)
2 tablespoons vegetable oil
175 ml (6 fl oz) first soup stock
2 teaspoons sugar
2 tablespoons soy sauce

Rinse the *hijiki* flakes in cold water, then put into a bowl with water to cover and soak for 1 hour. Drain, drop into a saucepan of boiling water and blanch for 1 minute. Drain, and set aside.

Wash the fried bean curd pieces in hot water to remove the excess oil, pat dry and slice into lengthways halves. Stack and cut into 1 cm (½ in) slices. Set aside.

In a medium-sized saucepan, heat the oil, add the *hijiki* flakes, and sauté, stirring with chopsticks for about 1 minute. Add the bean curd and soup stock and simmer, uncovered, for 5 minutes. Stir in the sugar and soy sauce and continue to simmer, over low heat, uncovered, until the liquid has evaporated, about 10 minutes. Serve in small, deep bowls.

FREEZE-DRIED BEAN CURD WITH PRAWNS

KOYADOFU TO EBI NO NIMONO

This is a non-vegetarian version of Freeze-Dried Bean Curd with Vegetables (page 154).

SERVES 4
2 cakes dried bean curd (*koyadofu*)
700 ml (1¼ pints) first soup stock, about
2 tablespoons sugar
Salt
1 tablespoon *sake*
1 tablespoon light soy sauce (*usukuchi shoyu*)
250 g (8 oz) cooked frozen prawns, thoroughly defrosted and coarsely chopped
1 small egg white
1 tablespoon cornflour
8 young okra pods, trimmed
2 teaspoons *mirin*

Put the bean curd into a bowl with hot water to cover and weight so that they are submerged. Soak for 3 minutes, then lightly squeeze out in up to 6 changes of cold water until the water is clear. Squeeze them out and put into a saucepan in a single layer. Combine the soup stock, sugar, ½ teaspoon salt, *sake* and light soy sauce, and pour over the bean curd. Cover with an inner wooden lid (*otoshibuta*), or use a plate, and the saucepan lid and cook over low heat for 1 hour. Remove from the heat and let stand for 2 hours. After this time, combine the prawns, egg white, cornflour and ½ teaspoon salt in a blender or food processor and reduce to a paste. Squeeze out the bean curd, cut into quarters and set aside. Reserve the liquid.

Using 2 wet tablespoons, form the prawn mixture into 8 quenelles. Bring the reserved liquid to a simmer, adding a little soup stock if necessary, and drop in the quenelles. Simmer gently for about 3 minutes. They will rise to the top of the pan when cooked. Lift out with a slotted spoon and set aside. Reserve the liquid.

Drop the okra into a saucepan of briskly boiling salted water and simmer until tender but still crisp, about 8 minutes. Drain and sprinkle with the *mirin*.

Arrange the bean curd, prawn quenelles, and okra on 4 small plates. Pour 2 tablespoons of the liquid over each serving.

Omelettes and other egg dishes, imported from the West, are relative newcomers to the Japanese kitchen. However, the Japanese show the same originality in adopting and adapting egg dishes as they do in every other aspect of the cuisine, from the light and delicious egg custard to the rolled omelette. They have also invented a rectangular pan called a *tamago-yaki nabe* which makes the cooking of rolled omelettes extremely easy, but an ordinary omelette pan can be used, and the omelette trimmed. A bamboo mat (*sudare*) makes rolling and firming them up easy too, though a kitchen towel can be used instead.

There are not a great many egg dishes but they all have the elegance that characterizes the cuisine. These omelettes, in either a Western or a Japanese context, make a splendid appetizer or accompaniment to drinks. In a Japanese meal they are very versatile and may be served for breakfast, or with soup as the main course of a light lunch or supper. They are also great favourites for picnics.

EGG DISHES AND OMELETTES

OMELETTE WITH SHRIMPS AND MUSHROOMS

FUKUSA YAKI

The *fukusa* dishes are very old traditional ones whose name signifies tender or happy. They are universally popular.

SERVES 4
1 bean curd (*momen tofu*) weighing about 250 g (8 oz)
4 dried Japanese mushrooms (*shiitake*)
4 large eggs
½ teaspoon salt
2 teaspoons *mirin*
1 teaspoon light soy sauce (*usukuchi shoyu*)
1 teaspoon sugar
⅛ teaspoon MSG
150 g (5 oz) tiny peeled shrimps
1 tablespoon cooked green peas
1 tablespoon vegetable oil
75 g (3 oz) white radish (*daikon*)

Roll the bean curd in a bamboo mat (*sudare*) or kitchen cloth and weight with 2 plates for about 5 minutes to press out the excess liquid. Pat dry. Soak the mushrooms in warm water for 30 minutes, drain, squeeze out, cut away the hard stems and slice into julienne strips.

Mash the bean curd in a bowl with a fork. Break the eggs into another bowl and stir with chopsticks until they are well-blended but not foamy. Stir into the bean curd with the salt, *mirin*, light soy sauce, sugar and MSG. Stir well to mix then gently fold in the mushrooms, shrimps and peas.

Heat a rectangular frying-pan (*tamago-yaki nabe*) or a 20 cm (8 in) frying-pan, preferably non-stick, with the oil. Pour in the bean curd mixture, smoothing the surface, and cook, covered, over low heat for about 7 minutes. Turn the omelette and cook for 5 minutes longer. Slide the omelette out of the pan onto a chopping board and cut it into slices about 3.5 × 5 cm (1½ × 2 in). Arrange on 4 small dishes. Finely grate and squeeze out the radish and put a little of it on top of each slice of omelette. Serve at room temperature.

ROLLED OMELETTE STUFFED WITH SPINACH

HORENSO TAMAGO MAKI

The omelettes are sliced and served at room temperature so that they can be made ahead of time, ideal as an accompaniment to drinks, or for a buffet. They look very attractive with the green of spinach in contrast with the yellow of the egg.

SERVES 4
300 g (10 oz) trimmed spinach
2 teaspoons soy sauce
⅛ teaspoon MSG
2 large eggs
½ teaspoon salt
Vegetable oil

Wash and drain the spinach and drop it into a saucepan of briskly boiling water. Bring back to a boil on high heat and cook for 2 minutes. Rinse immediately in cold water and drain. Form the spinach into a roll and lay it on a bamboo mat (*sudare*) or use a kitchen towel, roll up to squeeze out the excess moisture. Put the spinach into a bowl and sprinkle it with the soy sauce and MSG. Mix lightly, divide into 2 rolls and set aside.

Break the eggs into a bowl, add the salt and stir with chopsticks until they are well-blended but not foamy. Heat a rectangular frying-pan (*tamago-yaki nabe*) or a 20 cm (8 in) frying-pan, preferably non-stick, and add just enough oil to lightly film the surface. Pour in half of the egg and tilt the pan quickly so that the egg covers the whole surface. When the egg is set and lightly browned on the bottom, a minute or less, lift it out carefully on to a bamboo mat (*sudare*) or a cloth. Lay one of the spinach rolls along the short edge of the omelette. If using an ordinary frying-pan, trim the omelette into a rectangle. Using the bamboo mat, or a cloth, roll up the spinach in the omelette and squeeze lightly to firm. Lift it out on to a cutting board. Repeat with the remaining egg and spinach. Cut the rolls into 2.5 cm (1 in) slices and arrange on a platter, or on individual small plates. Serve at room temperature.

ROLLED OMELETTE WITH SOUP STOCK

DASHI-MAKI TAMAGO

This omelette, which is easy to make especially with a rectangular frying-pan (*tamago-yaki nabe*), looks impressive and is a perennial favourite for breakfast, as an appetizer, as an accompaniment to drinks, as part of a meal and for picnics.

SERVES 4
6 large eggs
First soup stock
Salt
1 teaspoon light soy sauce (*usukuchi shoyu*)
2 teaspoons *mirin*
⅛ teaspoon MSG
Vegetable oil
125 g (4 oz) sliced white radish (*daikon*)
4 teaspoons soy sauce

Break the eggs into a bowl and stir with chopsticks until they are well-blended but not foamy. Measure the eggs in a jug. Add ¼ the amount of soup stock to the eggs, add salt to taste, light soy sauce, *mirin* and MSG and stir again to mix.

Heat a rectangular omelette pan (*tamago-yaki nabe*), or a 20 cm (8 in) frying-pan, preferably non-stick, and add just enough oil to film the surface. Pour in ⅓ of the egg mixture, tilt the pan so that the egg covers the whole surface, and cook over moderate heat just until the egg is set.

Off the heat, using chopsticks, roll up the omelette to the end of the pan. Add enough oil to again film the surface of the pan on moderate heat. Pour in another ⅓ of the egg mixture, tilting the pan as before so that the egg runs down to the cooked omelette. Cook until the second omelette is set. Take off the heat. Starting at the end with the first omelette, begin to roll towards the handle of the pan so that the first omelette incorporates the second. Repeat with the remaining egg, rolling the three omelettes towards the end of the pan.

Carefully lift the omelette roll out of the pan on to a bamboo mat (*sudare*) or a kitchen cloth, and roll it up very gently. Weight it with a plate until it is cold, unwrap and cut into 12 slices. Serve 3 slices per person on small plates or platters. Finely grate the radish, squeeze out and put a small mound on each plate. Pour 1 teaspoon of soy sauce over each mound of radish.

VARIATION: For Rolled Omelette (*Tamago Yaki*), make in the same way as above, but instead of soup stock add 75 g (3 oz) freshly cooked garden peas, 2 tablespoons *sake*, 2 teaspoons sugar and ½ teaspoon of salt to the stirred eggs. SERVES 4.

EGGS AND BAMBOO SHOOTS

TAKENOKO NO TAMAGO-TOJI

This is an unusual and delicious dish that takes very little time to make.

SERVES 4
4 medium-sized mushrooms
300 g (10 oz) whole bamboo shoots, tinned
125 g (4 oz) boned and skinned chicken breast
1 medium-sized onion
475 ml (16 fl oz) first soup stock
75 ml (3 fl oz) soy sauce
125 ml (4 fl oz) *mirin*
⅛ teaspoon MSG
12 mangetout
4 large eggs

Wipe the mushrooms with a damp cloth, trim the stems and slice thinly. Halve the bamboo shoots lengthways, then slice thinly. Slice the chicken breast thinly on the diagonal. Halve the peeled onion lengthways, then slice finely. Put the mushrooms, bamboo shoots, chicken and onion in a saucepan with the soup stock, soy sauce, *mirin* and MSG. Simmer over low heat, uncovered, for 4 minutes. Slice the mangetout finely on the diagonal and add to the pan. Break the eggs into a bowl and stir until they are well-blended but not foamy. Pour the eggs in a thin stream over the whole surface of the pan, cover and cook over very low heat for 1 minute, or until the eggs are set. Serve in bowls.

PRAWN OMELETTE

EBIIRI-TAMAGO-YAKI

This is another rolled omelette that makes a very good appetizer, and can also be made ahead of time.

SERVES 4
8 medium-sized raw prawns, peeled and
deveined, *or* **use cooked frozen prawns,**
thoroughly defrosted
75 ml (3 fl oz) first soup stock
1 teaspoon salt
2 large eggs
1 teaspoon sugar
1 tablespoon *sake*
1 teaspoon arrowroot
Vegetable oil

Chop the prawns to a paste with the back of a heavy knife, or reduce to a paste in a food processor or blender. Put into a small saucepan with the soup stock and ½ teaspoon of the salt, bring to a simmer and cook over low heat for 1 minute. Cook, drain and set aside.

Break the eggs into a bowl and stir with chopsticks until they are well-blended but not foamy. Stir in the sugar, *sake* and remaining ½ teaspoon salt. Mix the arrowroot with a teaspoon of water, stir into the eggs. Stir in the reserved prawns.

Heat a rectangular omelette pan (*tamago-yaki nabe*) or a 20 cm (8 in) frying-pan, preferably non-stick, and add just enough oil to film it lightly. Pour in the egg mixture and tilt the pan so that it covers the whole surface. When the omelette is lightly browned on one side, turn it and brown the other side. Slide the omelette out onto a bamboo mat (*sudare*) or a cloth and roll it up. Squeeze gently to firm it. Leave the omelette in the mat or cloth until it is cool, transfer it to a chopping board and cut into 1 cm (½ in) slices. Serve on an oblong platter or on small individual plates as an appetizer.

STEAMED EGG CUSTARD

CHAWAN-MUSHI

In Japan this delicate egg custard is made in special lidded soup cups as graceful and attractive to look at as the contents are appetizing. Any lidded soup pot holding about 250 ml (8 fl oz), or a ramekin covered with foil, can be used. This is one of the few Japanese dishes that is eaten with a spoon.

SERVES 4

4 small dried Japanese mushrooms (*shiitake*), *or* 4 medium-sized fresh mushrooms
125 g (4 oz) boned and skinned chicken breast
1 teaspoon *sake*
1 tablespoon light soy sauce (*usukuchi shoyu*)
4 large spinach leaves
4 medium-sized uncooked prawns, if frozen thoroughly defrosted
4 eggs
½ teaspoon salt
600 ml (1 pint) first soup stock
4 small pieces lime peel (optional)

Soak the mushrooms in warm water for 30 minutes, drain, squeeze out and cut away the tough stems. If using fresh mushrooms, wipe the caps with a damp cloth and trim the stems. Cut the chicken breast into diagonal slices about 1 × 2.5 cm (½ × 1 in). Put the mushrooms and chicken into a small bowl with the *sake* and soy sauce and mix lightly. Drop the spinach leaves into a saucepan of boiling water, bring back to a boil over high heat and cook for 1 minute. Drain, rinse in cold water and squeeze out lightly. Peel and devein the prawns leaving the tails on. Divide these ingredients among 4 small, lidded soup bowls.

Break the eggs into a bowl and stir with chopsticks until they are well-blended but not foamy. Stir in the salt and soup stock, strain and divide among the soup bowls. If there are any bubbles on the surface, break them with chopsticks as they will otherwise pit the finished surface. Garnish with the lime peel, if using. Cover and arrange in a steamer over boiling water, cover the steamer and steam over moderate heat for 15 to 20 minutes or until set. Eat with a spoon.

Pickles are immensely popular in Japan, where they play a far more important role than they do in the Western world. They are a vital accompaniment to rice served at the end of a meal, their sharp flavour in contrast with the blandness of the rice. They are also used with many dishes as a garnish to enhance both appearance and taste. Mouth-puckering small pickled plums (*umeboshi*), ginger shoots, red pickled ginger (*beni-shoga*), the edible shoots of bracken (*warabi*) and a great many others can be bought ready prepared (*tsukemono*) in shops selling Japanese foods. These commercial pickles are prepared in rice bran (*nuka*). Vegetables like white radish (*daikon*) or Chinese cabbage, sold as Chinese leaves, (*hakusai*) are air dried then buried in rice bran for about 3 weeks. This is not a practical form of pickling for the average household but there are a number of pickles that can be made easily at home. Many vegetables can be pickled in *miso* (bean paste), *sake*, or rice vinegar, many taking very little time.

Serve a variety of pickles at a meal. Rinse and dry the pickles, cut them into bite-size pieces and serve on small individual dishes with a little soy sauce. A bowl of rice and an assortment of pickles can make an adequate breakfast or simple lunch.

PICKLES

TSUKEMONO

CHINESE CABBAGE AND CARROT PICKLES

HAKUSAI TO NINJIN NO KAORIZUKE

SERVES 4 to 6
**900 g (2 lb) Chinese cabbage (Chinese leaves)
(*hakusai*)**
1 medium-sized carrot
1 large clove garlic
1 dried hot red chilli pepper
2 tablespoons salt
10 cm (4 in) square kelp seaweed (*kombu*)

Trim the base of the cabbage, rinse, drain and pull away the leaves. Stack the leaves and cut them into 2.5 cm (1 in) crossways slices. Trim and scrape the carrot and cut into julienne strips. Have ready a large saucepan of briskly boiling water, add the cabbage and carrot, bring back to a boil over high heat and cook, stirring with chopsticks for 1 minute. Drain and cool. Squeeze in a bamboo mat (*sudare*) or kitchen towel, or by hand to remove the excess liquid. Transfer to a bowl.

Crush the garlic clove with the back of a knife, then chop finely. Cut the stem end away from the pepper, shake out the seeds and chop finely. Mix the garlic and pepper with the cabbage and carrot. Mix in the salt. Wipe the seaweed with a damp cloth, cut into a 1 cm (½ in) fringe along one side and bury in the cabbage mixture. Cover the cabbage with an inner wooden lid (*otoshibuta*) or a plate and put a weight, about 1.4 kg (3 lb) on top. Stand bowl in a cool place overnight or refrigerate. When ready to use, drain and discard the seaweed. The pickles can be eaten after 24 hours, but will keep, refrigerated in a covered container, for a week. Serve the pickles in 4 small individual bowls with rice.

RICE VINEGAR CABBAGE PICKLE

HAKUSAI NO SUZUKE

The delicate flavour of rice vinegar adds something special to these easy-to-make cabbage pickles.

SERVES 4
**500 g (1 lb) Chinese cabbage (Chinese leaves)
(*hakusai*)**
Salt
3 dried hot red chilli peppers
2 tablespoons vegetable oil
3 tablespoons soy sauce
125 ml (4 fl oz) rice vinegar

Trim the end of the cabbage and pull away the leaves. Rinse, drain and stack the leaves then cut crossways into 2.5 cm (1 in) slices, then cut into approximately 2.5 cm (1 in) squares. To do this, cut the narrow part of the leaf in half, and the wide part in thirds. Drop the cabbage into a large saucepan of briskly boiling water, bring back to a boil on high heat and cook, uncovered, for 2 minutes. Drain in a colander and sprinkle with a little salt. Put into a bowl.

Cut the stem end from the chillies and shake out the seeds, or poke them out with chopsticks. Rinse, dry and chop finely. Put them into a small saucepan with the oil and soy sauce. Bring the mixture to a simmer, remove from the heat and stir in the vinegar. Pour over the cabbage and mix well with chopsticks. Cool, transfer to a covered container, and refrigerate for 3 days. Eat as an accompaniment to rice.

SALT-PICKLED VEGETABLES

SHIOZUKE

This is a quick and very good way of making pickles. Use sea salt if possible, as this helps to produce a crisp and delicious pickle. In Japan a lidded wooden pickle barrel would be used, but a bowl does very well.

SERVES 4
**1 Chinese cabbage (Chinese leaves) (*hakusai*), *or*
2 cucumbers, *or* 2 white radishes (*daikon*)
50 g (2 oz) salt
3 dried hot red chilli peppers (optional)
7 cm (3 in) square kelp seaweed (*kombu*)
(optional)**

Cut away the stem end of the cabbage, cut into lengthways quarters, then into 5 cm (2 in) slices. Peel and seed the cucumbers and cut into 1 cm (½ in) slices. Peel the white radish, cut into lengthways quarters, then into 5 cm (2 in) pieces. Pat all the vegetables dry with paper towels.

Layer whichever vegetable is being used with salt in a large glass or ceramic bowl, first sprinkling the bowl with salt and ending with a layer of salt. If using them, split the chillies and wipe the seaweed with a damp cloth, and bury them in the centre of the vegetables. Put an inner wooden lid (*otoshibuta*) on top, or use a plate, then top with a weight, 2.3 kg (5 lb) about. Put into a cool place or the refrigerator for 3 to 4 days. By this time the vegetables will have given off a lot of liquid and the brine will have risen above the level of the solids. To eat, lift out the required amount of pickle, rinse, squeeze out and cut into bite-size pieces if necessary, and sprinkle, if liked, with a little MSG and soy sauce. Serve with rice as an accompaniment to a main dish.

The pickles will keep, in the brine, for about 2 months.

PICKLED AUBERGINE

NASU NO SHOYUZUKE

Aubergine are a favourite vegetable in Japan and pickled aubergine even more so. Like so many of the homemade pickles, this one is easy to make and could almost call itself instant pickles.

SERVES 4
**500 g (1 lb) small purple aubergine
Salt
2 teaspoons Japanese horseradish (*wasabi*), *or* dry
Japanese or English mustard
2 tablespoons *mirin*
1 tablespoon sugar
3 tablespoons soy sauce**

Rinse and trim the aubergines and cut into fairly thick slices, about 2 cm (¾ in). Put into a glass or ceramic bowl and sprinkle generously with salt. Let stand for 1 hour. Drain the accumulated liquid, rinse quickly in cold water, squeeze lightly and return to the bowl.

Mix the horseradish powder or dry mustard with water to a paste, using cold water for the horseradish, boiling water for the mustard. Mix with the *mirin*, sugar, and soy sauce and pour over the aubergine slices. Toss gently so that they are well covered with the mixture. Cover, and refrigerate for 3 to 4 hours, turning once or twice. To serve, lift the aubergine out of the marinade and cut into bite-size pieces. Arrange on individual plates and serve with rice.

QUICK BEAN PASTE VEGETABLE PICKLES

SOKUSEKI MISOZUKE

This is an economical dish as the bean paste can be used more than once. The dish also allows for plenty of variations and personal choice, using favourite vegetables, and vegetables at their seasonal peak. It is ready to eat in a day.

SERVES 4, or more
250 g (8 oz) red *miso* (bean paste)
2 tablespoons soy sauce
2 tablespoons *mirin*
½ medium-sized cucumber
1 small aubergine, 7 to 10 cm (3 to 4 in) long
4 small white or red radishes
4 small okra, *or* 1 medium-sized sweet green pepper, *or* 4 stalks asparagus, preferably green

Mix the bean paste, soy sauce and *mirin* and put into a glass or ceramic bowl large enough to hold all the vegetables comfortably. Wash and dry the vegetables, leaving them whole, and gently fold into the bean paste. Leave for a day in a cool place, covered, or in the refrigerator.

To eat, lift the vegetables out of the bean paste mixture, scraping the paste off with chopsticks. Rinse quickly in cold water and pat dry, if liked. Slice the vegetables into bite-size pieces and arrange some of each one on 4 small dishes. Eat with rice.

Reserve the bean paste to use again. To re-use, pour off any accumulated liquid from the vegetables and put the bean paste into a small saucepan. Stir over low heat and add a little more bean paste until the paste is again of the original consistency. It can be used several times to make these pickles.

CHICKEN AND VEGETABLES PICKLED IN BEAN PASTE

NIKUMISO

This pickle is eaten as a garnish on rice or served in small bowls accompanied by rice. It is a popular ingredient in lunch boxes. It may also be eaten by putting a little rice on a lettuce leaf, adding some pickle, folding up the lettuce and eating by hand, a custom that shows a Korean influence on the Japanese kitchen.

SERVES 8
1 medium-sized onion
1 medium-sized sweet green pepper
4 dried Japanese mushrooms (*shiitake*)
1 medium-sized carrot
2.5 cm (1 in) slice fresh ginger root
2 tablespoons fresh green peas
Vegetable oil
250 g (8 oz) ground chicken meat, using any part
175 g (6 oz) red *miso* (bean paste)
⅛ teaspoon ground hot red pepper (*togarashi*)

Peel and finely chop the onion. Seed and finely chop the green pepper. Soak the mushrooms for 30 minutes in warm water, drain, squeeze out, cut away the hard stems and chop finely. Scrape and finely chop the carrot. Peel and finely chop the ginger root. Drop the peas into boiling water and simmer for 4 minutes. Drain. Set all these ingredients aside.

Film the bottom of a medium-sized saucepan with oil. Add the chicken and cook over moderate heat, stirring, with 4 or 5 chopsticks held in a bunch in one hand for about 3 minutes. Add the onion, green pepper, mushrooms, carrot and ginger, one by one and cook, stirring, for 2 to 3 minutes after each addition. Stir in the bean paste and cook for 4 minutes longer, or until the mixture is smooth and well-blended. Add the peas and cook for 2 minutes longer. Season with the hot pepper. Cool and store in a covered container. It will keep for up to 3 weeks, refrigerated.

PICKLED GINGER

SHOGA NO SUZUKE

This delicious pickle, which is sharp and sweet at the same time, is always served with *sushi*. Very young ginger shoots, which are not easy to find, can be pickled in the same way and make a decorative as well as flavourful garnish to grilled fish and other dishes. Ginger turns a very light, delicate pink when it is pickled. For *Beni-Shoga* (Red Pickled Ginger) the Japanese add a little pickled plum juice. Pickled ginger can be bought, ready prepared, in Japanese groceries and supermarkets but it is easy to make at home.

MAKES 175 g (6 oz)
125 g (4 oz) fresh ginger root
Salt
125 ml (4 fl oz) rice vinegar
1 tablespoon sugar
Red vegetable colouring (optional)

Wash and peel the ginger and cut with the grain into the thinnest possible slices. Put into a bowl, pour in cold water to cover and stand for 30 minutes. Drain, drop into a saucepan of briskly boiling water, bring back to a boil on high heat, drain and cool. Put back into the bowl and sprinkle with a little salt.

In a saucepan, combine the vinegar and sugar and simmer to dissolve the sugar. Add a little red colouring, if liked. Pour over the ginger, mixing well. Cover the bowl, or transfer to a jar and refrigerate for about a week before using. The ginger will keep, refrigerated, for several months.

PICKLED CUCUMBERS

KYURI NO INROZUKE

Inro is a small box that was used to hold pills in the days of old Tokyo then called Edo, before the city became the imperial and administrative capital of modern Japan. The cucumbers, halved and seeded, are put together like small boxes, hence *inrozuke*.

SERVES 6–8
4 ridge cucumbers, weighing about 625 g (1¼ lb)
Salt
4 large cabbage leaves
2.5 cm (1 inch) slice fresh ginger root
2 tablespoons *shiso* seeds (beefsteak plant),
optional
⅛ teaspoon MSG
***Kombu* (kelp)**

If the cucumbers are waxed, peel them, otherwise leave unpeeled. Wash thoroughly, dry, halve lengthways and scrape out the seeds. Sprinkle them inside with 2 teaspoons salt. Put the cucumbers, cut side down, on a large flat plate, or platter, cover with another plate and weight. The weight should be about double the weight of the cucumbers. Leave for 1 hour.

Rinse and dry the cabbage leaves then shred them finely. Peel the ginger and cut it into julienne strips. In a bowl combine the cabbage and ginger with 2 teaspoons salt, mixing well. Rinse in cold water and drain. Mix in the *shiso* seeds, if available, and a dash of MSG.

Remove weight from the cucumbers and pat them dry. Stuff the seed cavity of half the cucumbers with the cabbage mixture, pressing it down firmly, then top with the other half to make a little box.

Line a large shallow dish that will hold the cucumbers in a single layer with *kombu* (kelp) wiped with a damp cloth. Arrange the cucumbers on top, sprinkle with a little salt and the MSG. Cover with more seaweed. Cover with a plate and weight with a 1.8 kg (4 lb) weight. Leave for 4 or 5 hours in a cool place. Remove the seaweed, lift out the cucumbers and cut into 1 cm (½ inch) slices. Serve on small plates.

Puddings, as we know them, do not exist in the Japanese kitchen. At the end of a meal, fruit, exquisitely cut, is served – its presentation as elegant as all the other dishes in this most elegant cuisine. The Japanese, however, do enjoy sweet things. These take the form of cakes or sweets that are served with tea when guests call or between meals or at any time of the day. Most cakes are bought ready-made and are very beautiful to look at. They may be made in the shape of maple leaves or plum blossoms according to the seasons. Their appearance is of great importance perhaps even more than their taste. Some of the dishes are more in the nature of snacks.

Nowadays in Japan all the usual Western drinks are served, and wine is becoming increasingly popular. However, *sake* (rice wine) remains the national drink. *Sake* sets consisting of tiny china bowls and a matching flask holding about 250 ml (8 fl oz) are traditionally used. The drink is served lukewarm, either before or during meals.

Tea is the other great drink of Japan, from *matcha,* the powdered green tea of the formal tea ceremony, to the green tea of everyday use. This stimulating and refreshing unfermented tea is always taken plain. There are a number of grades: *Gyokuro,* the first new leaves on the tea bush, is the best, with *sencha* the second best. *Bancha* or *hojicha* are the grades used for everyday drinking. *Mugicha,* made from roasted barley and served chilled is a popular summer drink.

SWEETS — OKASHI — AND DRINKS

STRAWBERRY SNOW FOAM JELLY

ICHIGO NO AWAYUKIKAN

This is a light and pretty sweet, lovely for summer meals. It is simple to make and since agar-agar sets much more quickly than gelatine, needs little time. If Agar Flakes are available use them as they need less preparation than the bar form. It is also available in strand and powder form. Derived from Gelidium and other similar seaweed species, it is often sold under its Japanese name, *kanten*. The more familiar agar is a Malay word meaning jelly.

SERVES 8
3 tablespoons agar flakes *or* 7 g (¼ oz) bar agar-agar (*kanten*)
150 g (5 oz) sugar
2 large egg whites
1 tablespoon lemon juice
8 whole, or 4 halved, large strawberries

Shake the agar flakes into a saucepan with 475 ml (16 fl oz) cold water, stir, bring to a simmer over moderate heat and cook, stirring until the agar is dissolved, about 2 minutes. If using bar agar, wash in cold water, squeeze out, shred with the fingers, and soak for at least 30 minutes before cooking. Strain into a bowl, rinse out the saucepan and return the liquid to it. Add the sugar and stir over moderate heat until the sugar has dissolved. Cool. Stir in the lemon juice.

Beat the egg whites until they stand in firm peaks, then fold them into the agar mixture, lightly but thoroughly. Pour into a loaf tin, about 19 × 10 cm (7½ × 4 in), rinsed out in cold water. Stand in a bowl of cold water to set, or refrigerate until set, about 30 minutes. To serve, unmould, halve lengthways then cut into 2.5 cm (1 in) slices. Top each slice with a halved strawberry, serve on small plates and eat with cake forks, or push the whole strawberries into the pan of jelly before putting it to set, at approximately 2.5 cm (1 in) intervals in 2 rows, leaving the tip of the berry showing to make cutting easier. Unmould when set and reverse before cutting.

VARIATION 1: Snowdrop Jelly (*Ebisu-Tamago*) is a New Year dish special to the holiday. Cook the agar as in the main recipe. Add 2 tablespoons sugar, 1 teaspoon light soy sauce (*usukuchi shoyu*), and ½ teaspoon salt. Break 1 large egg into a bowl and stir with chopsticks until well-blended but not foamy. Holding 4 or 5 chopsticks at the edge of the bowl, pour the eggs in a very thin stream into the saucepan, or pour through a small coarse sieve so that the eggs, when they fall into the hot liquid, will set in threads. Remove the pan from the heat. Cool and pour into a loaf tin as in the main recipe. Unmould and slice. SERVES 8.

VARIATION 2: For a much simpler dish, Snow Foam Jelly (*Awayukikan*), prepare the agar in the same way as in the main recipe. Strain the dissolved agar into a bowl, rinse out the saucepan and return the agar to it with 250 g (8 oz) sugar and cook, stirring, until the sugar has dissolved. Cool slightly and stir in 1 teaspoon vanilla. Cool thoroughly, then fold in the egg whites, gently but thoroughly. Pour into the loaf tin and leave to set in a bowl of cold water, or in the refrigerator, about 30 minutes. To serve, unmould, halve lengthways, then cut into 2.5 cm (1 in) slices. Serve on small plates and eat with small forks. Serve with tea. SERVES 6 to 8.

RED BEAN PASTE

KOSHI-AN

This bean paste is the basis for many Japanese-style puddings. It may be bought ready-prepared in powder form needing only the addition of water to reconstitute it. It is easy to make, though somewhat time consuming. Using a food processor instead of the traditional earthenware mortar (*suribachi*) with the wooden pestle (*suri-kogi*) speeds things up without loss of flavour or texture as the homemade article is better than the ready-prepared version.

MAKES ABOUT 750 g (1½ lb)
300 g (10 oz) red adzuki (*azuki*) beans

Wash and pick over the beans and put them into a large saucepan with 1.4 litre (2½ pints) cold water. Cover and bring to a boil over high heat. Cook until the beans begin to rise to the surface, reduce the heat to moderate, add 175 ml (6 fl oz) cold water and bring back to a boil. Add another 175 ml (6 fl oz) cold water, bring back to a boil and repeat this process twice more, adding 4 lots of cold water in all. Reduce the heat to low and cook, covered, until the beans are tender, about 30 minutes.

Drain the beans, reserving the cooking liquid. In the traditional method, the beans are pushed through a coarse sieve and the skins discarded. They are then pounded to a paste in the mortar and mixed with the reserved cooking liquid and put through a fine sieve to remove any skins that may have gone through the coarse sieve. Instead, strain the beans, reserve the liquid and put the beans into a food processor adding as much of the liquid as needed. Process to a purée then push this through a fine sieve, adding the rest of the cooking liquid to help the process.

Pour the resulting heavy bean liquid, produced by whichever method, through a sieve lined with a double layer of dampened cheesecloth set over a large saucepan. After the liquid has dripped through, twist the cloth to remove any remaining liquid, leaving a firm paste. Put the paste in a covered dish and refrigerate until ready to use. It will keep for about 4 days refrigerated or frozen for several weeks.

RED BEAN JELLY

MIZUYOKAN

This is a summer sweet and one of the most popular. Small slices are served on plates and eaten with cake forks. Traditionally they would be garnished with a pickled cherry leaf, though today a plastic leaf might be used at the side of the plate. The sweet is served with roasted barley tea (*mugicha*) to family and visiting friends.

SERVES 8 to 10
**7 g (¼ oz) bar agar-agar (*kanten*), or 2½
tablespoons agar flakes
250 g (8 oz) sugar
250 g (8 oz) red bean paste (*koshi-an*) (left)
¼ teaspoon salt**

If using bar agar, wash it in cold water, squeeze out and shred with the fingers. Put into a saucepan with 400 ml (14 fl oz) cold water and soak for at least 30 minutes. If using flakes, stir them into the water. Cook over moderate heat, stirring from time to time until the agar has dissolved. Add the sugar and continue to cook, stirring, until the sugar has dissolved. Strain the mixture through a fine sieve, return to the saucepan and stir in the bean paste and salt. Cook, stirring, over moderate heat until the mixture comes to a boil. Remove from the heat, cool slightly then pour into a loaf pan about 19 × 10 cm (7½ × 4 in), rinsed out in cold water. Set in a pan of cold water or refrigerate until set, about 1 hour. Unmould and cut into 2.5 × 5 cm (1 × 2 in) slices. Serve on small plates and eat with cake forks.

SWEET POTATOES AND CHESTNUTS

KINTON

This is one of the New Year dishes that is served to visitors – family and friends – who call during the 3-day holiday. Use white sweet potatoes, not the orange kind known as Lousiana yams.

SERVES 8 to 10
900 g (2 lb) sweet potatoes (*satsuma-imo*)
250 g (8 oz) sugar
½ teaspoon salt
75 ml (3 fl oz) *mirin*
500 g (1 lb) tin whole chestnuts in syrup

Wash the sweet poatoes, peel and cut into 5 mm (¼ in) slices and drop into a bowl of cold water. Drain and cook in boiling water for 5 minutes. Drain, return to the saucepan, cover with cold water and cook, partially covered, until tender, about 15 minutes. Add the sugar and salt and cook, stirring and mashing with the back of a wooden spoon, until the mixture forms a heavy paste, about 15 minutes. Push the mixture through a sieve and put into a casserole or heavy saucepan. Stir in the *mirin* and 125 ml (4 fl oz) syrup from the tinned chestnuts. Cook, stirring, over moderate heat until thick, about 10 minutes. Halve the chestnuts and fold into the sweet potato mixture. Transfer to a covered dish. Serve on small dishes, 1 or 2 chestnuts to a serving. Eat with chopsticks.

SWEET BEAN SOUP WITH RICE CAKES

ZENZAI

This is a favourite winter snack. The thick, sweet bean soup with sticky rice cakes can be wonderfully appetizing in cold weather. Rice cakes are available packaged from Japanese shops.

SERVES 4
150 g (5 oz) red adzuki (*azuki*) beans
175 g (6 oz) sugar
1 teaspoon arrowroot
4 rice cakes (*mochi*)

Wash and pick over the beans, put in a saucepan with 1 litre (1¾ pints) water. Bring to a boil, covered, over high heat, reduce the heat to moderate and simmer for about 1 hour or until the beans are very tender. Drain and set aside.

In a small saucepan, combine the sugar with 50 ml (2 fl oz) water and cook, stirring, over low heat until the sugar has dissolved making a syrup. Combine the beans and syrup in a saucepan and mash over very low heat into a heavy paste. Gradually stir in 475 ml (16 fl oz) water. Mix the arrowroot with a little water and stir into the bean mixture. Cook until lightly thickened.

Grill the rice cakes until they are lightly browned and tender. Put a rice cake into each of 4 small bowls. Pour the hot bean soup over them. Eat the rice cakes, which may be cut into quarters before grilling, if liked, with chopsticks and drink the bean soup from the bowl.

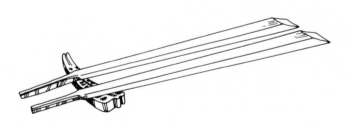

SWEET RICE EGGS

OHAGI

This is a favourite snack for the autumn equinox holiday, *Shubun No Hi*, on September 24. This was formerly a Buddhist festival but is now a public holiday. Rice eggs can, of course, be eaten at any time. Sweet rice, often called sticky rice or glutinous rice, can be bought in any shops selling Asian foods.

SERVES 4 to 12 (according to appetite)
175 g (6 oz) sweet rice
40 g (1½ oz) short-grain rice
500 g (1 lb) red bean paste (*koshi-an*), page 173
250 g (8 oz) sugar
¼ teaspoon salt

Mix the two lots of rice together, wash, drain and put into a saucepan with 350 ml (12 fl oz) water and soak for 1 hour. Bring to a boil over high heat, reduce the heat to moderate and cook for 5 minutes, then reduce the heat to low and cook for 10 minutes. Let the rice stand for 10 minutes, then mash it to a paste with a pestle, or reduce it to a paste in a food processor. While it is still warm form it, with wet hands, into 12 egg-shaped balls.

In a saucepan, combine the bean paste, sugar and salt and cook over low heat, stirring, until it forms a firm paste. Let it cool a little then form it into 12 balls. Fold a length of cheesecloth, wrung out in cold water, into a square. Flatten a ball of bean paste on the cloth and put a rice egg in the centre. Carefully pat the paste all over the rice to cover it using the cloth to help smooth it. Continue until all the rice balls are covered. Serve on the small square platters traditionally used for snacks, or on small plates.

JAPANESE TEAS

BEST TEA

GYOKURO

Put 1½ tablespoons tea into a small teapot. Warm 4 small tea bowls. Bring water to a boil in a tea kettle, then cool it for 3 minutes as it should be under boiling point. Pour 250 ml (8 fl oz) into the teapot and let it stand for about 1 minute. Pour it into the bowls. SERVES 4.

SECOND-BEST TEA

SENCHA

Put 2 tablespoons tea into a teapot. Bring water to a boil in a tea kettle and cool it for about 2 minutes as it should be just under boiling point. Pour 475 ml (16 fl oz) water into the teapot and let it stand for about 1 minute. Pour into 4 medium-sized bowls. SERVES 4.

EVERYDAY TEA

BANCHA OR HOJICHA

Put 3 tablespoons tea into a teapot. Bring water to a boil in a tea kettle and pour 600 ml (1 pint) boiling water into the teapot. Let it stand for about 30 seconds then pour into large tea bowls. SERVES 4.

Barley Tea (*Mugicha*) is made in the same way as *bancha* and is served chilled as a summer drink.

GLOSSARY OF JAPANESE FOODS

Aburaage, deep-fried bean curd sold in packages in Japanese markets. Will keep, refrigerated. Freezes well.

Aemono, literally, mixed things such as poultry, fish and vegetables in a sauce or dressing. It is a type of salad and accompanies a main dish.

Agar-Agar, see *kanten*.

Agemono, deep-fried foods, including *tempura*.

Aji-ni-moto, MSG (monosodium glutamate) powder used to enhance flavour. In Chinese markets it may be called *mei jiung*. It is sold in supermarkets under the name of the compound or under brand names which are more expensive. Widely sold in Japanese and other markets. It should be used, as the Japanese do, very sparingly. It may be omitted, if preferred, from any recipe.

Ajitsuke warabi, fernbrake, bracken, fiddleheads, seasoned with soy sauce, sugar, MSG, etc. Available in vacuum-sealed plastic bags in Japanese markets.

Amazu-shoga, see *beni-shoga*.

Azuki beans (*Phaseoulus angularis*), an Asian species of legume called *adzuki* in Chinese markets, varies in colour from dark red to black, mottled and cream. Available in Japanese and Chinese markets and in health food shops.

Beni-shoga, red pickled ginger, available bottled or in vacuum-sealed plastic bags in Japanese markets. Will keep, refrigerated. **Amazu-shoga** is pickled ginger without extra colouring. It is light pink.

Chikuwa, see *naruto-maki*.

Dai dai, see *ponzu*.

Daikon (*Raphanus sativus*), the Oriental white radish is a large cylindrical root sold fresh in Japanese markets and often in supermarkets and greengroceries where it may be called *mooli*. It varies in size and is sold by the piece to be used both cooked and raw, often grated as a garnish and added to sauces. It will keep, refrigerated, for as long as 2 weeks.

Dashi, is the basic Japanese soup and cooking stock made from dried kelp seaweed (*kombu*) and dried bonito flakes (*hana-katsuo*). Both ingredients are available in Japanese shops and sometimes in health food shops. An instant version needing only the addition of water is available, packaged, in Japanese shops.

Dembu, see *soboro*.

Fu, wheat gluten cake available in Japanese markets, packaged in a number of sizes and shapes. Used mostly as a garnish in soups and one-pot dishes. **Shonaifu**, is packaged in sheets which may be cut to the size needed.

Ganmodoki, fried bean curd balls, available packaged in Japanese shops.

Ginnan, gingko (or ginkgo) nuts available in Oriental markets and speciality food shops, cooked and bottled or tinned. The nuts will keep, refrigerated, in a closed container, for several weeks.

Gobo, the root of burdock (*Arctium lappa*) of the Daisy Family, is a long, slender root sold fresh in Japanese markets usually under its Japanese name. It will keep, refrigerated, for up to 2 weeks. It can also be bought tinned. The best substitutes, close botanical relatives, are salsify and scorzonera.

Goma, sesame seed, both black (*kuro goma*) and white (*shiro goma*) are available, packaged, in Japanese shops. The white sesame is sold in the spice section of supermarkets and both types are often available in Chinese markets and health food shops.

Hakusai, Chinese cabbage, Chinese Leaves or Celery cabbage, sold fresh by the pound in Japanese and Chinese markets, supermarkets and most greengroceries. It has broad-ribbed, pale green leaves 30 to 40 cm (12 to 16 in) long, and will keep, refrigerated in a plastic bag, for a week or more. It is used a great deal in Japanese cooking.

Hana-katsuo or **-gatsuo**, see *katsuobushi*.

Harusame, literally 'spring rain', bean gelatine noodles, also called cellophane or transparent noodles. Available packaged in Chinese and Japanese markets.

Hijiki, flaked dried seaweed that looks rather like dry tea leaves but which expands by as much as four or five times in a liquid. It is a member of the order *Fucales* and is related to the rockweed kelps, *Fucus*. Traditionally it is supposed to bring the eater health, wealth and beauty.

Hiyamugi, thin white, pink and green wheat-flour noodles, usually eaten cold in summer dishes. Available packaged in Japanese shops.

Ika, squid, cuttlefish, sold in fishmongers and in Japanese shops.

Itazuri, is the method of cutting a thin slice off the ends of cucumbers, then rubbing the cut surfaces with the slices, after which the cucumber is rolled in salt. This is said to remove any bitter taste.

Kabocha, Japanese pumpkin. Any pumpkin, especially West Indian pumpkin, available in Caribbean markets, is a good substitute.

Kamaboko, fish sausage made from pounded white fish mixed with cornflour, formed into a sausage shape and cooked. It is sold, ready-made, in Japanese shops and comes in many shapes and sizes. Some are coloured pink or green. See also *naruto-maki*.

Kanpyo, dried strips of the winter melon, also called dried gourd strips, used for tying various foods. Sold packaged in Japanese shops.

Kanten (*Gelidium amansii*), a red alga high in gelatine, is manufactured into colourless *kanten*, better known as *agar-agar*, and used as gelatine in Japanese cooking. Available packaged in Japanese and Chinese shops and in health food shops.

Karashi, mustard, sold dried and ground in small tins in Japanese shops. It is mixed with boiling water to a stiff paste and is very hot. Dried English mustard is very similar.

Karashina, mustard greens, (genus *Brassica* of the Crucifer Family). Available in Japanese shops and in supermarkets and greengroceries.

Katakuriko, flour made from the root of the Japanese dog-toothed violet (*Erythronium japonicum*), closely resembles arrowroot, used to thicken sauces and as a coating for foods. Available in Japanese shops and labelled 'potato starch'.

Katsuobushi, dried bonito fillet, used to make soup stock (*dashi*) and as a garnish. Looks like a piece of wood and traditionally is shaved into flakes with a *kezuriki*, a special box with sharp blades set in the top. This is a tedious chore with the special tool and almost impossible without it. However, pre-flaked dried bonito is sold in Japanese shops in boxes or plastic bags as *hana-katsuo*, or *hana-gatsuo*, as the spelling varies slightly from brand to brand. Keeps indefinitely, unrefrigerated.

Kikurage, jelly mushroom, available packaged, dried in Chinese and Japanese shops. Sometimes called black fungus or Tree Ear mushrooms.

Kinako, soy bean flour available, packaged, in Japanese shops and in health food shops.

Kinome, Japanese pepper leaf used as a garnish. Not usually available, no substitute leaf. For cooking purposes use the ground version, see *kona sansho*.

Kinugoshi tofu, silky bean curd, a custard-like cake made from white soy beans, sold fresh from the refrigerator section of Japanese and health food shops and sometimes from supermarkets. Will keep for several days if put into a container with water that is changed daily. This is a more delicate form of bean curd than *momen tofu*, often called cotton bean curd.

Kiriboshi daikon, dried white radish strips, available in Japanese shops.

Kishimen, broad, flat, wheat-flour noodles. Available in Japanese shops and in health food shops.

Kisu, smelt. Japanese varieties are available, frozen, in some Japanese shops. Otherwise use local smelt.

Koji, malted rice. Available in Japanese shops.

Kombu, kelp, sometimes spelled *konbu* (*Laminaria japonica*) also called oarweed, tangle and Japanese kelp, is a large marine plant that plays an important role in the Japanese kitchen. The leathery fronds of the seaweed, sold dried and packaged in Japanese shops, are used principally in *dashi*, the basic soup and cooking stock. The seaweed is also sold flaked and shredded, see *tororo kombu*.

Kona sansho, Japanese pepper, used as a table condiment, is made from the ground leaf of the prickly ash, (*Zanthoxylum piperatum* of the Citrus Family). Available, packaged, in Japanese shops. *Kinome*, the pretty pinnate leaf, is used whole as a garnish, but is seldom available. The ground pepper may be used instead.

Konnyaku, translucent oblong cake made from the tubers of an aroid known as Devil's Tongue or Snake Palm, sold packaged in Japanese shops. Will keep, refrigerated, for several days.

Koridofu, see *koyadofu*.

Koshi-an, red (*azuki*) bean paste in powder form. Available, packaged, in Japanese shops.

Koyadofu, freeze-dried bean curd, also called *koridofu*. Koya is the name of the place where it was first made, *kori* is ice, hence the two names. Available, packaged, in Japanese shops.

Kuzu shirataki, dried green bean noodles, sometimes used in *sukiyaki* instead of *shirataki*. Available, packaged, in Japanese shops.

Kuzu-ko, made from the roots of kudzu (*Pueraria lobata*), is a delicate starch used to thicken sauces and for coating foods for deep-frying. Arrowroot is an excellent substitute. Available, packaged, in Japanese shops and often labelled '*Kuzu*, arrowroot', though arrowroot is made from the rhizome of *Maranta arundinacea*, another tropical plant.

Kyuri Narazuke, *Nara*-style pickled cucumber. Available in vacuum-sealed plastic bags in Japanese shops.

Matsutake (*Armillaria edocles*), the pine mushroom found in Japan's pine forests in autumn. The large mushroom is highly prized as a delicacy. Sometimes available, tinned, in Japanese shops.

Mirin, sweet rice wine used in cooking. Available in Japanese shops. No substitute.

Miso, paste made from fermented, cooked, soy beans. Two main types, *aka miso* (red bean paste) and *shiro miso* (white bean paste), are available in vacuum-sealed plastic bags in Japanese shops and sometimes in health food shops. When *miso* appears in a recipe without specifying either red or white *miso*, either may be used.

Misozuke, meat, fish, or vegetables pickled in bean paste.

Mitsuba (*Cryptotaenia canadensis* of the carrot Family). Trefoil is a herb with a distinctive flavour, used in soups and as a garnish. Sometimes available in Japanese shops. Substitutes are indicated in recipes.

Mochigome, see *sweet rice*.

Momen tofu, sometimes called cotton bean curd, custard-like cake made from white soy beans, sold fresh from the refrigerator section of Japanese shops, health food shops and some supermarkets. Will keep for several days, refrigerated, in water that is changed daily. It is firmer than the delicate *kinugoshi tofu* (silky bean curd) and is the most used of all forms of bean curd.

Momiji-oroshi, which means autumn maple leaves, is made by stuffing a slice of Japanese white radish (*daikon*) with dried, hot, red chillies, then grating them together. The resultant mix of red and white is said to look like maple leaves turning in autumn.

Mooli, see *daikon*.

Moromi miso, soy beans and malted rice, available bottled in Japanese shops.

MSG, monosodium glutamate; see *aji-ni-moto*.

Nabemono, one-pot cookery. An electric frying-pan or a fireproof earthenware casserole (*donabe*), heavy frying-pan, or shallow, round, cast-iron pot (*sukiyaki-nabe*) on an electric or other type of table heater, or a charcoal-burning *hibachi* can all be used for these dishes where the food is cooked at the table.

Nama udon, fresh noodles, ready-cooked in 200 g (7 oz) packages needing only to be reheated in hot water. Also uncooked *nama udon*, to be cooked in the same way as dry noodles. Available in the refrigerator section of Japanese shops.

Namaage, type of fried bean curd, available in Japanese shops.

Na-No-Hana, rape blossoms, the yellow flowers found on sprigs of *Brassica napus* of the Crucifer Family, known as broccoli di rapa, colza, rape or rape greens. Available in summer and autumn in Chinese and Japanese shops, and sometimes in supermarkets, especially in Italian markets.

Naruto-maki, a popular fish sausage, has a spiral pattern of pink or yellow running through it, very attractive when sliced. *Naruto* means whirlpool, the spiral pattern. There are whirlpools off the coast at Naruto, hence the poetic name of the sausage. **Chikuwa**, another type of fish sausage, has a hole running through its length. For practical purposes, any fish sausage will substitute for another.

Natto, fermented soy beans, eaten as a garnish with rice. Available packaged in Japanese shops.

Nimono, simmered foods cooked in a number of differently flavoured stocks. Meats, poultry, fish and vegetables are all cooked by this method.

Nori, purple laver seaweed pressed into thin sheets, greenish-black in colour, used principally as a garnish, and for *sushi*. Available packaged in Japanese shops. Keeps indefinitely.

Oysters are harvested from Japan's Inland Sea in winter and are sometimes available in fishmongers and Japanese shops, frozen.

Ponzu, pon vinegar, made from *dai dai*, a lime-like Japanese citrus fruit. Available bottled in Japanese shops. Use lime or lemon juice as a substitute, though they will lack the fragrance of *ponzu*.

Renkon, lotus root, available fresh in Chinese and Japanese shops at times. The root may be as long as 1.4 m (4 ft) and about 7 cm (3 in) in diameter. It is sold in sections. It is more readily available tinned. The root is perforated by holes throughout its length and when sliced looks like a flower with ten petal-shaped holes. This makes it ideal for stuffing.

Sake, rice wine, Japan's traditional drink, usually served slightly warm in small handleless cups (*sakazuki*), poured from a small china flask. *Sake* flasks and cups are available from Japanese shops. *Sake* is available from Japanese shops and from Off-Licence shops.

Sashimi, sliced raw fish, served with garnishes and very popular in Japan.

Sato-imo, taro, the name given to a diverse group of tropical root vegetables of the Arum Family. Available fresh or tinned in Japanese markets as *sato-imo*, they are sometimes called Japanese potatoes. They look like medium-sized potatoes with a rough brown skin marked by prominent rings. They may also be found in Caribbean markets called by a number of names, usually eddo, yautía, dasheen or tannia.

Satsuma-age, oval fish cakes available packaged in Japanese shops.

Satsuma-imo, sweet potato, one of the white or yellow-fleshed varieties, not the orange (Louisiana yam) sweet potato. Widely available in supermarkets, greengroceries and in Caribbean markets where it may be called boniato.

Seri, water dropwort (*Oenanthe stolonthe*), belonging to the same family as celery, is best described as a kind of aquatic parsley. Sometimes available fresh in Japanese shops. Flat (continental) parsley is the best substitute.

Shichimi-togarashi, seven-flavour spice, is a seasoning powder made from ground hot red chillies, ground Japanese pepper leaf, sesame, mustard, rape and poppy seeds, and dried tangerine peel. Available in Japanese shops in containers to be used as an on-the-table condiment.

Shiitake, Japanese mushrooms, available dried (*hoshi-shiitake*) in Japanese shops. To use soak for 30 minutes in warm water, then squeeze out and cut away the tough stems. When fresh mushrooms (*namo-shiitake*) are called for in a recipe, use fresh local mushrooms, or use the dried Japanese ones.

Shirataki, literally 'white waterfall', translucent noodles made from the roots of the Devil's Tongue, or Snake Palm plant called *konnyaku* in Japan, a member of the Arum Family. Available water-packed in tins or vacuum-sealed plastic bags in Japanese shops.

Shiratama-ko, rice cake flour, available packaged in Japanese shops.

Shiso, *Perilla frutescens* of the Mint Family, commonly known as the beefsteak plant. The leaves are used mainly as a garnish and in pickles. Sometimes available fresh in Japanese shops. Grows easily from seeds. Substitutes, where possible, are indicated in recipes.

Shoga, ginger. Fresh ginger root is very widely available, in most greengroceries and in Oriental, Caribbean and Japanese shops. Will keep, refrigerated, for some weeks. To make ginger juice, grate finely and squeeze out the juice (which freezes well).

Shoyu, soy sauce, available in Japanese shops and in supermarkets and groceries, is lighter and less salty than Chinese soy sauce.

Shungiku, the edible or Garland chrysanthemum (*Chrysanthemum coronarium*), whose leaves are used, principally as a garnish, in Japanese cooking. Often available in Chinese and Japanese markets. The plant should not be confused with the ordinary Western garden varieties of chrysanthemum, which are not edible.

Soba, buckwheat noodles, available packaged in health food shops and Japanese shops.

Soboro, also called *dembu*, cooked pink-coloured fish or prawn sweetened garnish sold packaged or in jars in Japanese shops.

Somen, thin wheat-flour noodles, available packaged in Japanese shops and sometimes in health food shops.

Stir-fry, a Chinese cooking technique also used in the Japanese kitchen in which cut-up food is fried in shallow fat over high heat while being stirred constantly and quickly.

Su, rice vinegar, available bottled in Japanese shops. It is very delicately flavoured. Cider vinegar is probably the best substitute.

Sunomono, foods in a vinegared dressing, salads. This category overlaps with *aemono*, dressed salads. Both types of dish are served as accompaniments to main courses.

Sushi, vinegared rice dishes usually topped with raw fish.

Sweet rice, sticky, sweet, glutinous rice (*mochigome*), a short-grained rice that sticks together when cooked. Used in Far Eastern cooking and in Japanese cooking. Available in Chinese and Japanese shops.

Takenoko, bamboo shoots. Tinned whole shoots are available in Chinese and Japanese shops and sometimes in groceries and supermarkets. Once opened, will keep, refrigerated, in a covered container in the liquid from the tin, for about a week.

Teriyaki, the technique of glazing food in a soy sauce and *mirin* mixture either in a frying-pan or under a grill.

Tofu, soy bean curd, usually refers to *momen tofu*.

Togarashi, whole dried hot red chillies. When ground and put into containers the peppers are called *togarashi-ko* and are used as an on-the-table condiment. Available in Japanese shops. Any dried hot red chilli may be used. For the ground pepper, cayenne is a good substitute.

Tori-sasami, bamboo-leaf chicken breasts. These are the two smaller fillets of the skinned and boned whole chicken breast and in Japan are considered the best part. Save the two larger fillets for another use.

Tororo kombu, shredded kelp (seaweed), sold packaged in Japanese shops. Keeps indefinitely.

Toso, cold spiced *mirin*, a traditional New Year drink. In Japan, *toso*, made with *sake*, giving a much drier drink, is becoming increasingly popular.

Tsukemono, pickled vegetables available bottled or in vacuum-sealed plastic bags in Japanese shops.

Udon, medium-sized wheat-flour noodles, available packaged in Japanese shops and sometimes in health food shops.

Umeboshi, small pickled plums available bottled in Japanese shops. Will keep indefinitely, refrigerated.

Uni, sea urchins, available in Japanese shops as a prepared paste in jars. Used as a stuffing for *onigiri* (rice balls).

Usukuchi shoyu, light soy sauce available bottled in Japanese shops.

Uzura tamago, quail eggs, ready cooked and tinned, available in Japanese shops.

Wakame, lobe-leaf seaweed sold dried in packages in the form of long, dark green strands that expand rapidly in water to a lighter green. Used in soups and salads. Will keep indefinitely. Available in Japanese shops.

Warabi, the young edible sprout of fernbrake, bracken or fiddleheads. Sometimes pickled or salted, used in soups and salads and available in vacuum-sealed plastic bags in Japanese shops.

Wasabi (*Eutrema wasabi* of the Cabbage Family), Japanese horseradish. In Japan the freshly grated root, used to make a pungent green-coloured condiment rather like horse-radish, is preferred. However, the dried powdered form, which is mixed with water to make a green paste, is also used and is available tinned in Japanese shops.

Yakidofu, grilled soy bean curd, available in Japanese shops.

Yuba, dried soy bean curd packaged in rolls or in flat sheets. Available in Japanese shops.

Yuzu, a lime-like citrus fruit, very fragrant, used in Japanese cooking. Use lime or lemon juice as a substitute.

GLOSSARY OF JAPANESE COOKING EQUIPMENT

Chopsticks, *hashi* in Japanese, are used for both eating and cooking in the Orient. Cooking chopsticks are usually made of wood or bamboo, of various lengths up to about 30 cm (12 in), with small holes at the top ends so that they can be tied loosely together in pairs with kitchen string. Eggs are stirred with chopsticks instead of being beaten, and chopsticks are used to turn foods when frying and for mixing foods together, taking the place of cooking spoons and forks. Five or six chopsticks, held in a bunch in the right hand, are used to stir certain dishes. They are so useful for any type of cooking that it is worth the small effort required to learn how to use them.

Chopsticks for the table may be made of wood or bamboo, plain or lacquered, plastic, ivory and sometimes metal. In Japanese shops 20 cm (8 in) bamboo chopsticks are sold in joined pairs in individual paper wrapping and must be broken apart for use. Almost all Japanese food is eaten with chopsticks of this type. They can, of course, be washed and re-used.

Chawan-mushi, tall, straight-sided lidded soup pots for *chawan-mushi*, savoury steamed custard. Available in Japanese shops.

Donabe, lidded earthenware casserole unglazed outside, glazed inside. Comes in various sizes and can be used over direct heat. The larger sizes are used for one-pot dishes cooked at the table, such as Simmered Beef and Vegetables (*Shabu-Shabu*). The casseroles should be heated and cooled slowly to prevent cracking. Available in Japanese shops. Other domestic and imported fireproof casseroles can be used.

Donburi, large individual ceramic bowls, often with lids, used for noodle and rice dishes. Available in Japanese shops.

Hibachi, Japanese charcoal grill available in various sizes. Can be used indoors or out. From Japanese shops.

Kana-gushi, long and short metal skewers used for grilling many types of food, including whole fish. In Japanese shops.

Knives. Japanese kitchen knives (*hocho*) are magnificent tools, and though good sharp Western knives can be used for cutting in the Japanese manner, a set of 4 *hocho* is worth investing in as they can be used for cutting in any cuisine. There is a long, thin-bladed *sashimi-hocho* for slicing raw fish; a cutting knife for vegetables (*nakiri-hocho*) useful for chopping, slicing and paring; a long, blunt-ended slicing knife for fish, meat and poultry; and a basic kitchen knife for all general cutting. Available made of stainless steel in sets from Japanese shops.

Kushi, small bamboo or metal skewers, available in Japanese shops.

Mushiki, bamboo stacking steamers are available from Chinese shops. Both bamboo and metal steamers are used in Japan, but any good steamer will do.

Nagashikan, resembles an aluminium loaf tin with an inserted sideless tray that lifts out, making it easy to remove and slice delicate custards and similar dishes that would be hard to unmould. Available in Japanese shops in various sizes.

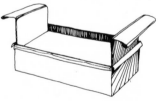

Oroshi-gane, a very fine grater made of aluminium or ceramic with a well at the end for collecting juices. This is ideal for grating ginger for juice and for grating Japanese white radish, *daikon*.

Oshiwaku, an oblong wooden box about 15 × 10 cm (6 × 4 in), with a removable top and bottom used for pressing vinegared rice when making certain kinds of *sushi*. May come in other sizes. Available in Japanese shops.

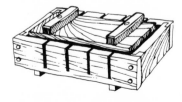

Otoshibuta, an inner wooden lid that fits closely on top of the food being cooked in a saucepan. Made in several sizes, they are sometimes available in Japanese shops. A smaller saucepan lid, or a plate may be used as a substitute.

Shamoji, a round wooden spatula used for stirring and serving rice. It does not break up the rice grains. Available in Japanese shops.

Sudare, a bamboo mat made of thin slats of bamboo very like a bamboo place mat, which may be used as a substitute, used for rolling omelettes, *sushi* and vegetables such as spinach. Available in Japanese shops.

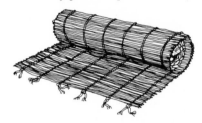

Sukiyaki-nabe, a round, cast-iron pan used for cooking *sukiyaki*. Available in Japanese shops. A cast-iron frying-pan is a good substitute.

Suribachi, a serrated earthenware or ceramic mortar used with a **surikogi**, a wooden pestle. Makes grinding nuts and other foods easy. Use chopsticks to scrape down the sides. Available in Japanese shops. A small coffee mill or nut grinder is a good substitute.

Sushioke, also called a **bandai**, is a round, shallow wooden dish for *sushi* (vinegared rice dishes). In Japanese shops.

Takegushi, small bamboo skewers resembling large toothpicks. Available in Japanese shops.

Tamago-yaki nabe, rectangular frying-pan used specially for making rolled omelettes. Available in Japanese shops. Though any frying-pan may be used, the oblong shape makes rolling the omelettes easier and gives them a neater look.

Tempura pan, round iron pan for deep-fat frying with a built-in draining rack on one side. Ideal for all *agemono* (deep-fried dishes). Available in Japanese markets. A deep-fat fryer, or a heavy iron frying-pan may be used instead.

Zaru, plate-like bamboo strainers used for straining foods, especially noodles for summer dishes. They may also be used as serving plates. Available in Japanese shops, round, oblong, or square.

USEFUL ADDRESSES

JAPANESE FOOD SHOPS AND SUPPLIERS

LONDON

A & K Mori Ltd
Setsu Japan
11 Gilda Court
Watford Way
Mill Hill
London NW7 2QN
Tel: 01 203 4268
(Countrywide delivery of Japanese foods)

Clearspring
Natural Grocer
196 Old Street
London EC1V 9BP
Tel: 01 250 1708
Mail Order: please send 3 first-class stamps to cover cost
of catalogue.

Cheong-Leen Supermarket
4–10 Tower Street
London WC2H 9NR
Tel: 01 836 5378
(Not exclusively Japanese)

Cornucopia
Branches at:
64 St Mary's Road
Ealing
London W5 5EX
Tel: 01 579 9431

70 Pitshanger Lane
Ealing
London W5 1QE
Tel: 01 997 3382
(Not exclusively Japanese)

Furusato (Fish Shop)
67A Camden High Street
London NW1
Tel: 01 388 3979

J. A. Centres
Branches at:
348 Regents Park Road
Finchley
London N3 2LJ
Tel: 01 349 0011/01 346 1042

250 Upper Richmond Road
London SW15
Tel: 01 789 3980

Japan Centre
66 Brewer Street
London W1R 3PJ
Tel: 01 437 6445

Mikado-ya
193 Upper Richmond Road
London SW15 6SG
Tel: 01 788 3905

Mitsukiku
Branches at:
90 Regent Street
London W1
Tel: 01 437 5582
(Food and equipment)

15 Old Brompton Road
London SW7 3HZ
Tel: 01 589 1725
(Food and equipment)

157 Victoria Street
London SW1
Tel: 01 828 0158
(Equipment only)

Neal Street East
5 Neal Street
Covent Garden
London WC2 9PU
Tel: 01 240 0135
(Equipment only)

Ninjin
Branches at:
244 Great Portland Street
London W1
Tel: 01 388 2511

140 Brent Street
Hendon
London NW4
Tel: 01 202 6292

Oriental Food and Wine
241 Camden High Street
London NW1 7BU
Tel: 01 485 2533
(Not exclusively Japanese)

Osaka, Oriental Grocer
17/17a Goldhurst Terrace
London NW6 3HX
Tel: 01 624 4983

Takē
45–46 Chalk Farm Road
London NW1 8AJ
Tel: 01 267 4124
(Equipment only)

Tokyo-ya
20 North End Road
Golders Green
London NW11 7PH
Tel: 01 458 8333

Yamato-ya
55 Church Road
Hendon
London NW4
Tel: 01 203 4773

Yoshino & Co (UK) Ltd
15–16 Monkville Parade
Temple Fortune
Finchley Road
London NW11
Tel: 01 209 0966

KENT

J.A. Centres
70 Croydon Road
Coney Hall
West Wickham
Kent BR4 9HY
Tel: 01 462 3404

STAFFORDSHIRE

Sunwheel Foods Ltd
Granary House
Wetmore Road
Burton-on-Trent DE14 1TE
Tel: 0283 43221 44611
(Wholesale only)

SURREY

Miura Foods
40 Coombe Road
Norbiton
Surrey KT2 7AF
Tel: 01 549 8076

SCOTLAND

Nastiuks
International Food Specialists
10 Gillespie Place
Edinburgh EH10 4HS
Tel: 031 229 7054

AUSTRALIA

NEW SOUTH WALES

Anegawa Enterprises
16A Deepwater Road
Castle Cove
Tel: 406 5452

Coles Supermarket
Chatswood Chase, Shop C
Cnr. Victoria & Archer Streets
Chatswood
Tel: 419 2888
Have small Japanese grocery section.

Ichibankan
36 Nurses Walk
The Rocks
Sydney
Tel: 27 2667
All groceries, frozen food, cigarettes; speciality *Sake* –
they have the only licence in Sydney.

Mrs June Hazell
The Bay Tree, Imports Pty Ltd
40 Holdsworth Street
Woolahra
Tel: 328 1101
Supply Iwatani gas tabletop 'Casette Feu' and
rectangular tabletop grills.

Supa Sakura
Shop 9
100 Edinburgh Road
Castlecraig
Tel: 95 1947

Tokyo Mart
Shop 27
Northbridge Plaza
Sailors Bay Road
Northbridge
Tel: 95 6860

QUEENSLAND

Nikko International
Queens Arcade
77 Queen Street
Brisbane 4000
Tel: 229 3069
All Japanese groceries.

SOUTH AUSTRALIA

Ingredients available at variety of stalls and shops in the
Adelaide Central Market, Grote Street, Adelaide.

Japanese
Cookery

The Japanese Foods Centre
113 Murray Street
Perth 6000
Tel: 325 3929

VICTORIA

The Miyajima Food Centre
2 Sanicki Court
East Bentley
Melbourne 3165
Tel: 570 3321
Most Japanese groceries.

Tokyo Mart
584 Glenhuntry Road
Esterwick
Melbourne 3185
Tel: 523 6200
All Japanese groceries and frozen food.

NEW ZEALAND
Soung Yueen & Co Ltd
235 Hobson Street
Auckland
Tel: 734 936/778 361/397 994

Calico Pie
Square Edge
Church Street
Palmerston North
Tel: 80361

WELLINGTON

Cathay Trading Co Ltd
14–16 Courtenay Place
Wellington
Tel: 848 545

Manawatu Farmers Meat Co
134 Cuba Street
Wellington
Tel: 847 646

Ocean Commodities Ltd
65 Taranaki Street
Wellington
Tel: 851 064

Wellington Fisheries
173 Cuba Street
Wellington
Tel: 842 560

Wellington Trawling Co
218–220 Cuba Street
Wellington
Tel: 844 056

INDEX